Public and Private Schools

HOW MANAGEMENT AND FUNDING
RELATE TO THEIR SOCIO-ECONOMIC PROFILE

This work is published on the responsibility of the Secretary-General of the OECD. The opinions expressed and arguments employed herein do not necessarily reflect the official views of the Organisation or of the governments of its member countries.

This document and any map included herein are without prejudice to the status of or sovereignty over any territory, to the delimitation of international frontiers and boundaries and to the name of any territory, city or area.

Please cite this publication as:
OECD (2012), *Public and Private Schools: How Management and Funding Relate to their Socio-economic Profile*, OECD Publishing.
http://dx.doi.org/10.1787/9789264175006-en

ISBN 978-92-64-17491-7 (print)
ISBN 978-92-64-17500-6 (PDF)

The statistical data for Israel are supplied by and under the responsibility of the relevant Israeli authorities. The use of such data by the OECD is without prejudice to the status of the Golan Heights, East Jerusalem and Israeli settlements in the West Bank under the terms of international law.

Photo credits:
Getty Images © Ariel Skelley
Getty Images © Geostock
Getty Images © Jack Hollingsworth
Stocklib Image Bank © Yuri Arcurs

Corrigenda to OECD publications may be found on line at: *www.oecd.org/publishing/corrigenda*.
© OECD 2012

You can copy, download or print OECD content for your own use, and you can include excerpts from OECD publications, databases and multimedia products in your own documents, presentations, blogs, websites and teaching materials, provided that suitable acknowledgement of OECD as source and copyright owner is given. All requests for public or commercial use and translation rights should be submitted to *rights@oecd.org*. Requests for permission to photocopy portions of this material for public or commercial use shall be addressed directly to the Copyright Clearance Center (CCC) at *info@copyright.com* or the Centre français d'exploitation du droit de copie (CFC) at *contact@cfcopies.com*.

Foreword

The OECD's Programme for International Student Assessment (PISA) represents a commitment by governments to monitor student achievement within an internationally agreed framework. In the decade since its first report was issued, PISA has become the most comprehensive and rigorous student assessment programme in the world. The countries participating in PISA together make up close to 90% of the global economy.

PISA 2009 focused on reading literacy, although students' skills in mathematics and science were also assessed. This report uses data from the *PISA 2009 Database* and *Education at a Glance 2011: OECD Indicators* to investigate public and private involvement in managing and funding schools, and examines how these types of involvement are related to socio-economic stratification between publicly and privately managed schools. It also shows that in those countries with less socio-economic stratification between publicly and privately managed schools, privately managed schools receive higher proportions of public funding. However, the results of the analyses do not suggest that providing more public funding for privately managed schools will reduce stratification between publicly and privately managed schools in all countries. The mechanisms used to finance privately managed schools with public funds vary across school systems, and they may also be related to stratification in different ways. Furthermore, other school characteristics, such as a school's student-admittance criteria, academic performance, policies, practices and learning environment are also partly related to stratification. These aspects, which are not related to funding, also need to be considered when devising policies to reduce stratification between publicly and privately managed schools.

This publication was prepared at the OECD Directorate for Education with the support of the countries and economies participating in PISA and various experts. This publication was drafted by Miyako Ikeda and Soojin Park in collaboration with Guillermo Montt and Anna Pons. Marilyn Achiron, Elizabeth Del Bourgo, and Elisabeth Villoutreix provided editorial support and oversaw production. Alejandro Gomez Palma, Giannina Rech, Andreas Schleicher and Jean Yip reviewed and offered many helpful suggestions. Fung-Kwan Tam conducted the layout design. Our special thanks to Mark Berends, University of Notre Dame and Henry M. Levin, Teachers College, Columbia University for their analytical guidance and critical insights. The development of the report was steered by the PISA Governing Board, which is chaired by Lorna Bertrand (United Kingdom).

The report is published on the responsibility of the Secretary-General of the OECD.

Lorna Bertrand
Chair of the PISA Governing Board

Barbara Ischinger
Director for Education, OECD

Table of Contents

EXECUTIVE SUMMARY 7

INTRODUCTION 9

READER'S GUIDE 15

CHAPTER 1 **MANAGEMENT AND FUNDING** 17
Management of schools 18
Funding for schools 20

CHAPTER 2 **ASPECTS OF SOCIO-ECONOMIC STRATIFICATION** 25
How socio-economic stratification varies across countries 26
Socio-economic stratification and overall performance 27
Some system characteristics and socio-economic stratification 28
Socio-economic stratification before and after accounting for public funding 30

CHAPTER 3 **SCHOOL VOUCHERS AND STRATIFICATION** 33
School vouchers 34
Various voucher systems and socio-economic stratification 35

CHAPTER 4 **OTHER SCHOOL CHARACTERISTICS RELATED TO STRATIFICATION** 39
School-admittance criteria 40
Parental choice for better education 42

CONCLUSION AND POLICY IMPLICATIONS 47

Country Box A: A brief history of public and private involvement in schools in Ireland 49
Country Box B: A brief history of public and private involvement in schools in Chile 53
Country Box C: A brief history of public and private involvement in schools in the Netherlands 59

ANNEX A **TECHNICAL BACKGROUND** 63
Annex A1: Construction of reading scales and indices from the student, school and parent context questionnaires 64
Annex A2: Technical notes on preliminary multilevel regression analysis for performance 70
Annex A3: Standard errors, significance tests and subgroup comparisons 76

ANNEX B **DATA TABLES** 77

TABLE OF CONTENTS

BOX
Box 1.1 PISA 2009 questions: public and private involvement in managing and funding schools 18

FIGURES
Figure 1.1 Public and private management of schools 19
Figure 1.2 How school autonomy, resources, climate and performance differ between publicly and privately managed schools 20
Figure 1.3 Public funding for schools 21
Figure 1.4 Public and private involvement in managing and funding schools 22

Figure 2.1 How socio-economic stratification varies across countries 26
Figure 2.2 Attaining both small stratification and high performance is possible 27
Figure 2.3 Relationship between stratification and public funding for privately managed schools 29
Figure 2.4 How socio-economic stratification varies across countries, before and after accounting for the proportion of public funding for schools 30
Figure 2.5 Countries with and without stratification, before and after accounting for the proportion of public funding for schools 31

Figure 3.1 Various voucher systems 34
Figure 3.2 Stratification by type of vouchers 36

Figure 4.1 How stratification varies across countries, after accounting for various school-admittance criteria 41
Figure 4.2 The likelihood that socio-economically advantaged students will attend privately managed schools 43

TABLES
Table A1.1 Levels of parental education converted into years of schooling 67

Table A2.1 Descriptive statistics of explanatory and background variables 71
Table A2.2 Relationship between public and private involvement in schools and performance in reading 73

Table B1.1 Public and private involvement in managing schools 78
Table B1.2 School autonomy, resources, climate and performance, by publicly and privately managed schools 79
Table B1.3 Public and private involvement in funding schools 82
Table B1.4 Public and private involvement in funding schools, by publicly and privately managed schools 83

Table B2.1 Socio-economic stratification between students who attend publicly and privately managed schools 84
Table B2.2 Socio-economic stratification, by lower and upper secondary education 85
Table B2.3 Summary of stratification and countries' socio-economic and education characteristics 86
Table B2.4 Correlation between stratification and various system characteristics 86
Table B2.5 Relationships between stratification and various system characteristics 87
Table B2.6 Socio-economic stratification, by the proportion of public and private funding for schools 88
Table B2.7 Socio-economic stratification, after accounting for school funding 89

Table B3.1 Financial incentives for parents to choose their child's school (2009) 90
Table B3.2 School vouchers only available for students from socio-economically disadvantaged backgrounds (2009) 91
Table B3.3 Relationships between stratification and various voucher systems 92

Table B4.1 Student socio-economic background, by schools with various school-admittance criteria 94
Table B4.2 Various school-admittance criteria, by school type 96
Table B4.3 Socio-economic stratification, after accounting for the proportion of public funding for schools and various school-admittance criteria 98
Table B4.4 Relationship between student socio-economic background and school autonomy, resources, climate and performance 100
Table B4.5 Likelihood that socio-economically advantaged students will attend privately managed schools 101
Table B4.6 Likelihood that socio-economically advantaged students will attend privately managed schools, after accounting for the proportion of public funding for schools 102

Executive Summary

In recent years, an increasing number of education systems in OECD and partner countries have welcomed the involvement of private entities, including parents, non-governmental organisations and enterprises, in funding and managing schools. Part of the interest in broadening the responsibility for schools beyond the government is to provide greater choice for parents and students and to spur creativity and innovation within schools, themselves. This report examines how private involvement in managing and funding schools is related to socio-economic stratification between publicly and privately managed schools.

Stratification, which, in this report, means creating "classes" of students according to their socio-economic backgrounds, can lead to unequal educational opportunities and outcomes, and can undermine social cohesion. Students who attend schools that have access to more resources and offer a supportive learning environment are more likely to perform better than students who attend schools with neither of these advantages. How children perform in school can have a great impact on their prospects in life later on. This report examines whether those countries that manage to have low levels of socio-economic stratification in their education systems – and thereby maximise equity and social cohesion – can, at the same time, have efficient – that is, high-performing – education systems as well.

Why do more advantaged parents tend to send their children to privately managed schools than disadvantaged parents do? One reason could be that parents believe that these schools offer a better education, an environment more conducive to learning, additional resources, and better policies and practices; and advantaged parents are more informed or aware of the differences in quality across schools. Indeed, results from PISA show that, in most countries, privately managed schools tend to have more autonomy, better resources, and perform better on the PISA reading scale than publicly managed schools. However, PISA finds that, in all countries, privately managed schools seem to attract advantaged students largely because their student bodies are advantaged. Indeed, **in most PISA-participating countries and economies, the average socio-economic background of students who attend privately managed schools is more advantaged than that of those who attend public schools.** Why, then, is socio-economic stratification more pronounced in some countries than in others?

Results show that while the prevalence of privately managed schools in a country is not related to stratification, the level of public funding to privately managed schools is. In Sweden, Finland, the Netherlands, the Slovak Republic and the partner economy Hong Kong-China, principals in privately managed schools reported that over 90% of school funding comes from the government, while in Slovenia, Germany, Belgium, Hungary, Luxembourg and Ireland, between 80% and 90% of funding for privately managed school does. In contrast, in the United Kingdom, Greece, the United States, Mexico, and the partner countries and economies Albania, Kyrgyzstan, Tunisia, Uruguay, Dubai (UAE), Qatar and Jordan, 1% or less of funding for privately managed schools comes from the government; in New Zealand and the partner countries and economies Panama, Brazil, Chinese Taipei, Kazakhstan, Peru and Shanghai-China, between 1% and 10% does.

In those countries where privately managed schools receive higher proportions of public funding, there is less stratification between publicly and privately managed schools. Across OECD countries, 45% of the variation in stratification can be accounted for by the level of public funding to privately managed schools; across all participating countries, 35% of the variation in stratification can be accounted for in this way.

EXECUTIVE SUMMARY

There are many ways of providing public funding to privately managed schools. One way is through vouchers and tuition tax credits, which assist parents directly. The two types of voucher systems considered in this report, universal voucher systems, in which vouchers are available to all students, and targeted voucher systems, in which vouchers are provided only to disadvantaged students, have different effects on socio-economic stratification.

If school vouchers are available for all students, they could help to expand the choice of schools available to parents and promote competition among schools. School vouchers that target only disadvantaged students address equity issues, but they have a limited effect on expanding school choice and promoting competition among schools overall. An analysis of PISA data shows that **universal voucher systems tend to have twice the degree of stratification as targeted voucher systems.**

However, an analysis of PISA findings also shows that **providing more public funding for privately managed schools will not necessarily eliminate stratification between publicly and privately managed schools in all countries.** In some countries, socio-economic stratification is mainly explained by the fact that parents must pay more to send their children to privately managed schools; but in other countries, school fees do not explain stratification completely. Other school characteristics, such as a school's student-admittance criteria, academic performance, policies, practices and learning environment are also partly related to stratification. These aspects, which are not related to funding, also need to be considered when devising policies to reduce stratification between publicly and privately managed schools.

Crucially, PISA results also show that those countries that have low levels of socio-economic stratification also tend to have better overall performance. That means that policy makers – and ultimately parents and students – do not have to choose between equity/social cohesion and strong performance in their school systems. The two are not mutually exclusive.

Introduction

The great public benefits of education have historically prompted governments to assume the primary role in managing and funding schools. Recently, a growing interest in improving school quality and student outcomes, and a quest for greater school choice for parents and students, and for more creativity and innovation in the schools, themselves, have challenged the notion of government's primacy in education (OECD, 2006; Brewer and Hentschke, 2009). This trend, emerging in a number of countries, is based on the belief that the public interest in education can be better served by also involving private entities, including parents, non-governmental organisations and enterprises, in addition to government agencies, in managing and funding schools.

This report focuses on public and private involvement in managing and funding schools, and examines how this is related to socio-economic stratification between publicly and privately managed schools. The report uses data from the *PISA 2009 Database* (OECD, 2010) and *Education at a Glance 2011: OECD Indicators* (OECD, 2011).

Stratification, which, in this report, means creating "classes" of students according to their socio-economic backgrounds, can lead to unequal educational opportunities and outcomes, and can undermine social cohesion. For example, if certain types of schools have more resources or a better learning environment, students who attend these types of schools are more likely to perform better. Conversely, those students who attend schools with fewer resources and disruptive environments tend to perform poorly, which could ultimately limit their prospects in life. In addition, as learning environments and peers play important roles not only in students' academic performance but also in their socialisation in a broader sense, school systems that are highly stratified along socio-economic lines could inadvertently undermine social cohesion. Socio-economic stratification, as well as how students' educational experiences differ depending on whether they attend publicly or privately managed schools, are examined in detail in Chapters 1 and 2.

Policies designed to avoid stratification and the consequent stigmatisation of disadvantaged schools and students will be important. Experience has shown that some policy designs are better than others when it comes to addressing the objectives of efficiency, equity, social cohesion and freedom of choice in education (Levin, 2002). This report also examines whether those countries that manage to minimise socio-economic stratification, and thus maximise *equity* and *social cohesion*, in their education systems, can at the same time also attain another major goal of education, *efficiency*, which is measured as countries' overall performance.

Advocates of private schools argue that private involvement in school management leads to more efficiency and responsiveness to parents' demands. Principals in these schools have more autonomy to manage than public school principals do, although the extent of school autonomy varies across countries. Privately managed schools may have the authority to hire and compensate teachers and staff, and thus can select better-prepared teachers and introduce incentives for performance. Privately managed schools may also have more discretion on curricula and instructional methods, and so can adapt them to the interests and abilities of their students. In addition, privately managed schools have greater incentives to reduce costs and may be subject to more flexible regulations. The need to attract students means that privately managed schools must be more sensitive to parents' demands concerning curricula, teaching methods, facilities and discipline, and more responsive to students' needs.

INTRODUCTION

Advocates also argue that the existence of private schools creates a useful competition that can improve the productive efficiency of public schools, as well, and benefit the entire system. The families, non-profit organisations or enterprises that fund private schools are more likely to demand better student outcomes and hold the school accountable. Parents of children in public schools – and staff in these schools – may then begin comparing the quality of education available in other schools and start demanding higher standards too. Advocates also point out that more funding from families and private institutions would ease governments' obligation to invest in education.

Those who oppose private schools argue that private schools threaten equity and social cohesion and are subject to market failures. For example, a public monopoly can be replaced by a private one, and consumers may have incomplete information about the schools or may be discriminated against during admissions procedures. Private schools, they argue, have no incentives to look at the broader picture of education, such as the negative impact of stratification. Indeed, one of the greatest concerns about private schools is that these schools tend to "skim off" the best students and leave average or struggling students to be educated in public schools. In addition, they argue, granting greater discretion over curricula can mean that schools could opt out of teaching certain core social values. In many countries, private schools have been created with the explicit intent of catering only to specific groups of students, identified by religion, ethnicity, academic ability or socio-economic status. While the prevalence of these kinds of schools offers parents greater choice, it undermines social cohesion and erodes a sense of community among different social groups.[1]

Providing public funding to privately managed schools could help to strike a balance between various education goals (Levin, 2009). For example, tuition fees are usually an obstacle to attending private schools, particularly for students from low-income families. In settings where private schools provide more effective learning environments, public funding can level the playing field for disadvantaged students. If all students are eligible for funding, regardless of their socio-economic background, then parents can choose from a larger number of schools. That, in turn, can reduce the pressure to move residence and increase competition among schools.

Although public funding may create opportunities for those who could not afford tuition fees, those who oppose public funding argue that it necessarily increases public spending and can lead to higher fixed costs per student, as schools often cannot adapt quickly to drops in enrolment and also must continue paying for such non-instructional items as marketing and transport. Detractors argue that the benefits of competition depend on whether all students can exercise school choice. If only advantaged students can freely choose their school because disadvantaged students have only limited access to relevant information, lack adequate transportation, or have different levels of motivation or aspiration, then any competition created will only increase stratification, to the detriment of disadvantaged schools and their students. In addition, public funding may reduce the pressure on schools to be accountable for student outcomes, since parents would be less likely to exert this pressure, given that they do not directly bear the cost of education in these schools.

The evidence on the impact of public and private involvement on performance is mixed. Cross-country studies conducted by Woessmann (2006 and 2009) based on the OECD's Programme for International Student Assessment (PISA) 2000 and by Woessmann, et al. (2009) and West and Woessmann[2] (2010) based on PISA 2003 concluded that countries that combine private management and public funding tend to have better overall academic performance. Studies in Chile (Lara, Mizala and Repetto, 2009), the Czech Republic (Filer and Münich, 2003), Sweden (Sandström and Bergström, 2005), the United Kingdom (Green, et al., 2011) and the United States (Couch, Shugart and Williams, 1993; Peterson, et al., 2003) showed that higher private school enrolments are related to better performance based on cross-sectional or longitudinal data or the data before and after structural changes.

But the debate on performance is far from conclusive, as other studies report little, negative or insignificant effects, and the results often depend on methodological choices. For example, other studies based on the data of US states concluded that higher private school enrolment is not significantly related to performance (Wrinkle, et al. 1999; Geller, Sjoquist and Walker, 2006; Sander, 1999); a few reported only small negative effects (Smith and Meier, 1995), negative effects for low-income districts (Maranto, Milliman and Scott, 2000), or that the relationship depends on the student educational outcome measured (Greene and Kang, 2004). Preliminary evidence from PISA 2009 also points to mixed results (see Annex A2).

Private schools represent an "exit option" from public systems for more advantaged parents; they also exacerbate socio-economic stratification. Students' ability, family income and parents' education, and ethnic background are associated with private school enrolment (Epple, Figlio, and Romano, 2004; Bifulco, Ladd and Ross, 2009). Cross-country evidence indicates that private schools can also reinforce inequities in learning outcomes. Using data from PISA 2000 and PIRLS 2001, Ammermuller (2005) found that a system with a large private school sector showed greater inequality in scores, although

the estimation did not distinguish between public and private funding. However, Schuetz, Ursprung and Woessmann (2009), using data from TIMSS and TIMSS-Repeat, and Woessmann, et al. (2009), using PISA 2003 data comparing public to private funding, concluded that higher shares of private management and public funding were related to lower impacts of socio-economic background on performance. Studies in Sweden (Böhlmark and Lindhal, 2007), Chile (Hsieh and Urquiola, 2006) and New Zealand (Fiske and Ladd, 2000) provide evidence that public funding that does not specifically target disadvantaged students leads to greater stratification. These findings highlight the importance of establishing targeted approaches and ensuring that private providers use public funds in the interest of the public when designing policies to enhance the private sector's role in education (OECD, 2012).[3]

Chapter 1 of this report describes public and private involvement in schools in each country from the perspectives of management and funding. Chapter 2 presents the differences in the socio-economic backgrounds of students who attend publicly and privately managed schools (hereafter referred to as "socio-economic stratification" or "stratification"), and how these differences vary across countries. It also examines how countries' public and private involvement in school management and funding, as well as other country-level characteristics, are related to socio-economic stratification. Chapter 3 discusses how different types of public funding are related to socio-economic stratification by comparing universal and targeted voucher systems. Chapter 4 examines other aspects that may explain why privately managed schools tend to attract socio-economically advantaged students, focusing on school-admittance criteria and the quality of education in the schools.

Care should be taken when interpreting relationships. First, it is difficult to define "private school". The historical, cultural and socio-economic contexts of each country must be taken into account in international comparisons (for example, see Country Box A at the end of this report). The definition is discussed in detailed in the following section. Second, in some federal systems, such as Germany and many other countries, the system-level indicators reported at the country level could vary within each country. Third, since the analyses in this report are based on cross-sectional data (e.g. from a single point in time), they are intended to describe and identify patterns and relationships, rather than determine the causality of those relationships.

References

Ammermuller, A. (2005), "Educational Opportunities and the Role of Institutions", *ZEW Discussion Paper*, No. 44, Centre for European Economic Research, Mannheim.

Brewer, D. and **G. Hentschke** (2009), "An international perspective on publicly-financed, privately-operated schools", in M. Berends (ed.) *Handbook of Research on School Choice*, Routledge, New York, pp. 227-246.

Böhlmark, A. and **M. Lindahl** (2007), "The impact of school choice on pupil achievement, segregation and costs: Swedish evidence" in A. Böhlmark (ed.), *School Reform, Educational Achievement and Lifetime Income,* Department of Economics, Stockholm University, Stockholm, pp. 1-63.

Bifulco, R., H.F. Ladd and **S.L Ross** (2009), "The effects of Public School Choice on Those Left Behind: Evidence from Durham, North Carolina", *Peabody Journal of Education*, Vol. 84, No. 2, pp. 130-149.

Couch, J., W. Shugart and **A. Williams** (1993), "Private school enrollment and public school performance", *Public Choice*, Vol. 76, pp. 301-312.

Epple, D., D.N. Figlio and **R.E. Romano** (2004), "Competition between private and public schools: testing stratification and pricing predictions", *Journal of Public Economics*, Vol. 88, No. 7, pp. 1215-1245.

Geller, C.R., D.L. Sjoquist and **M.B. Walker** (2006), "The effect of private school competition on public school performance in Georgia", *Public Finance Review*, Vol. 34, No. 1, pp. 4-32.

Green, F., et al. (2011), "The Changing Economic Advantage from Private Schools", *Economica*, Digital Object Identifier: *10.1111/j.1468-0335.2011.00908.x.*

Greene, K.V. and **B.G. Kang** (2004), "The effect of public and private competition on high school outputs in New York state", *Economics of Education Review*, No. 23, pp. 497-506.

Fiske, E.B. and **H.F. Ladd** (2000), *When Schools Compete: A Cautionary Tale,* Brookings Institution Press, Washington.

Filer, R.K. and **D. Munich** (2003), Public Support for Private Schools in Post-Communist Europe: Czech and Hungarian Experiences" in D.N. Plank and G. Sykes (eds.), *Choosing Choice: School Choice in International Perspective,* Teachers College Press, New York, pp. 196-222.

Hsieh, C-T. and **M. Urquiola** (2006), "The effects of generalized school choice on achievement and stratification: Evidence from Chile's voucher program", *Journal of Public Economics*, Vol. 90 (8-9), pp. 1477-1503.

Lara, B., A. Mizala and **A. Repetto** (2009), "The Effectiveness of Private Voucher Education: Evidence from Structural School Switches", Working Paper No. 263, CEA, Universidad de Chile.

Levin, H.M. (2002), "A comprehensive framework for evaluating educational vouchers", *Educational Evaluation and Policy Analysis*, Vol. 24(3), pp.159-174.

Levin, H. (2009), "An Economic Perspective on School Choice", in M. Berends, M. Springer, D. Ballou and H. Walberg (eds.), *Handbook of Research on School Choice*, Lawrence Erlbaum Associations, pp.19-34.

Maranto, R., S. Milliman and **S. Scott** (2000), "Does Private School Competition Harm Public Schools? Revisiting Smith and Meier's: The Case Against School Choice", *Political Research Quarterly*, Vol. 53, No. 1, pp. 177-192.

OECD (2006), *Demand-Sensitive Schooling? Evidence and Issues, Schooling for Tomorrow,* OECD Publishing.

OECD (2011), *Education at a Glance 2011: OECD Indicators*, OECD Publishing.

OECD (2012), *Equity and Quality in Education: Supporting Disadvantaged Students and Schools*, OECD Publishing.

Peterson, P., et al. (2003), "School Vouchers: Results from Randomized Experiments", in C. Hoxby (ed.), *The Economics of School Choice*, University of Chicago Press, Chicago, pp. 107-144.

Sander W. (1999), "Private Schools and Public School Achievement", *Journal of Human Resources*, Vol. 34, No. 4, pp. 697-709.

Sandström, M. and **F. Bergström** (2005), "School vouchers in practice: Competition will not hurt you", *Journal of Public Economics*, Vol. 89, No. 2–3, pp. 351-380.

Schuetz, G., H. Ursprung and **L. Woessmann** (2008), "Education Policy and Equality of Opportunity", *Kyklos*, Vol. 61, No. 2, pp. 279-330.

Smith, K. and **K. Meier** (1995), "Public Choice in Education: Markets and the Demand for Quality Education", *Political Research Quarterly*, Vol. 48, pp. 461-478.

West, M.R. and **L. Woessmann** (2010), "Every Catholic Child in a Catholic School: Historical Resistance to State Schooling, Contemporary School Competition, and Student Achievement across Countries", *Economic Journal*, Vol. 120 (546), pp. 229-255.

Woessmann, L. (2006), "Public-private partnerships and schooling outcomes across countries", Cesifo Working Paper, No. 1662, Center for Economic Studies, Institute for Economic Research, Munich.

Woessmann, L., et al. (2009), *School Accountability, Autonomy, and Choice around the World*, Edward Elgar, Cheltenham.

Wrinkle, R., et al. (1999), "Public school quality, private schools, and race", *American Journal of Political Science*, Vol. 43, No. 4, pp. 1248-1253.

Notes

1. Socio-economic stratification between public and private schools is not the only form of stratification. Stratification can also occur among private schools, as in the case of elite schools or when it is related to residential segregation. Stratification can also be related to attributes other than socio-economic background, such as by ability, ethnicity, gender or religion.

2. West and Woessmann (2010) account for the share of Catholic schools, which have historically fostered the expansion of private schools, and address concerns related to omitted variables in the demand and supply of private schooling.

3. Regulations often limit the ability of schools to select students, for example by limiting top-up fees and admissions criteria, and create financial incentives to enrol disadvantaged students. Regulations may also encompass employment or other operational issues. Governments play a key role in ensuring quality by setting standards and monitoring compliance on curricula and teacher credentials and by enacting more stringent accountability frameworks.

Reader's Guide

Data underlying the figures
The data referred to in this volume are presented in Annex B and, in greater detail, on the PISA website (*www.pisa.oecd.org*).

Five symbols are used to denote missing data:

a The category does not apply in the country concerned. Data are therefore missing.

c There are too few observations or no observation to provide reliable estimates (i.e. there are fewer than 30 students or less than five schools with valid data).

m Data are not available. These data were not submitted by the country or were collected but subsequently removed from the publication for technical reasons.

w Data have been withdrawn or have not been collected at the request of the country concerned.

x Data are included in another category or column of the table.

Country coverage
This publication features data on 65 countries and economies, including all 34 OECD countries (indicated in black in the tables and figures) and 31 partner countries and economies (indicated in blue in the tables and figures), which implemented the PISA assessment in 2009.

The statistical data for Israel are supplied by and under the responsibility of the relevant Israeli authorities. The use of such data by the OECD is without prejudice to the status of the Golan Heights, East Jerusalem and Israeli settlements in the West Bank under the terms of international law.

Calculating international averages
An OECD average was calculated for most indicators presented in this report. The OECD average corresponds to the arithmetic mean of the respective country estimates. Readers should, therefore, keep in mind that the term "OECD average" refers to the OECD countries included in the respective comparisons.

Rounding figures
Because of rounding, some figures in tables may not exactly add up to the totals. Totals, differences and averages are always calculated on the basis of exact numbers and are rounded only after calculation. All standard errors in this publication have been rounded to one or two decimal places. Where the value 0.00 is shown, this does not imply that the standard error is zero, but that it is smaller than 0.005.

Reporting student data
The report uses "15-year-olds" as shorthand for the PISA target population. PISA covers students who are aged between 15 years 3 months and 16 years 2 months at the time of assessment and who have completed at least 6 years of formal schooling, regardless of the type of institution in which they are enrolled and of whether they are in full-time or part-time education, of whether they attend academic or vocational programmes, and of whether they attend public or private schools or foreign schools within the country.

Reporting school data
The principals of the schools in which students were assessed provided information on their schools' characteristics by completing a school questionnaire. Where responses from school principals are presented in this publication, they are weighted so that they are proportionate to the number of 15-year-olds enrolled in the school.

Focusing on statistically significant differences
This volume discusses only statistically significant differences or changes. These are denoted in darker colours in figures and in bold font in tables. See Annex A3 for further information.

READER'S GUIDE

Abbreviations used in this report

ESCS   PISA index of economic, social and cultural status
GDP   Gross domestic product
ISCED International Standard Classification of Education
PPP   Purchasing power parity
S.D.   Standard deviation
S.E.   Standard error

Further documentation

For further information on the PISA assessment instruments and the methods used in PISA, see the *PISA 2009 Technical Report* (OECD, 2012) and the PISA website (*www.pisa.oecd.org*).

Management and Funding

This chapter describes public and private involvement in schools from the perspectives of management and funding.

MANAGEMENT AND FUNDING

In PISA 2009, school principals were asked to respond to questions regarding the public and private involvement in both managing and funding schools as shown in Box 1.1.

Box 1.1 PISA 2009 questions: public and private involvement in managing and funding schools

Q2 **Is your school a public or a private school?**
(Please tick only one box)

A public school	☐₁
(This is a school managed directly or indirectly by a public education authority, government agency, or governing board appointed by government or elected by public franchise.)	
A private school	☐₂
(This is a school managed directly or indirectly by a non-government organisation; e.g. a church, trade union, business, or other private institution.)	

Q3 **About what percentage of your total funding for a typical school year comes from the following sources?**
(Please write a number in each row. Write 0 (zero) if no funding comes from that source.)

		%
a)	Government (includes departments, local, regional, state and national)	
b)	Student fees or school charges paid by parents	
c)	Benefactors, donations, bequests, sponsorships, parent fund raising	
d)	Other	
	Total	**100%**

MANAGEMENT OF SCHOOLS

School principals were asked whether the school is managed directly or indirectly by a public education authority, government agency, or governing board appointed by government or elected by public franchise, or managed directly or indirectly by a non-government organisation, such as a church, trade union, business, or other private institution.[1] In the reminder of this report, the former are referred to as *publicly managed schools*, and the latter are referred to as *privately managed schools*. Figure 1.1 shows that across OECD countries, 82% of 15-year-old students attend publicly managed schools while 18% attend privately managed schools. In 18 OECD countries and 14 partner economies, over 90% of 15-old-students attend publicly managed schools. In Turkey, Iceland, Norway and the partner countries the Russian Federation, Azerbaijan, Romania, Montenegro, Latvia, Lithuania, Serbia, Tunisia, Singapore, Croatia and Bulgaria, over 98% of students attend publicly managed schools. In contrast, over 50% of students attend privately managed schools in Belgium (70%), the Netherlands (66%), Ireland (62%), Chile (58%) and the partner economies Macao-China (96%), Hong Kong-China (93%) and Dubai (UAE) (79%) (Table B1.1).

In general, privately managed schools tend to have more autonomy, better resources, better school climate and better performance levels than publicly managed schools as shown in Figure 1.2. In 26 OECD countries and 19 partner countries and economies principals in privately managed schools tend to report greater school autonomy in resource allocation than principals in publicly managed schools reported (Table B1.2). Only in the Czech Republic, the Slovak Republic, Austria and the Netherlands there is no difference in school autonomy in resource allocation between publicly and private managed schools.

In 16 OECD countries and 16 partner countries and economies, principals in privately managed schools tend to report greater school autonomy in curricula and assessments than principals in publicly managed schools reported. In 12 OECD countries and 13 partner countries and economies, principals in privately managed schools tend to report that they have better educational resources than principals in publicly managed schools reported. In 13 OECD countries and 12 partner countries and economies, principals in privately managed schools reported fewer teacher shortages; only in Korea, Slovenia and the partner country Indonesia is the opposite observed. In 16 OECD countries and 4 partner countries and economies, students in privately managed schools tend to report better disciplinary climate than students in publicly managed schools do. Only in Italy and Japan and the partner economy Chinese Taipei is the opposite observed.

MANAGEMENT AND FUNDING

■ Figure 1.1 ■
Public and private management of schools

	Percentage of students who attend:	
	Publicly managed schools	Privately managed schools
Macao-China	4	96
Hong Kong-China	7	93
Dubai (UAE)	21	79
Belgium	31	69
Netherlands	34	66
Ireland	39	61
Chile	42	58
Indonesia	57	43
Australia	60	40
Korea	63	37
Chinese Taipei	64	36
Argentina	64	36
Spain	66	34
Qatar	69	31
Japan	71	29
Panama	77	23
Denmark	77	23
Peru	78	22
Colombia	81	19
Jordan	81	19
OECD average	**82**	**18**
Uruguay	82	18
Israel	82	18
Thailand	83	17
Luxembourg	85	15
Portugal	86	14
Hungary	87	13
Austria	87	13
Brazil	88	12
Mexico	88	12
Albania	89	11
Trinidad and Tobago	89	11
Shanghai-China	90	10
Sweden	90	10
Slovak Republic	91	9
United States	91	9
Canada	93	7
Switzerland	94	6
United Kingdom	94	6
Italy	94	6
New Zealand	94	6
Liechtenstein	94	6
Greece	95	5
Germany	95	5
Finland	96	4
Czech Republic	96	4
Estonia	97	3
Kazakhstan	97	3
Kyrgyzstan	97	3
Slovenia	97	3
Poland	98	2
Bulgaria	98	2
Croatia	98	2
Singapore	98	2
Tunisia	98	2
Norway	99	1
Serbia	99	1
Lithuania	99	1
Iceland	99	1
Turkey	99	1
Latvia	99	1
Montenegro	99	1
Romania	100	0
Azerbaijan	100	0
Russian Federation	100	0

Countries are ranked in ascending order of the percentage of students in publicly managed schools.
Source: OECD, *PISA 2009 Database*; Table B1.1.

MANAGEMENT AND FUNDING

■ Figure 1.2 ■
How school autonomy, resources, climate and performance differ between publicly and privately managed schools

	Difference between privately and publicly managed schools (private – public)						
	Index of school responsibility for curriculum and assessment	Index of school responsibility for resource allocation	Index of the school's educational resources	Index of teacher shortage	Index of disciplinary climate	Performance in reading
	(Index points)	(Index points)	(Index points)	(Index points)	(Index points)	(Score points)
OECD average	0.36	1.08	0.43	-0.24	0.16	30
The number of countries and economies where the difference is in the same direction as that of the OECD average (the number of OECD countries are in parentheses)	32 (16)	45 (19)	25 (12)	25 (13)	20 (16)	29 (16)
The number of countries and economies where the difference is in the opposite direction of the OECD average (the number of OECD countries are in parentheses)	0 (0)	0 (0)	0 (0)	3 (2)	3 (2)	5 (1)

Source: OECD, *PISA 2009 Database*; Table B1.2.

In 16 OECD countries and 13 partner countries and economies, students in privately managed schools tend to perform better in reading than students in publicly managed schools, while the opposite is observed only in Italy, the partner countries Tunisia and Indonesia and the partner economies Chinese Taipei and Hong Kong-China (Table B1.2).

However, on average across OECD countries, over three-quarters of the score-point difference in performance between publicly and privately managed schools can be attributed to the capacity of privately managed schools to attract socio-economically advantaged students (OECD, 2011). This raises the question of why the difference in socio-economic background between students who attend publicly managed schools and those who attend privately managed schools, or stratification, is more pronounced in some countries than in others.

FUNDING FOR SCHOOLS

Schools' budgets may come from difference sources. School principals were asked to report the percentage of their schools' total annual funding that came from: (a) the government, including departments, local, regional, state and national authorities; (b) student fees or school charges paid by parents; (c) benefactors, donations, bequests, sponsorships, and parent fundraising; and (d) other.[2] Figure 1.3 shows that, on average across OECD countries, 85% of total school funding for a typical school year comes from government sources; 10% from parents, in student fees or school charges paid by parents; 2% from benefactors; and 2% from other sources. In Sweden, Finland, Norway, Iceland, Estonia, and the partner countries Azerbaijan and Lithuania, the average student attends a school where over 98% of school funding comes from government sources, while over 30% of school funding comes from parents in Korea (48%), Mexico (46%), and the partner countries and economies Dubai (UAE) (82%), Peru (39%), Colombia (32%), Chinese Taipei (31%) and Indonesia (30%). In all countries and economies except Turkey and Greece and the partner countries Peru, Argentina and Indonesia, over 90% of school funding comes from either government sources or parents (Table B1.3).

The levels of public funding for privately managed schools differ greatly across countries. In Sweden, Finland, the Netherlands, the Slovak Republic and the partner economy Hong Kong-China, principals in privately managed schools reported that over 90% of school funding comes from the government, while in Slovenia, Germany, Belgium, Hungary, Luxembourg and Ireland, between 80% and 90% of funding for privately managed school does (Table B1.4). In contrast, in the United Kingdom, Greece, the United States, Mexico, and the partner countries and economies Albania, Kyrgyzstan, Tunisia, Uruguay, Dubai (UAE), Qatar and Jordan, 1% or less of funding for privately managed schools comes from the government; in New Zealand and the partner countries and economies Panama, Brazil, Chinese Taipei, Kazakhstan, Peru and Shanghai-China, between 1% and 10% does.

MANGEMENT AND FUNDING

■ Figure 1.3 ■
Public funding for schools
Percentage of total school funding for a typical school year comes from government, including departmental, local, regional state and national authorities

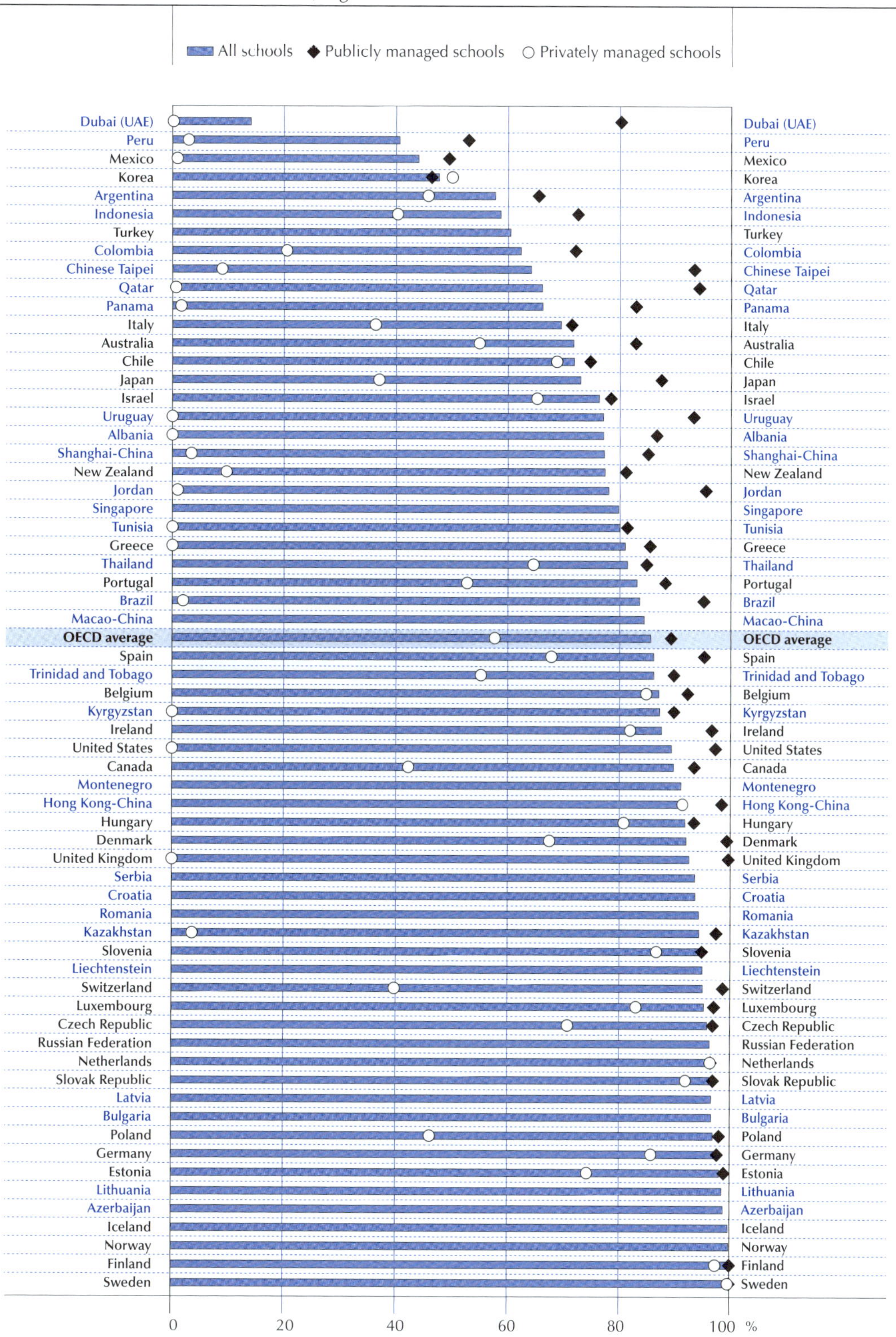

[Bar chart showing percentage of public funding for all schools, publicly managed schools (black diamonds), and privately managed schools (open circles) across countries, ranked in ascending order of percentage of public funding for all schools: Dubai (UAE), Peru, Mexico, Korea, Argentina, Indonesia, Turkey, Colombia, Chinese Taipei, Qatar, Panama, Italy, Australia, Chile, Japan, Israel, Uruguay, Albania, Shanghai-China, New Zealand, Jordan, Singapore, Tunisia, Greece, Thailand, Portugal, Brazil, Macao-China, OECD average, Spain, Trinidad and Tobago, Belgium, Kyrgyzstan, Ireland, United States, Canada, Montenegro, Hong Kong-China, Hungary, Denmark, United Kingdom, Serbia, Croatia, Romania, Kazakhstan, Slovenia, Liechtenstein, Switzerland, Luxembourg, Czech Republic, Russian Federation, Netherlands, Slovak Republic, Latvia, Bulgaria, Poland, Germany, Estonia, Lithuania, Azerbaijan, Iceland, Norway, Finland, Sweden. X-axis: 0 to 100%]

Note: The percentages of public funding for privately and publicly managed schools are shown only for those countries with results available for both privately and publicly managed schools.
Countries are ranked in ascending order of the percentage of public funding for all schools.
Source: OECD, *PISA 2009 Database*; Tables B1.3 and B1.4.

PUBLIC AND PRIVATE SCHOOLS: HOW MANAGEMENT AND FUNDING RELATE TO THEIR SOCIO-ECONOMIC PROFILE © OECD 2012

MANAGEMENT AND FUNDING

As expected, countries that provide more public funding to privately managed schools tend to require less funding from parents.[3] In Sweden, Finland, Hungary, the Netherlands, Slovenia, the Slovak Republic, Germany and the partner economy Hong Kong-China, principals in privately managed schools reported that 10% or less of school funding comes from student fees or school charges paid by parents, while in the United Kingdom, Greece, Mexico, and the partner countries and economies Tunisia, Dubai (UAE), Uruguay, Shanghai-China, Panama, Peru and Qatar, 90% or more does (Table B1.4).

Management and funding of schools can be dissociated from each other. In most countries, publicly managed schools have high levels of public funding; but countries with a greater number of publicly managed schools are not necessarily those with high levels of public funding for schools. This is because in these countries, publicly managed schools receive funding not only from the government, but also from parents; and privately managed schools receive funding not only from parents, but also from government sources. Countries in the bottom right section of Figure 1.4 are those with higher levels of public involvement in both managing and funding schools. Countries in the top left section are those with lower levels of public involvement in both managing and funding schools (see Country Box B at the end of this report for a brief history of public and private involvement in schools in Chile as an example of the countries in this section). Countries in the top right section are those with lower levels of public involvement in managing schools but higher levels of public involvement in funding them (see Country Box C at the end of this report for a brief history of public and private involvement in schools in the Netherlands as an example of the countries in this section). Countries in the bottom left section are those with higher levels of public involvement in managing schools but lower levels of public funding for schools. Thus, it is important to examine the public and private involvement in schools from both perspectives: management and funding.

■ Figure 1.4 ■
Public and private involvement in managing and funding schools

		FUNDING Percentage of total school funding from public sources (OECD average = 85%)		
		Below OECD average	**Around OECD average**	**Above OECD average**
MANAGEMENT Percentage of students who attend publicly managed schools (OECD average = 84%)	**Below OECD average**	Australia (60%, 71%) Chile (42%, 72%) Japan (71%, 73%) Korea (63%, 48%) Argentina (64%, 58%) Dubai (UAE) (21%, 14%) Indonesia (57%, 59%) Jordan (81%, 78%) Panama (77%, 66%) Peru (78%, 41%) Qatar (69%, 66%) Chinese Taipei (64%, 64%)	Belgium (31%, 87%) Ireland (39%, 87%) Spain (66%, 86%)	Denmark (77%, 92%) Netherlands (34%, 96%) Hong Kong-China (7%, 92%) Macao-China (4%, 84%)
	Around OECD average	Israel (82%, 76%) Colombia (81%, 62%) Uruguay (82%, 77%)	Portugal (86%, 83%) Thailand (83%, 81%)	Hungary (87%, 92%)
	Above OECD average	Greece (95%, 81%) Italy (94%, 69%) Mexico (88%, 44%) New Zealand (94%, 77%) Turkey (99%, 60%) Albania (89%, 77%) Shanghai-China (90%, 77%) Singapore (98%, 80%) Tunisia (98%, 80%)	Brazil (88%, 84%) Kyrgyzstan (97%, 87%)	Canada (93%, 90%) Czech Republic (96%, 96%) Estonia (97%, 98%) Finland (96%, 100%) Germany (95%, 97%) Iceland (99%, 100%) Luxembourg (85%, 95%) Norway (99%, 100%) Poland (98%, 97%) Slovak Republic (91%, 96%) Slovenia (97%, 95%) Sweden (90%, 100%) Switzerland (94%, 95%) United Kingdom (94%, 93%) United States (91%, 89%) Azerbaijan (100%, 99%) Bulgaria (98%, 97%) Croatia (98%, 94%) Kazakhstan (97%, 94%) Latvia (99%, 97%) Liechtenstein (94%, 95%) Lithuania (99%, 99%) Montenegro (99%, 91%) Romania (100%, 94%) Russian Federation (100%, 96%) Serbia (99%, 94%) Trinidad and Tobago (89%, 86%)

Note: The percentage of students who attend publicly managed schools and the percentage of total school funding from public source are indicated in parentheses.
Source: OECD, *PISA 2009 Database*; Tables B1.1 and B1.3.

Reference

OECD (2011), "Private schools: Who benefits?" *PISA in Focus*, No. 7, OECD Publishing.

Notes

1. In Ireland, all schools that have been classified as privately managed are those managed by religious organisations. Most of these schools are publicly funded, and only a minority charge student fees. In the United States, the question in the PISA 2009 school questionnaire asked if the school was public or private, but did not include the parenthetical text regarding management. This is because in the United States, school type (public or private) is determined by the primary funding source, not the management model. Thus, the data from the United States show the percentage of students in publicly funded and privately funded schools. In general, publicly-funded schools are also publicly managed. However, the United States has a small but growing number of "charter schools" that are primarily funded with public money but may be (but not always) managed privately. These schools would be considered "public" and would be so categorised in the data file even if they are managed by a private institution. There are also instances in which a public school system or schools may be led by a private institution, but are not "charter schools"; these too would be considered public schools.

2. Privately managed schools are grouped into government-dependent and government-independent private schools based on the level of public funding. A government-dependent private institution is one that receives more than 50% of its core funding from government agencies or whose teaching personnel are paid by a government agency; a government-independent private institution is one that receives less than 50% of its core funding from government agencies and whose teaching personnel are not paid by a government agency.

3. Correlation coefficient between these two indicators is -0.97 across OECD countries.

2

Aspects of Socio-economic Stratification

This chapter examines the differences in the socio-economic backgrounds of students who attend publicly and privately managed schools, and how these differences vary across countries. The chapter also analyses how various system characteristics are related to socio-economic stratification.

2 ASPECTS OF SOCIO-ECONOMIC STRATIFICATION

HOW SOCIO-ECONOMIC STRATIFICATION VARIES ACROSS COUNTRIES

Students who attend privately managed schools tend to be those from more socio-economically advantaged backgrounds (Table B2.1). In most PISA-participating countries and economies, the average socio-economic background of students who attend privately managed schools is more advantaged than that of those who attend public schools. The exceptions are Luxembourg, the Netherlands, Korea, Israel, Finland, the Slovak Republic, Estonia and the partner countries and economies Indonesia, Chinese Taipei, Hong Kong-China and Shanghai-China, where the average socio-economic background of students who attend privately managed schools is not more advantageous than that of those students who attend publicly managed schools.

Figure 2.1 shows the socio-economic stratification between students attending publicly and privately managed schools by country and how this stratification varies across countries.[1] In Mexico, Poland, Greece, the United States, Chile, New Zealand, the United Kingdom, Spain, Slovenia, Canada and the partner countries and economies Panama, Brazil, Uruguay, Colombia, Peru, Kyrgyzstan, Argentina, Albania, Dubai (UAE), Tunisia, Kazakhstan and Jordan, the difference in socio-economic background between these two groups of students is 0.5 index points or more, favouring privately managed schools. This is equivalent to over half a standard deviation of the index. In contrast, in Luxembourg and the partner economy Chinese Taipei, the socio-economic background of students who attend publicly managed schools tends to be more advantaged than that of students who attend privately managed schools. In the Netherlands, Korea, Israel, Finland, the Slovak Republic, Estonia, the partner country Indonesia and the partner economies Hong Kong-China and Shanghai-China, there is no difference in the socio-economic backgrounds of students who attend publicly and privately managed schools.

■ Figure 2.1 ■
How socio-economic stratification varies across countries
Difference in socio-economic background between students in privately and publicly managed schools, as measured by the PISA index of economic, social and cultural status (ESCS)

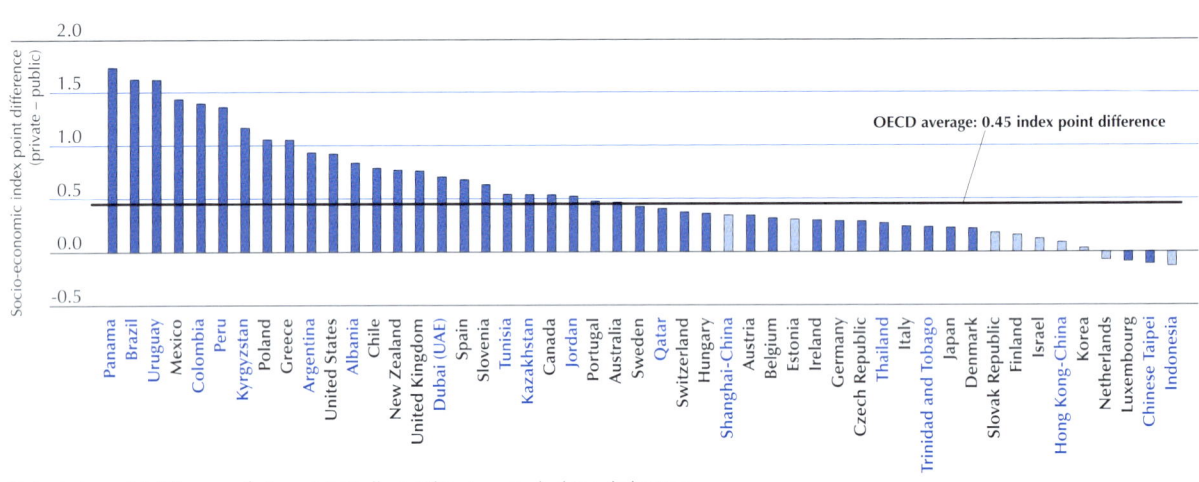

Note: Index-point differences that are statistically significant are marked in a darker tone.
Countries are ranked in descending order of the index point of difference.
Source: OECD, *PISA 2009 Database;* Table B2.1.

As the student samples of PISA are based on age, the 15-year-old students who participated in PISA 2009 attended either lower secondary or upper secondary levels. In most countries, the stratification within each of these levels is similar to the overall stratification at the country level (Table B2.2). However, in Switzerland and the Czech Republic, the overall stratification favours privately managed schools, that is, in general in these countries, more advantaged students attend privately managed schools, but no socio-economic stratification is observed at the upper secondary level. In contrast, in the partner country Trinidad and Tobago, overall stratification favours privately managed schools, but no such stratification is observed at the lower secondary level. In Thailand, overall stratification favours privately managed schools, but no stratification is observed at the lower or upper secondary level. In Indonesia, there is no overall stratification, but there is at the upper secondary level, and it favours publicly managed schools.

ASPECTS OF SOCIO-ECONOMIC STRATIFICATION

Another way of looking at socio-economic stratification is to examine the percentage of students who attend privately managed schools by quarters (i.e. quartiles) of the *PISA index of economic, social and cultural status*. For example, in Chile, 80% of the country's most-advantaged quarter of students attend privately managed schools, while 38% of the country's least-advantaged quarter of students attend such schools (Table B2.1), a difference of 42 percentage points. There is a 20 percentage points, or greater, difference between these two groups of students in Chile, Australia, Spain, Mexico, Ireland, the United States and the partner countries and economies Panama, Uruguay, Argentina, Peru, Colombia, Brazil, Dubai (UAE), and Qatar. In contrast, in Chinese Taipei, 31% of the country's most-advantaged quarter of students attend privately managed schools, while 41% of the country's least-advantaged quarter of students attend such schools.

SOCIO-ECONOMIC STRATIFICATION AND OVERALL PERFORMANCE

Is it possible for countries to minimise stratification while achieving high overall performance? Do countries have to choose between the two? Figure 2.2 shows that countries with less stratification tend to have higher scores in reading, while countries with more stratification tend to have lower scores.[2]

■ Figure 2.2 ■
Attaining both small stratification and high performance is possible
Stratification: Difference in socio-economic background between students in privately and publicly managed schools, as measured by the PISA index of economic, social and cultural status (ESCS)

Source: OECD, *PISA 2009 Database;* Tables B2.1 and B2.3.

ASPECTS OF SOCIO-ECONOMIC STRATIFICATION

This cross-sectional analysis does not prove any causal relationship, and it is not possible to conclude that countries tend to have better overall performance if they provide all students, regardless of their socio-economic background, with the opportunity to attend privately managed schools, which, in general, have more autonomy, better educational resources and better school climates to maximise students' potential. There could be other aspects involved. Even though preliminary evidence from PISA 2009 does not provide any clear cross-country patterns in the relationships between public and private involvement in school management and funding and countries' average performance levels (see Annex A2), what these results do show is that minimising stratification and attaining high overall performance are not mutually exclusive.

SOME SYSTEM CHARACTERISTICS AND SOCIO-ECONOMIC STRATIFICATION

The difference in socio-economic background between students who attend publicly managed schools and those who attend privately managed schools varies greatly across countries. This section explores how public and private involvement in schools is related to stratification. Do countries with more privately managed schools have less socio-economic stratification? Do countries with higher levels of public funding to privately managed schools have less stratification?

If socio-economically disadvantaged families have more difficulties in sending their children to privately managed schools because of tuition fees, more public financial involvement in privately managed schools would ease that burden and more disadvantaged students would be able to attend privately managed schools. The extent to which public funding covers schooling costs matters. In some countries, such as the Netherlands, the government fully covers the cost of tuition and schools can only ask for voluntary contributions from parents. In other countries, public money does not fully cover tuition costs and schools are allowed to charge top-up fees, which not only make some choices less affordable for disadvantaged parents, but can also result in significant differences in school resources and, consequently, differences in the quality of education offered (Hirsch, 2002). For this report, the average percentage of private schools' funding that comes from the government is used as a proxy for the level of public financial commitment to private schooling in a given country.[3]

This chapter also explores how stratification is related to country-level background characteristics, such as variations in students' socio-economic backgrounds and countries' average socio-economic level, and some characteristics of the countries' school systems, such as the prevalence of privately managed schools or of competition among schools.[4] Countries with wider socio-economic variations among students might be more likely to have greater stratification between publicly and privately managed schools. Countries with more students from disadvantaged backgrounds might be more likely to have greater stratification as the financial burden that parents must bear to send their children to privately managed schools would be even heavier in these countries. Countries with more school competition might be more likely to have greater stratification as well.

Results show that stratification does not seem to be related to the prevalence of privately managed schools or to the prevalence of school competition (see correlation results in Table B2.4 and multilevel regression results in Model 2 in Table B2.5). One could argue that the relationship would not be linear, but a U shape. This means that countries with only a small proportion of students in privately managed schools or countries where most students attend privately managed schools tend to have greater stratification than countries with similar numbers of students in publicly and privately managed schools. The most advantaged students might attend privately managed schools where only a very few privately managed schools are available, while the most disadvantaged students might attend publicly managed schools when privately managed schools are available for almost everyone. However, there is no even non-linear relationship between the prevalence of privately managed schools and the magnitude of socio-economic stratification across OECD countries.[5]

In contrast, the level of public funding to privately managed schools is related to the magnitude of socio-economic stratification. Figure 2.3 shows that in those countries where private schools receive higher proportions of public funding, there is less stratification between public and private schools. Across OECD countries, 45% of the variation in stratification can be accounted for by the level of public funding to privately managed schools; across all participating countries,[6] 35% of the variation in stratification can be accounted for in this way (Table B2.4).[7] Even after accounting for the prevalence of private schools (Model 7 in Table B2.5) and other country-level characteristics, such as variations in the socio-economic backgrounds of students, the average socio-economic background of countries and the level of school competition (Model 8 in Table B2.5), the magnitude of stratification between publicly and privately managed schools

ASPECTS OF SOCIO-ECONOMIC STRATIFICATION

is still related to the level of public funding for privately managed schools. The coefficient of -0.06 for public funding for privately managed schools in Model 8 means that a 10 percentage-point increase in public funding for privately managed schools is associated with a 0.06 index-point reduction in stratification.

■ Figure 2.3 ■
Relationship between stratification and public funding for privately managed schools
Stratification: Difference in socio-economic background between students in privately and publicly managed schools, as measured by the PISA index of economic, social and cultural status (ESCS)

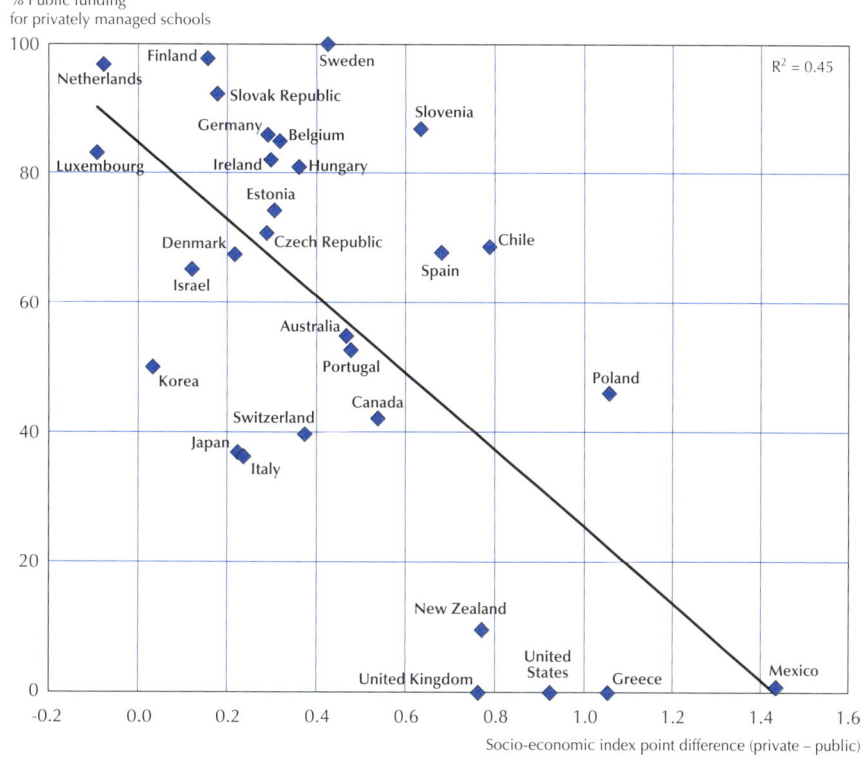

Source: OECD, *PISA 2009 Database;* Tables B1.4 and B2.1.

Among OECD countries, those with greater variations in the socio-economic backgrounds of students and that are more disadvantaged overall tend to have greater stratification (Table B2.4). But, after accounting for other country-level characteristics, these aspects do not seem to be significantly related to stratification (Model 8 in Table B2.5). The level of school competition is also not related to stratification among OECD countries (Table B2.4).

In sum, the level of public funding for privately managed schools is related to the magnitude of stratification, even after accounting for various country-level characteristics. These results should be interpreted cautiously. Despite the association, this result does not suggest that providing more public funding for privately managed schools will automatically result in reducing stratification between publicly and privately managed schools. First, cross-country data do not indicate any causal relationships. Second, about 55% of the variation in socio-economic stratification is not accounted for by the level of public funding for privately managed schools. For example, as shown in Figure 2.3, Finland, Japan and Italy have similar levels of stratification; but while Italy and Japan spend similarly low levels of public funding on private education (about 35%), in Finland, practically all funding for private schools comes from public sources. Finally, the design of funding schemes can influence the degree of stratification. This is examined in detail in Chapter 3.

ASPECTS OF SOCIO-ECONOMIC STRATIFICATION

SOCIO-ECONOMIC STRATIFICATION BEFORE AND AFTER ACCOUNTING FOR PUBLIC FUNDING

In some countries, socio-economic stratification is mainly explained by the fact that parents must pay more to send their children to privately managed schools; but in other countries, school fees do not explain stratification completely.

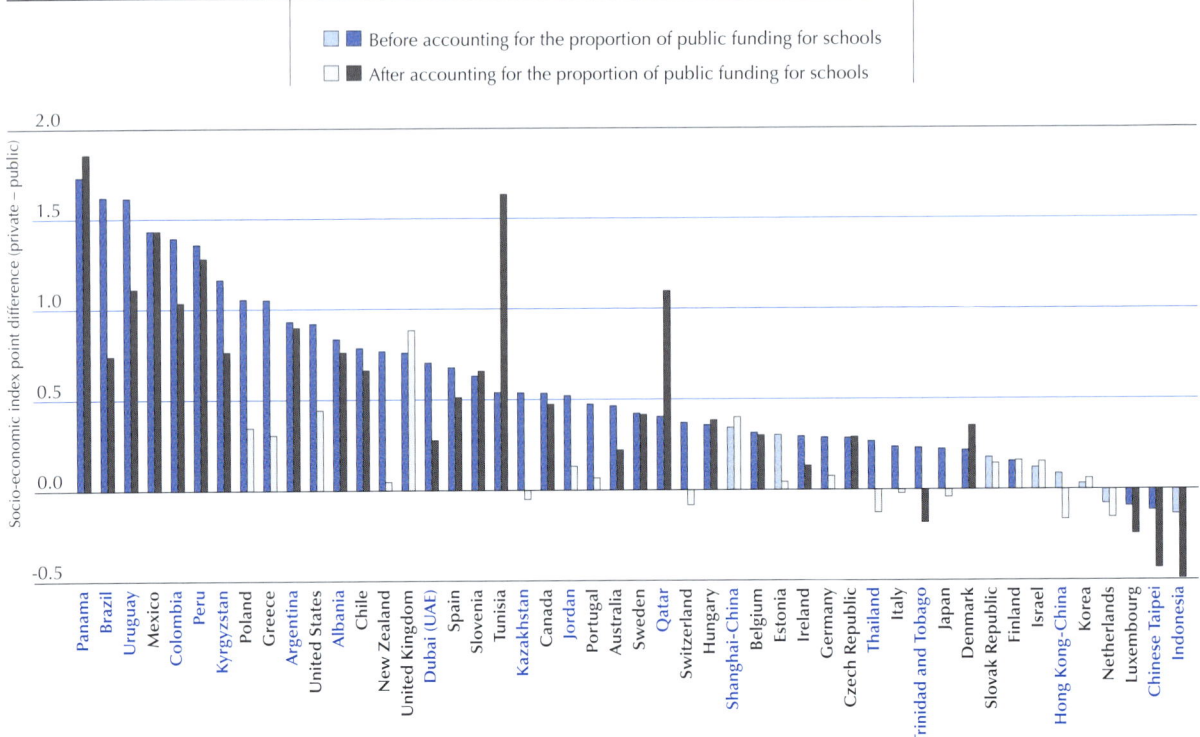

■ Figure 2.4 ■
How socio-economic stratification varies across countries, before and after accounting for the proportion of public funding for schools
Stratification: Difference in socio-economic background between students in privately and publicly managed schools, as measured by the PISA index of economic, social and cultural status (ESCS)

Note: Index-point differences that are statistically significant are marked in a darker tone.
Countries are ranked in ascending order of the index-point difference before accounting for the proportion of public funding for schools.
Source: OECD, *PISA 2009 Database*; Tables B2.1 and B2.7.

As shown in Figure 2.4, stratification between publicly and privately managed schools is reduced in most countries and economies after the level of public funding has been accounted for, as socio-economically advantaged schools tend to receive a greater proportion of funding from parents, and less funding from the government, than disadvantaged schools (Table B2.6). Among 25 OECD countries and 16 partner countries that show stratification in favour of privately managed schools, after accounting for the proportion of public funding invested in individual schools, 13 OECD countries and 4 partner countries show no difference in socio-economic background between students who attend publicly managed schools and those who attend privately managed schools (Figure 2.5). This means that, in these countries, stratification between publicly and privately managed schools is mainly driven by the different levels of public funding for schools. However, 12 OECD countries and 11 partner countries (Mexico, Chile, Slovenia, Spain, Canada, Sweden, Belgium, Hungary, Denmark, the Czech Republic, Australia, Ireland, the partner countries Panama, Tunisia, Peru, Uruguay, Qatar, Colombia, Argentina, Kyrgyzstan, Albania, Brazil, and the partner economy Dubai [UAE]) show socio-economic stratification in favour of privately managed schools even after accounting for the level of public funding invested in individual schools.

So what other aspects, in addition to funding, can explain these differences in stratification? Two of these, namely school admissions criteria and school quality, are examined in Chapter 4.

ASPECTS OF SOCIO-ECONOMIC STRATIFICATION

■ Figure 2.5 ■
Countries with and without stratification, before and after accounting for the proportion of public funding for schools

BEFORE accounting for the proportion of public funding for schools		AFTER accounting for the proportion of public funding for schools
Socio-economic stratification *in favour of publicly managed schools*	Luxembourg Chinese Taipei	Socio-economic stratification *in favour of publicly managed schools*
	Indonesia	
No socio-economic stratification	Finland Korea Netherlands Hong Kong-China	No socio-economic stratification
Socio-economic stratification *in favour of privately managed schools*	Trinidad and Tobago	Socio-economic stratification *in favour of publicly managed schools*
	Estonia Germany Greece Israel Italy Japan New Zealand Poland Portugal Slovak Republic Switzerland United Kingdom United States Jordan Kazakhstan Shanghai-China Thailand	No socio-economic stratification
	Australia Belgium Canada Chile Czech Republic Denmark Hungary Ireland Mexico Slovenia Spain Sweden Albania Argentina Brazil Colombia Dubai (UAE) Kyrgyzstan Panama Peru Qatar Tunisia Uruguay	Socio-economic stratification *in favour of privately managed schools*

Source: OECD, *PISA 2009 Database*; Tables B2.1 and B2.7.

Reference

Hirsch, D. (2002), "What Works in Innovation in Education, School: A Choice of Directions", *CERI Working Paper,* OECD Publishing.

Notes

1. The difference in the average socio-economic background of students who attend privately managed schools and those who attend publicly managed schools is used as a measure of socio-economic stratification. Stratification measures are often contingent on some contextual conditions, such as overall disparities in students' socio-economic background within countries, differences in students' socio-economic background between schools within countries, and the size of the private sector. Thus, more elaborated measures of stratification are developed after accounting for these contextual conditions. The results show that the more elaborated measures of stratification (i.e. the percentage of ESCS variance accounted for by schools being managed publicly or privately) are highly correlated with the simple stratification measure used in this report. Thus, the findings based on this simple stratification measure will be robust.

2. Among OECD and partner countries, 25% of the variation in performance can be explained by the different levels of socio-economic stratification. Among OECD countries only, 15% of performance variation can be explained by the different levels of stratification.

3. Strictly speaking, the percentage of funding for private schools that comes from government sources (asked in Question 03 of the PISA 2009 School Questionnaire) would not include the costs that governments cover through tuition tax credits (i.e. governments pay the costs of private schools through foregone revenues); but this percentage shows the general level of countries' financial commitment to private schools.

4. A summary of these system-level characteristics is presented in Table B2.3.

5. Across OECD countries, stratification is regressed on the prevalence of private schools (i.e. the percentage of 15-year-old students who attend privately managed schools) and the square of this. Only 7% of the variation in stratification is explained.

6. Excluding the extreme case, Mexico, 37% of the variation in stratification across countries can be accounted for by the level of public funding for privately managed schools.

7. These percentages are obtained by squaring the correlation coefficients (i.e. 45=-0.67*-0.67*100). In those countries where privately managed schools receive higher proportions of funding from parents, stratification between public and private schools tends to be more pronounced. Across OECD countries, 42% of the variation in the stratification across countries can be accounted for by the level of funding from parents; across all participating countries, 35% of the variation in stratification can be accounted for in this way.

School Vouchers and Stratification

This chapter discusses how different types of public funding, particularly universal and targeted voucher systems, are related to socio-economic stratification.

3 SCHOOL VOUCHERS AND STRATIFICATION

This chapter examines the relationship between stratification and the manner in which public funding is provided to private schools. Are there more (and less) equitable ways of providing public funding to privately managed schools?

There are many ways of providing public funding to privately managed schools. This chapter considers funding provided directly to parents through vouchers. It compares universal voucher systems and targeted voucher systems, and examines how these two types of funding are related to the magnitude of stratification.[1]

SCHOOL VOUCHERS

Education reforms over the past decades have tended to give more autonomy and authority to parents and students to choose schools that better meet their educational needs or preferences (Heyneman, 2009). In order to increase the financial incentives for parents to facilitate school choice, some school systems make public funding available so that parents can send their children to private schools. Public funding to schools can be provided by allocating funding directly to parents (e.g. through student-based vouchers), the focus of this report, or to the selected school (e.g. through government subsidy).

School vouchers (or *scholarships*), are certificates issued by the government with which parents can pay for the education of their children at a school of their choice.[2] *Tuition tax credits*, another mechanism to make it easier for parents to choose a school for their children, allow parents to subtract educational expenses, including private-school tuition, from their taxes. As a result, governments pay the costs of private schools through foregone revenues. Tuition tax credits are sometimes regarded as a sort of new vouchers, which are known as "Neovouchers" (Welner, 2008). In this analysis, tuition tax credits are also considered as a part of school vouchers.

According to Levin (2002), the key elements to be considered in designing voucher programmes are: finance, regulation and support services. This chapter focuses one of these elements, *finance*, as this is directly related to public funding. Finance refers to the overall resources of the school-voucher programme, how these are allocated, and whether schools can charge tuition fees that exceed the value of the voucher (Levin, 2002). If school vouchers are available for all students, they could expand school choice and promote competition among schools. School vouchers targeting only disadvantaged students address equity issues, but they have a limited effect on expanding school choice and promoting competition among schools overall.

■ Figure 3.1 ■
Various voucher systems

	School vouchers (also referred to as scholarships) and/or tuition tax credits are available and applicable at the secondary school level	Vouchers are only available for socio-economically disadvantaged students at the secondary school level
Belgium (Fl.)	YES	YES
Belgium (Fr.)	YES	YES
Chile	YES	NO
Czech Republic	NO	NO
Denmark	NO	NO
England	NO	NO
Estonia	YES	NO
Finland	NO	NO
Germany	YES	YES
Greece	NO	NO
Hungary	NO	NO
Ireland	NO	NO
Israel	YES	YES
Italy	NO	NO
Japan	NO	NO
Korea	NO	NO
Luxembourg	NO	NO
Netherlands	NO	NO
New Zealand	NO	NO
Poland	YES	NO
Portugal	YES	NO
Slovak Republic	YES	YES
Spain	YES	NO
Sweden	NO	NO
Switzerland	NO	NO

Source: OECD, *PISA 2009 Database*; Tables B3.1 and B3.2.

SCHOOL VOUCHERS AND STRATIFICATION

Table B3.1 and Figure 3.1 show the availability of school vouchers and tuition tax credits for lower or upper secondary education in publicly and privately managed schools, by school system.[3] The data are drawn from *Education at a Glance 2011: OECD Indicators* (OECD, 2011).

In this report, the term *voucher systems* is defined as school systems where either school vouchers (also referred to as scholarships) or tuition tax credits are available to both public and private schools (i.e. government-dependent and/or independent private schools).[4] In other words, in this analysis, the concept of "voucher system" also includes tuition tax credits, but not other forms of funding, since it is intended to measure *the availability of public funding that directly increases the financial incentives for parents to choose private schools*. When vouchers for both public and private schools are available, they encourage parents and students to choose schools regardless of whether those schools are public or private; they also give disadvantaged students the opportunity to benefit from attending private schools.

As Table B3.1 shows, in all countries where vouchers or tuition tax credits are available for public schools, they are also available for government-dependent and/or independent private schools, except in Italy, where school vouchers are available only for public schools. Differences between lower- and upper-secondary levels of education are found only in Denmark, where upper secondary education is considered to be a voucher system while lower secondary education is considered to be a non-voucher system (Table B3.1). Since over 99% of the 15-year-old students in Denmark who participated in PISA 2009 are in lower secondary schools, the information on the availability of vouchers in Denmark is drawn from lower secondary education (Table B2.2). In New Zealand and Switzerland, data from lower secondary level are used, as data from upper secondary level are missing.

According to this report's definition, 10 OECD school systems are classified as *voucher systems* and 15 OECD school systems are classified as *non-voucher systems* (see Column 15 in Table B3.1). The Flemish and French Communities of Belgium, Chile, Estonia, Germany, Israel, Poland, Portugal, the Slovak Republic and Spain are defined as being *voucher systems*. The Czech Republic, Denmark, England, Finland, Greece, Hungary, Ireland, Italy, Japan, Korea, Luxembourg, the Netherlands, New Zealand, Sweden and Switzerland are defined as being *non-voucher systems*. This classification is used throughout the remainder of this report.

However, some caution is advised when examining these voucher systems, as they are complex and difficult to capture in a general survey. Data collected at the national level may vary considerably at the local level, and funding may be provided through other mechanisms that may have similar effects in practice, even if the systems are considered as those that do not use vouchers. The results of this chapter need to be carefully interpreted, since they are drawn from only a subset of 25 OECD school systems with available data.[5] Some systems provide funding at the level of schools, communities or regions rather than directly to parents, and target those schools, communities or regions that accommodate greater numbers of disadvantaged students. The examination of this type of public funding is beyond the scope of this report due to the limitation of the data availability.

Figure 3.1 and Table B3.2 present data from *Education at a Glance 2011: OECD Indicators* (OECD, 2011) on whether school vouchers are only available for students from low-income families. The data are presented by school type and by the level of education (lower or upper secondary). Systems are regarded as *voucher systems targeting disadvantaged students* if school vouchers are only available for students from socio-economically disadvantaged backgrounds for both public and private schools (i.e. government-dependent and/or independent private schools). Based on this definition, six school systems, namely those in the Flemish and French Communities of Belgium, Germany, Israel and the Slovak Republic, are regarded as *targeted voucher systems* that target disadvantaged students. The other five voucher systems in Chile, Estonia, Poland, Portugal and Spain are regarded as *universal voucher systems* that do not target disadvantaged students (i.e. these are the countries with "1" in Column 15 in Table B3.1 and "0" in Column 7 in Table B3.2).

VARIOUS VOUCHER SYSTEMS AND SOCIO-ECONOMIC STRATIFICATION

The relationships between stratification and the different types of voucher systems are examined with a three-level regression analysis.[6] As seen earlier in this report, across 25 OECD school systems with available data, private schools tend, on average, to have a more advantaged student body than public schools by 0.38 index points, equivalent to one-third of the standard deviation of the index (Model 1 in Table B3.3). Socio-economic stratification between publicly and privately managed schools varies significantly across systems. The variation in stratification is related to the levels of public funding for privately managed schools (Model 2 in Table B3.3). A 20 percentage-point increase in public funding to private schools is related to a 0.13 index-point reduction in stratification on the *PISA index of economic, social and cultural status*.[7]

SCHOOL VOUCHERS AND STRATIFICATION

When comparing systems with similar levels of public funding for privately managed schools (i.e. after accounting for the levels of public funding for privately managed schools), is providing more financial incentives to parents to choose their child's school related to less stratification? Results indicate that the answer is no. The index-point difference between *voucher systems* and *non-voucher systems* is 0.14, which is not significant (Model 3 in Table B3.3). Perhaps this is because *voucher systems* include many different types of voucher programmes. Thus, it is important to examine in greater detail the design elements of *voucher systems*.

Voucher systems are grouped into two categories: *universal voucher systems*, which do not target disadvantaged students, and *targeted voucher systems*, which target disadvantaged students. The results show that universal voucher systems tend to have twice the degree of stratification as targeted voucher systems do, as shown in Figure 3.2. The stratification observed in *targeted voucher systems* is 0.36 index points,[8] which is almost equivalent to the stratification observed in non-voucher systems, while the stratification in *universal voucher systems* is 0.63 index points[9] (Model 4 in Table B3.3).

These results stand even after other characteristics of school systems are taken into account. The results from Model 4 are further examined for their robustness in Models 5 through 8 (Table B3.3). Even before accounting for the level of public funding for privately managed schools (Model 5), and even after further accounting for socio-economic disparities in a given system, (Model 6), the main finding from Model 4 (i.e. that *universal voucher systems* tend to have greater stratification than *targeted voucher systems* and *non-voucher systems*) remains unchanged. Models 7 and 8 analyse how the relationship between stratification and voucher systems, and the relationship between stratification and *targeted voucher systems* vary according to the level of public funding for privately managed schools. These interactions are not significant, partly because there are only a limited number of cases at the system level.

■ Figure 3.2 ■
Stratification by type of vouchers
Stratification: Difference in socio-economic background between students in privately and publicly managed schools, as measured by the PISA index of economic, social and cultural status (ESCS)

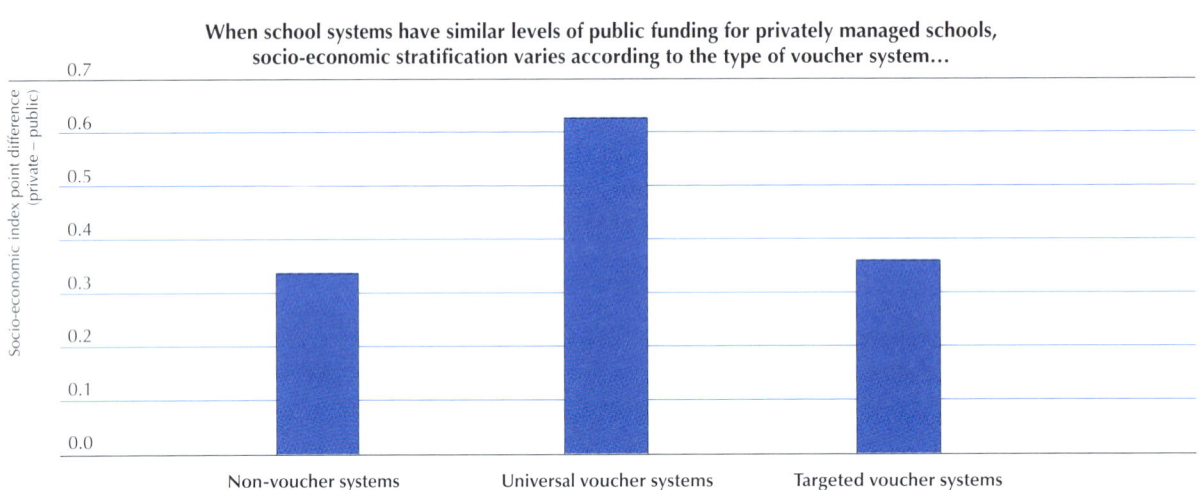

Source: OECD, *PISA 2009 Database;* Table B3.3.

References

Heyneman, S. (2009), "International perspectives on school choice", in M. Berends, et al. (eds.), *Handbook of School Choice*, Routledge, London.

Levin, H.M. (2002), "A comprehensive framework for evaluating educational vouchers", *Educational Evaluation and Policy Analysis*, Vol. 24(3), pp.159-174.

OECD (2011), *Education at a Glance 2011: OECD Indicators*, OECD Publishing.

Welner, K.G. (2008), *NeoVouchers: The Emergence of Tuition Tax Credits for Private Schooling*, Rowman & Littlefield, Maryland.

Notes

1. The question of whether systems that provide parents with more direct and obvious financial incentives to choose their children's school have less (or more) socio-economic stratification is beyond the scope of this paper.

2. This paper links data collected through PISA with that collected by the OECD's NESLI (network for the collection and adjudication of system-level descriptive information on educational structures, policies and practices). Thus, this paper applies the definition of school vouchers used in *Education at a Glance 2011: OECD Indicators* (OECD, 2011b). In most instances, parents do not actually receive a certificate or redeemable check; instead, schools verify that they are serving qualified students and the government provides funding to the school based on the number of qualified students enrolled. The definition of "qualified students" varies across school systems and often refers to the subgroup of students that is targeted by voucher or scholarship programmes. This may include ethnic minorities or students from low-income families.

3. School systems with only the valid data for the analysis are listed in Table B3.1.

4. A government-dependent private institution is one that receives more than 50% of its core funding from government agencies or whose teaching personnel are paid by a government agency; a government-independent private institution is one that receives less than 50% of its core funding from government agencies and whose teaching personnel are not paid by a government agency.

5. Belgium (Flemish Community), Belgium (French Community) and the United Kingdom (England) are regarded as individual school systems in this section's analysis.

6. The results from three-level regression models (i.e. student, school and system levels) are presented in Table B3.3. A dependent variable is the ESCS (*PISA index of economic, social and cultural status*) of students. Twenty-five school systems listed in Table B3.2 are included in the analysis. All systems are weighted equally. These are random-intercept, random-slope models. The slope of the variable PRIVATE is randomised at the system level. Models 2 to 8 are cross-level interaction models that estimate the slope of PRIVATE (school-level variable) by various system-level variables. The variables GFUNDP10 and ESSTD are grand-mean centred (i.e. the mean of GFUNDP10 across 25 school systems is set at zero).

7. This is computed as: -0.130 = -0.065*2.

8. This is computed as: 0.361 = 0.338+0.289-0.266.

9. This is computed as: 0.627 = 0.338+0.289.

Other School Characteristics Related to Stratification

Other reasons why privately managed schools tend to attract socio-economically advantaged students, including admittance criteria and the quality of education in the schools, are examined in this chapter.

OTHER SCHOOL CHARACTERISTICS RELATED TO STRATIFICATION

Public funding is not the only factor related to stratification. The cross-country analysis in Chapter 2 shows that about 45% of the variation in socio-economic stratification is accounted for by the level of public funding for privately managed schools, but the rest of the variation is related to other aspects. Why, for example, do privately managed schools tend to have more socio-economically advantaged students? In this final chapter, stratification is examined as a product of school policy, such as school-admittance criteria, and as a product of parents' choice, as parents seek schools that provide high-quality education.[1]

SCHOOL-ADMITTANCE CRITERIA

Some schools are free to select their own students by setting their own admittance criteria, such as students' academic level, religious affiliation, academic and/or non-academic interests, or relationship with other family members who have attended, or are attending, the school. The application of these criteria may inadvertently result in socio-economic stratification. If privately managed schools have more freedom than publicly managed schools to select their students based on academic achievement, then privately managed schools will tend to have more socio-economically advantaged students enrolled than publicly managed schools, since advantaged students tend to perform better in all countries (OECD, 2010).

In PISA 2009, school principals were asked to report whether the followings are "never", "sometimes" or "always" considered when students are admitted to their schools: (a) a student's record of academic performance, including placement tests; (b) recommendation of feeder schools; (c) parents' endorsement of the instructional or religious philosophy of the school; (d) whether the student requires or is interested in a special programme; and (e) preference given to family members of current or former students. Schools whose principals responded that at least either (a) or (b) is "always" considered are grouped as "schools admitting students based on academic performance". Schools whose principals responded that (c) is "always" considered are grouped as "schools admitting students based on parents' endorsement of the instructional or religious philosophy". Schools whose principals responded that (d) is "always" considered are grouped as "schools admitting students based on students' interest in a special programme". Schools whose principals responded that (e) is "always" considered are grouped as "schools admitting students based on family network".

First, the relationship between student socio-economic background and schools' admittance criteria is examined: whether socio-economically advantaged students are more likely to attend schools with certain admittance criteria. This is followed by an examination of the relationship between schools' admittance criteria and whether those schools are publicly or privately managed. The chapter then explores how admittance criteria are related to stratification.

In 15 OECD countries and 13 partner countries and economies, the socio-economic backgrounds of students who attend schools that admit students based on academic performance is more advantaged than that of students who attend schools that do not admit students based on this criterion (Table B4.1). Among these countries and economies, in 10 OECD countries and nine partner countries and economies, namely the United States, the United Kingdom, Canada, Greece, Germany, Chile, Slovenia, the Slovak Republic, Austria, Poland, Qatar, Dubai (UAE), Panama, Colombia, Peru, Argentina, Brazil, Uruguay and Trinidad and Tobago, privately managed schools are more likely than publicly managed schools to admit students based on their academic performance (Table B4.2).

In 12 OECD countries and 11 partner countries and economies, the socio-economic background of students who attend schools that admit students based on parents' endorsement of the instructional or religious philosophy is more advantaged than that of students who attend schools that do not admit students based on this criterion (Table B4.1). Among these countries and economies, in 10 OECD countries and nine partner countries and economies, namely the United States, Australia, New Zealand, Slovenia, Portugal, Ireland, Canada, Chile, Mexico, Spain, Argentina, Uruguay, Kazakhstan, Brazil, Albania, Colombia, Peru, Panama and Dubai (UAE), privately managed schools are more likely than publicly managed schools to admit students based on parents' endorsement of the instructional or religious philosophy (Table B4.2).

In four OECD countries and seven partner countries and economies, the socio-economic background of students who attend schools that admit students based on their interest in a special programme is more advantaged than that of students who attend schools that do not admit students based on this criterion (Table B4.1). Among these countries and economies, in the OECD countries Poland and Mexico, the partner country Colombia, and the partner economy Dubai (UAE), privately managed schools are more likely than publicly managed schools to admit students based on their interest in a special programme (Table B4.2).

OTHER SCHOOL CHARACTERISTICS RELATED TO STRATIFICATION

■ Figure 4.1 ■
How stratification varies across countries, after accounting for various school-admittance criteria
Stratification: Difference in socio-economic background between students in privately and publicly managed schools, as measured by the PISA index of economic, social and cultural status (ESCS)

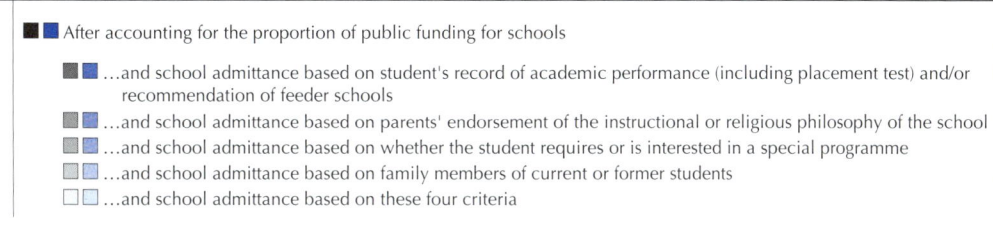

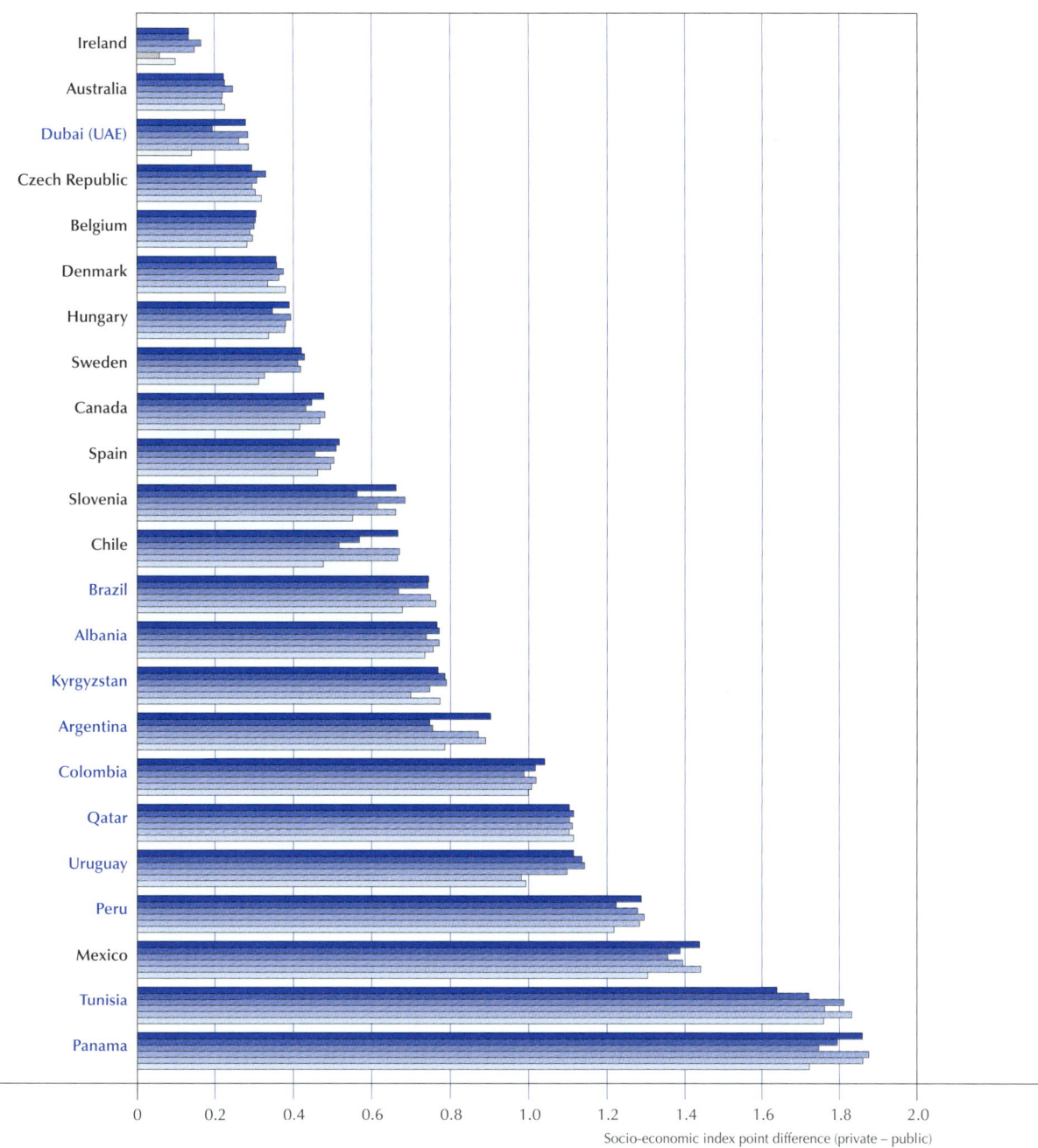

- After accounting for the proportion of public funding for schools
- ...and school admittance based on student's record of academic performance (including placement test) and/or recommendation of feeder schools
- ...and school admittance based on parents' endorsement of the instructional or religious philosophy of the school
- ...and school admittance based on whether the student requires or is interested in a special programme
- ...and school admittance based on family members of current or former students
- ...and school admittance based on these four criteria

Socio-economic index point difference (private – public)

Note: Index-point differences that are statistically significant are marked in a blue tone.
Countries are ranked in ascending order of the index-point difference before accounting for the proportion of public funding for schools.
Source: OECD, *PISA 2009 Database;* Tables B2.7 and B4.3.

PUBLIC AND PRIVATE SCHOOLS: HOW MANAGEMENT AND FUNDING RELATE TO THEIR SOCIO-ECONOMIC PROFILE © OECD 2012

In 15 OECD countries and seven partner countries and economies, the socio-economic background of students who attend schools that admit students based on a family network is more advantaged than that of students who attend schools that do not admit students based on this criterion (Table B4.1). Among these countries and economies, in eight OECD countries and five partner countries and economies, namely Sweden, Australia, Ireland, Canada, Spain, Chile, New Zealand, United States, Dubai (UAE), Qatar, Uruguay, Jordan and Argentina, privately managed schools are more likely than publicly managed schools to admit students based on a family network (Table B4.2).

How are these school-admittance criteria related to socio-economic stratification between publicly and privately managed schools? If advantaged students are more likely to attend privately managed schools because of the schools' admission processes and criteria, there would be no stratification between publicly and privately managed schools after accounting for schools' admissions criteria. Figure 4.1 shows the stratification between publicly and privately managed schools after accounting for various admittance criteria and after accounting for the proportion of public funding for schools. This is done for the 12 OECD countries and 11 partner countries and economies where socio-economic stratification between publicly and privately managed schools is observed after accounting for the proportion of public funding for schools (i.e. countries and economies in the bottom section in Figure 2.5).

As Figure 4.1 shows, after accounting for school admittance based on family network, Ireland shows no stratification. In the partner economy Dubai (UAE), after accounting for all four admittance criteria, no stratification is observed. In most countries, stratification becomes smaller after accounting for school admittance based on the four criteria. However, in all other countries and economies, even after accounting for the various admittance criteria, socio-economic stratification between publicly and privately managed schools is evident.

PARENTAL CHOICE FOR BETTER EDUCATION

Why do more advantaged parents tend to send their children to privately managed schools than disadvantaged parents do? One reason could be that parents believe that these schools offer a better education, an environment more conducive to learning, additional resources, and better policies and practices; and advantaged parents are more informed or aware of the differences in quality across schools. As discussed in Chapter 1, in many countries, privately managed schools tend to enjoy more autonomy, better resources, better school climate and better performance than publicly managed schools (Table B1.2). In many countries, socio-economically advantaged students tend to enrol in schools with more autonomy in curricula and assessments and in resource allocation, more education materials, fewer teacher shortages, better school climate and better performance levels (Table B4.4).

This section focuses on the likelihood that advantaged students will attend privately managed schools, before and after accounting for various aspects of the quality of education in those schools. For example, if privately managed schools attract advantaged students because those schools offer better school resources, the likelihood (i.e. the odds) of attending privately managed schools would decrease if publicly and privately managed schools offered a similar level of school resources. The likelihood is also examined after accounting for the level of public funding for individual schools, in other words, after taking school fees into consideration.

Before accounting for any school characteristics, socio-economically advantaged students are more likely to attend privately managed schools than students from backgrounds that are similar to the national average in 18 OECD countries and 11 partner countries and economies.[2] The likelihood that advantaged students will attend privately managed schools is two times greater or more in Chile and the partner countries Panama, Uruguay, Peru, Argentina and Colombia (Model 1 in Table B4.5). The likelihood is over 1.8 times greater, but less than 2.0 times greater, in Australia and Spain, the partner country Brazil, and the partner economy Dubai (UAE).

In some of these countries and economies, the likelihood decreases after accounting for the proportion of public funding for schools. In other words, when the proportion of public funding for both publicly and privately managed schools is around the national average,[3] the likelihood that advantaged students will attend privately managed schools is not necessarily greater than the likelihood that students from backgrounds similar to the national average will do so. This is true in the United States, New Zealand, Japan, Portugal, Greece, Denmark, the United Kingdom, the partner country Jordan and the partner economy Dubai (UAE) (The first column in Figure 4.2 and Model 1 in Table B4.6). In Chile, Mexico, Spain, Australia, Belgium, Hungary, Sweden, Ireland, Canada, Slovenia and the partner countries Argentina, Peru, Qatar, Panama, Colombia, Uruguay, Albania and Brazil, socio-economically advantaged students are still more likely to attend privately managed schools.

Figure 4.2
The likelihood that socio-economically advantaged students will attend privately managed schools

	How much more likely is it for socio-economically advantaged students to attend privately managed schools compared with students whose socio-economic background is similar to the national average?						
	Before accounting for school characteristics	After accounting for:				
		School's average reading performance	Quality of school's educational materials	School's autonomy in curriculum and assessment	School's disciplinary climate	Average student socio-economic background
	Odds ratio	Odds ratio	Odds ratio	Odds ratio	Odds ratio	Odds ratio
Dubai (UAE)	0.60	0.54	0.66	0.66	0.61	1.00
Indonesia	**0.61**	**0.80**	**0.67**	**0.57**	**0.60**	1.00
Chinese Taipei	**0.61**	0.91	**0.59**	**0.61**	**0.68**	1.00
Netherlands	0.85	0.92	0.85	0.85	0.84	1.00
Switzerland	0.88	1.01	0.87	0.88	0.90	1.00
Luxembourg	**0.89**	**0.92**	**0.83**	**0.87**	**0.89**	1.00
Trinidad and Tobago	**0.92**	1.02	**0.91**	**0.92**	**0.92**	1.00
Hong Kong-China	0.92	0.96	0.92	0.93	0.92	1.00
Thailand	0.94	1.09	0.85	0.94	0.94	1.00
Estonia	0.98	1.00	0.98	0.98	0.98	1.00
Kazakhstan	0.99	0.98	0.98	0.99	0.99	1.00
Italy	1.00	**1.09**	0.99	1.00	1.03	1.00
Germany	1.01	1.06	1.01	1.02	0.96	1.00
Finland	1.01	1.01	1.00	1.01	1.01	1.00
Poland	1.02	1.01	1.02	1.02	1.02	1.00
United States	1.02	1.00	0.99	1.02	0.97	1.00
New Zealand	1.03	1.06	1.02	1.03	1.01	1.00
Japan	1.03	**1.39**	1.02	1.03	1.23	1.00
Jordan	1.03	1.06	1.02	1.03	1.04	1.00
Portugal	1.04	1.01	1.02	1.04	1.05	1.00
Greece	1.05	1.04	1.04	1.02	1.04	1.00
Czech Republic	1.05	1.01	1.04	1.05	0.99	1.00
Tunisia	1.05	1.09	1.06	1.05	1.05	1.00
Slovak Republic	1.06	1.03	1.06	1.05	1.04	1.00
Kyrgyzstan	1.07	1.02	1.06	1.08	1.07	1.00
Denmark	1.07	1.02	1.07	1.08	1.06	1.00
Korea	1.07	0.92	1.07	1.06	0.96	1.00
Slovenia	**1.08**	1.04	**1.08**	**1.08**	1.03	1.00
Israel	1.10	1.02	1.10	1.10	1.09	1.00
Shanghai-China	1.10	1.06	1.11	1.10	1.02	1.00
Canada	**1.13**	**1.08**	**1.13**	**1.13**	**1.12**	1.00
Ireland	1.18	0.99	1.17	1.18	1.14	1.00
Brazil	**1.18**	**1.26**	**1.16**	**1.18**	**1.16**	1.00
Albania	1.19	1.13	1.11	1.21	1.23	1.00
Sweden	**1.20**	**1.12**	**1.18**	**1.21**	**1.15**	1.00
Hungary	**1.21**	**1.23**	**1.20**	1.18	**1.24**	1.00
Belgium	**1.32**	w	**1.32**	**1.32**	**1.36**	1.00
Uruguay	**1.39**	**1.29**	**1.38**	**1.37**	**1.43**	1.00
Australia	**1.40**	**1.25**	**1.39**	**1.41**	**1.36**	1.00
United Kingdom	1.45	1.07	1.48	1.35	1.21	1.00
Spain	**1.50**	**1.27**	**1.45**	**1.51**	**1.53**	1.00
Mexico	**1.50**	**1.42**	**1.29**	**1.45**	**1.50**	1.00
Colombia	**1.68**	**1.43**	**1.49**	**1.63**	**1.68**	1.00
Panama	2.01	1.72	1.77	2.13	1.94	1.00
Qatar	**2.04**	**2.01**	**1.95**	**2.18**	**2.05**	1.00
Peru	**2.08**	**1.57**	**1.76**	**2.13**	**2.08**	1.00
Chile	**2.10**	**1.47**	**1.89**	**2.07**	**2.05**	1.00
Argentina	**2.24**	**1.54**	**2.10**	**2.16**	**2.19**	1.00

Notes: These are the results after accounting for the proportion of public funding for schools. Socio-economically advantaged students are those whose nationally standardised ESCS is equal to 1. Students whose socio-economic background is similar to the national average are those whose nationally standardised ESCS is equal to 0. Values that are statistically significant are indicated in bold.
Countries are ranked in ascending order of the likelihood before accounting for school characteristics.
Source: OECD, *PISA 2009 Database*; Table B4.6.

OTHER SCHOOL CHARACTERISTICS RELATED TO STRATIFICATION

In all of these countries where stratification is observed, even after accounting for the proportion of public funding for schools, the likelihood that advantaged students will attend privately managed schools decreases after accounting for the schools' average performance in reading. In other words, when the performance levels of both public and private are around the national average,[4] this likelihood decreases from 1.2 times to equally as likely in Ireland, 1.1 times to equally as likely in Slovenia, and 1.2 times to 1.1 times as likely in Albania (Model 2 is compared with Model 1 in Table B4.6). Even after accounting for schools' average performance, advantaged students are still more likely to attend privately managed schools; but that likelihood decreases considerably in Chile (from 2.10 times to 1.47 times as likely), Argentina (from 2.24 times to 1.54 times as likely) and Peru (from 2.08 times to 1.57 times as likely).

The quality of schools' educational resources seems to be less related to whether advantaged students attend privately managed schools. Model 3 accounts for the quality of schools' educational resources, which is measured by the *PISA index of school's educational* resources,[5] which, in turn, is derived from the perceptions of school principals about the aspects that may hinder instruction at their schools. Even after accounting for the quality of schools' educational resources, advantaged students are more likely to attend privately managed schools in 10 OECD countries and seven partner countries (Model 3 is compared with Model 1 in Table B4.6). In Albania, the likelihood that advantaged students will attend privately managed schools is about the same as that for students whose socio-economic backgrounds are around the national average, after accounting for the quality of schools' educational resources and the proportion of public funding invested in schools.

A more flexible and innovative curriculum may also attract students to privately managed schools. But PISA results show that schools' autonomy in deciding curricula and assessments, measured by the *index of school responsibility for curriculum and assessment,*[6] seems to have a limited relationship to whether advantaged students choose privately managed schools (Model 4 in Table B4.6). Even after accounting for schools' autonomy in these areas, and after considering the proportion of public funding invested in schools, advantaged students are more likely to attend privately managed schools in nine OECD countries and eight partner countries. Only in Hungary does the likelihood that advantaged students will attend privately managed schools decrease to around the same level as that for students from socio-economic backgrounds that are similar to the national average.

In many countries, schools' disciplinary climate, measured by the *index of disciplinary climate,*[7] which is derived from students' reports, seems to be unrelated to whether advantaged students choose to attend a privately managed school (Model 5 in Table B4.6). After accounting for schools' disciplinary climate and the proportion of public funding for schools, advantaged students are more likely to attend privately managed schools in eight OECD countries and eight partner countries. The exceptions are Slovenia and Ireland, where the likelihood that advantaged students will attend privately managed schools decreases to around the same level as that for students from socio-economic backgrounds that are similar to the national average.

Model 6 shows the likelihood of attending privately managed schools after accounting for the average socio-economic background of a school's student body.[8] After this factor is taken into consideration, there is no greater likelihood that advantaged students will choose privately managed schools; and this is observed in all countries. This suggests that privately managed schools are chosen partly because of the differences in their academic performance levels, policies, practices and learning environments, but mostly because of the composition of their student bodies. This finding suggests that stratification may increase over time unless some structural changes occur,[9] since an advantaged student body in a privately managed school attracts more advantaged students, which increases the socio-economic advantages of the privately managed school even further, so that greater numbers of advantaged students will want to attend.

Reference

OECD (2010), *PISA 2009 Results, Overcoming Social Background: Equity in Learning Opportunities and Outcomes* (Volume II), OECD Publishing.

Notes

1. If privately managed schools exist only in certain areas, and residential areas are related to families' socio-economic background, this also contributes to stratification. But given the limited data available, this issue is beyond the scope of this paper.

2. In Tables 5.5 and 5.6, the *PISA index of economic, social and cultural status* (ESCS) is standardised within each country to have national mean of zero and a standard deviation of one. The likelihood is for socio-economically advantaged students (i.e. students whose nationally standardised ESCS is 1, while the reference group is the group of students whose nationally standardised ESCS is 0) to attend privately managed schools.

3. The level of public funding for a school is centred on the national mean within each country; so the national mean of this variable is zero.

4. A school's average performance is centred on the national mean within each country; so the national mean of this variable is zero.

5. This index is centred on the national mean within each country; so the national average is zero on this index.

6. This index is centred on the national mean within each country; so the national average is zero on this index.

7. This index is centred on the national mean within each country; so the national average is zero on this index.

8. This is measured by the school average of the *PISA index of economic, social and cultural status* (ESCS), which is standardised within each country.

9. Structural changes could be local (e.g. emergence of new housing estates) and regional or national (e.g. shifts in the distribution of the immigrant population; changes to curricula or policy on educational equity).

Conclusion and Policy Implications

This report examines how public and private involvement in managing and funding schools is related to socio-economic stratification between publicly and privately managed schools. In a few countries, the average socio-economic background of students who attend privately managed schools is similar to that of students who attend publicly managed schools; in other countries, there is a great disparity in the socio-economic intake of publicly and privately managed schools.

The analysis presented here also shows that those countries that have low levels of socio-economic stratification also tend to have better overall performance. This means that countries do not have to choose between minimal stratification and high performance; these two goals can be achieved simultaneously.

The results show that while the prevalence of privately managed schools is not related to stratification, the level of public funding to privately managed schools is. Countries with higher levels of public funding for privately managed schools tend to have less stratification, even after accounting for disparities in students' socio-economic backgrounds. This signals that greater public funding is related to less stratification.

However, these cross-country data do not indicate any causal relationships, and results may vary, depending on how public funding is provided to private schools. Providing more public funding for privately managed schools will not necessarily eliminate stratification between publicly and privately managed schools. In fact, in some countries, tuition fees are not the only reason why advantaged students are more likely than disadvantaged students to attend privately managed schools. Other school characteristics, such as a school's student-admittance criteria, academic performance, policies, practices and learning environment are also partly related to stratification. Furthermore, in all countries, privately managed schools seem to attract advantaged students largely because their student bodies are advantaged. These aspects, which are not related to funding, also need to be considered in order to reduce stratification between publicly and privately managed schools. This is particularly true in Australia, Belgium, Canada, Chile, the Czech Republic, Denmark, Hungary, Ireland, Mexico, Slovenia, Spain, Sweden, the partner countries Albania, Argentina, Brazil, Colombia, Kyrgyzstan, Panama, Peru, Qatar, Tunisia, Uruguay, and the partner economy Dubai (UAE).

In addition, the mechanisms used to finance privately managed schools with public funds vary across school systems and they may have different effects on stratification. Vouchers and tuition tax credits are the most direct incentives for parents to choose their child's school. However, systems that use these mechanisms without targeting disadvantaged students tend to have more pronounced socio-economic stratification. This is perhaps because, when incentives are available for all students, advantaged parents tend to exercise their right to choose schools more than disadvantaged parents. In contrast, the degree of stratification found in systems that target vouchers to disadvantaged students is similar to that found in systems that do not use vouchers at all, after accounting for the level of public funding to privately managed schools. These results suggest that specific design options and policies, such as whether financial incentives are targeted to disadvantaged students or not, are critically important for voucher systems.

CONCLUSION AND POLICY IMPLICATIONS

In sum, the results suggest that public funding – and how that funding is provided – play an important role in limiting socio-economic stratification without sacrificing countries' overall performance. However, funding is only one of a range of aspects to be taken into account when trying to reduce stratification between publicly and privately managed schools. Other aspects to consider include schools' ability to select specific students and the disparities in parental choice, including but not limited to the financial capacities, between disadvantaged and advantaged parents.

Country Box A

A brief history of public and private involvement in schools in Ireland

OVERVIEW

In Ireland, the management of schools at second level is complex.[1] Virtually all second-level schools in Ireland were owned and controlled by religious entities until 1931. The establishment of Vocational Educational Committees (VECs) in 1931 (Government of Ireland, 1930) introduced a new and separate tier of vocational schooling. The introduction of free education in 1967 (Department of Education, 1966) occurred alongside rapid growth in participation in second-level education, and these developments, coupled with the fact that students in vocational schools could take the national examination, given after Grade 12, to obtain a Leaving Certificate, blurred the distinction between the education offered in privately owned and managed schools and vocational education. Community and comprehensive schools, which began appearing in the late 1960s, added other kinds of ownership arrangements to the education system, although they represent only a minority of schools at second level (Coolahan, 1981).

In popular discourse, "public education" became synonymous with education provided by schools in the free education scheme, while the term "private education" is frequently used to refer to second-level schools that charge tuition fees. In reality, most funding for second-level schools is provided by the Irish government. The only fully independent private schools are those providing courses on a commercial basis, and less than 1% of second-level students attend these types of schools (*www.education.ie*).

TYPES OF SCHOOLS

The *publicly-aided second-level sector* is composed of *four types* of schools. All provide a common curriculum prescribed by the Department of Education and Skills, enter their students in the same national examinations, are subject to inspection and evaluation by the Department of Education and Skills, and are regulated by the requirements of the Education Act of 1998, the Education (Welfare) Act of 2001, and other relevant legislation. All schools are required to put a management board in place whose functions are prescribed by the Education Act of 1998.

Hence, regardless of the type of school, all schools are managed under similar regulations. If school management is defined on the basis of the composition of schools' governing boards, then almost all second-level schools in Ireland would be classified as being privately managed; however, the authority of schools' governing boards is limited by regulations, as described above, which are in the public domain.

- **Voluntary secondary schools** are privately owned and managed but can receive public funding provided they comply with certain regulations. Originally, most of these schools were founded and owned by religious organisations. More recently, the management of these schools is being transferred to trusts. These trusts (non-trading, not-for-profit limited companies with charitable status) are run by religious orders, but will eventually be transferred to lay people. Secondary schools are largely publicly funded on a per capita basis. During the 2010-11 school year, about 52% of the second-level student population attended. An unusual feature of the Irish education system is that a majority of schools in this sector are single-sex. For example, 41% of all students who participated in PISA 2009 were enrolled in single-sex secondary schools (46% of girls and 37% of boys). In addition, 15% of these schools (or 8% of all schools) charge tuition fees; some 7% of the second-level student population attend these schools. The main difference between secondary schools that charge fees and those that do not is that those that charge fees do not receive government funding for running costs, while those that do not charge fees participate in the free-education scheme and are eligible for a range of subsidies and grants. Whether they charge fees or not, all secondary schools receive public funding for teachers' salaries, though schools that charge fees may employ additional teaching staff using funds from those fees.

COUNTRY BOX A: IRELAND

- **Vocational schools** traditionally emphasised vocational and technical education and are administered by the Vocational Education Committees (VECs), which are statutory bodies set up under the Vocational Education Act of 1930. In the 1960s, they were permitted to offer a five-year cycle of course work to cover national examinations taken at both lower and upper second levels. The boards of management for these schools are sub-committees of the VEC. Membership of the boards includes VEC representatives and parent, teacher and community representatives. Vocational schools and community schools/colleges (see below) are 90% funded by the Department of Education and Skills through a block-grant system. About 33% of the student population attend vocational schools.

- **Comprehensive schools** were introduced in the late 1960s. They incorporated schools that were under Catholic or Protestant ownership, and the various denominations continue to manage the school as patrons or trustees. Composition depends on whether the school is under Catholic or Protestant trusteeship. Just 2% of the student population attend this type of school.

- **Community schools/colleges** are funded individually and directly by the Department of Education and Skills. Their facilities are open to the community and these schools provide adult education in addition to normal programmes of education at the second level. They are managed by boards of management representative of local interests, including VEC nominees, nominees of the religious authorities and teacher and parent representatives. Most board members are nominated by non-public authorities. There are three types of community schools/colleges: those formed as the result of amalgamations, usually with one or more voluntary secondary schools; those established in response to demand for a new school; or long-established vocational schools whose name was changed to include the words "community college". The first two are not under VEC governance, while the third is. About 13% of second-level students in Ireland attend community schools/colleges.

There is a fifth category of second-level school: **private schools/colleges** are privately owned and managed. They receive no public funding and are not obliged to follow a set curriculum. Only six such schools exist, and less than 1% of the total second-level school population attends them. Most students who attend these schools do so to prepare for the Leaving Certificate (national examination at Grade 12) in order to gain the points required to enter a specific post-second-level course. About 13% of students in these schools are aged 15 and 16; 57% are aged 17 and 18; and 30% are over 18 years of age. To date, none of these schools has participated in PISA.

FUNDING AND CLASSIFICATION WITHIN PISA

Within PISA, secondary schools that do not charge fees and one secondary school that does are classified as government-dependent private schools.[2] Seven secondary schools that charge fees are classified as government-independent private schools. All other school types are classified as public schools. Of all the schools in Ireland that participated in PISA 2009, 88% of funding for these schools was from public sources, 9% was from student fees, and the remainder from other sources. When considering only those schools that do not charge fees, these percentages are 93% and 3%, respectively.

TARGETED FUNDING

Ireland does not provide funding directly to parents through vouchers, though allowances, such as those for school books and uniforms, and exemptions from examination fees, are available to low-income families (*www.hse.ie; www.welfare.ie*). Funding targeted to disadvantaged students is administered at the school level through the School Support Programme (SSP), under Delivering Equality of Opportunity in Schools (Department of Education and Science, 2005). The programme was introduced in order to streamline support programmes and ensure that the most disadvantaged schools benefit from a comprehensive range of supports. It covers both primary and second levels, and schools are eligible for the programme on the basis of the profile of their student population. Around 21% of second-level students are in the SSP. While an evaluation of the programme is ongoing (*www.erc.ie*), the SSP is not without its critics. For example, the method by which schools are assigned has been called into question. Some argue that a sliding scale, rather than a binary classification may be more appropriate (e.g. Sofroniou, Archer and Weir, 2004); others contend that the classification system may not go far enough in addressing the needs of disadvantaged students who are not enrolled in schools that participate in the programme (Smyth and McCoy, 2009).

DIFFERENCES IN PERFORMANCE BY MANAGEMENT AND FUNDING

The following Table, PISA 2009 student reading scores and socio-economic background levels, by school type, Ireland, shows the average performance in reading and the average socio-economic background of students as measured by the *PISA index of economic, social and cultural status* (ESCS), by school type. The average reading scores closely mirror average socio-economic index scores. The average reading score of students in vocational schools is 73 points lower than that of students in secondary schools that charge tuition fees; and their average position on the socio-economic index is just over one index point lower. Vocational schools also show the most variation in reading performance, as indicated by the standard deviation. Although similar regulations apply to all of these schools, there are large differences in their student populations.

PISA 2009 student reading scores and socio-economic background levels, by school type, Ireland

Type	Reading Mean score Mean	S.E.	Standard deviation S.D.	S.E.	PISA index of economic, social and cultural status (ESCS) Mean index Mean	S.E.	Standard deviation S.D.	S.E.
Community and comprehensive	486.9	(7.75)	96.6	(4.04)	-0.094	(0.061)	0.859	(0.028)
Secondary – no fees	504.0	(4.04)	89.0	(2.37)	-0.003	(0.036)	0.866	(0.015)
Secondary – fee-paying	538.8	(9.42)	80.9	(4.48)	0.752	(0.164)	0.820	(0.076)
Vocational	465.6	(6.47)	102.9	(5.66)	-0.287	(0.044)	0.832	(0.018)

References

Coolahan, J. (1981), *Irish education: History and structure,* Institute of Public Administration, Dublin.

Department of Education (1966), *Investment in education,* Stationery Office, Dublin.

Department of Education and **Science** (2005), *DEIS (Delivering Equality of Opportunity in Schools): An action plan for educational inclusion,* Department of Education and Science, Dublin.

Government of Ireland (1930), *Vocational Education Act,* Stationery Office, Dublin.

Government of Ireland (1998), *Education Act,* Stationery Office, Dublin.

Government of Ireland (2001), *Education Welfare Act,* Stationery Office, Dublin.

Smyth, E. and **S. McCoy** (2009), *Investing in Education: Combating educational disadvantage,* ESRI/Barnardos, Dublin.

Sofroniou, N., P. Archer and **S. Weir** (2004), "An analysis of the association between socioeconomic context, gender, and achievement", *Irish Journal of Education,* Vol. 35, pp. 58-72.

Notes

1. "Second-level" schools in Ireland are those that offer education to students in grades 7 to 12, while "secondary" refers to voluntary secondary schools, one of the five types of school – in addition to community, comprehensive, vocational and private – at second level.

2. Government-dependent private schools are schools that receive 50% or more of their core funding (i.e. funding that supports the basic educational services of the institution) from government agencies. Government-independent private schools are schools that receive less than 50% of their core funding from government agencies.

Country Box B

A brief history of public and private involvement in schools in Chile

In the 1980s, Chile reformed its education system by introducing profound changes in how schools are administered and funded. The aim of the reforms was to decentralise school management and introduce school choice (Beyer, 2000). The administration of state schools was devolved to municipalities, and special regulations for teachers' contracts were abolished.[1] Chile adopted demand-side subsidies to finance *municipal schools* and *government-funded private schools*.[2] This reform was guided by various principles: school choice improves the welfare of families who send their children to school; the social costs of implementing demand-side subsidies are minimal; privately managed education is inherently more efficient and cost-effective; municipal schools will also become more effective by competing for students; and a competitive education system is more likely to improve social mobility for children from low-income families (Carnoy, 1998; Hsieh and Urquiola, 2006; Cox, 2003; Beyer, 2008).

With this new system, both municipal and government-funded private schools would be administered locally (at the municipal level and by school owners, respectively) and funded on the basis of enrolment. Each school receives a fixed amount per child in attendance (a subsidy); the value of the subsidy depends on the ISCED level, the type of education (general, technical/professional or special), and the school's distance to an urban centre, among other considerations. Originally, the subsidies system did not differentiate among student characteristics. Consequently, municipal and government-funded private schools received the same per-student payment even if the characteristics of their students were different (municipal and government-funded private schools were not allowed to charge tuition until the 1993). Schools were allowed to select students on the basis of their achievement records or interviews with parents. Most municipal schools did not select students although some of them, mainly large urban schools focused on academic excellence, did. The monetary value of the subsidies system was set arbitrarily and no agency was established to review its value over time (Carnoy, 1998; Hsieh and Urquiola, 2006; Cox, 2003; Beyer, 2000 and 2008).

The introduction of these reforms created a dynamic educational market. More than 1 000 new schools were created by 1988, particularly in urban areas and in communities with greater income disparities; enrolments shifted from municipal schools to government-funded private schools. During this period, total enrolment increased, particularly for secondary education. At the beginning of the reform, some 20% of students attended government-funded private schools; at the end of the 1980s, this enrolment had increased to over 30%, and by 2009 more than half the students in Chile attended government-funded private schools (Cox, 2003; Hsieh and Urquiola, 2006; OECD, 2011; OECD, 2010). These reforms also implied a reduction in public expenditure on education because the government relied on the market incentives in place to finance education.

With the return to democracy in the 1990s, the centre-left government assumed a more direct role in public education, including all schools that are subsidised by the government. The government implemented compensatory programmes aimed at improving the performance of the lowest-performing schools (P-900 escuelas or LEM programme). The government also increased spending on public education, intervened through programmes like the *MECE*, and *Proyecto Montegrande*, created a teacher-evaluation system,[3] improved the standardised student-assessment system and published their results, and created incentives to improve teacher performance. The government also reformulated the curriculum and made full-day schooling mandatory (Cox, 2003; OECD, 2011).

In order to attract more funding for education, in 1993 the government introduced shared financing of schools, providing tax incentives for private donations to education.[4] As a result, municipal secondary schools and government-funded private schools were allowed to charge tuition fees to complement the subsidies they received (Cox, 2003). Under this new scheme, the subsidies that schools receive are worth less for schools that charge higher fees, but the reduction in the subsidy is lower than the increase in tuition fees, so total spending on higher-fee schools[5] is higher than that on lower-fee or no-fee schools. Under this scheme, low-income students cannot be charged tuition fees. This policy also includes

COUNTRY BOX B: CHILE

a mandatory scholarship scheme for disadvantaged schools. Although the subsidies are the same for all students, there is some evidence that the financing scheme is regressive after accounting for donations, tuition fees and other extra resources injected into schools by the municipalities or other government subsidies (Romaguera and Gallego, 2010).

In general, evidence on student performance as related to the demand-side subsidies is mixed. While some studies suggest that more competition in the community does not improve the performance of its schools (Hsieh and Urquiola, 2006), other studies do find that greater competition results in better test scores for students in both government-funded private schools and municipal schools (Gallego, 2006; Auguste and Valenzuela, 2004). Other studies suggest that the efficiency of municipal schools did not improve with the introduction of demand-side subsidies, and that government-funded private schools became more cost-efficient because they paid lower wages to teachers (McEwan and Carnoy, 2000). Nevertheless, none of these studies compares the situation before and after the reform in terms of academic performance measured by the same test instruments, since there are no such comparable tests. Thus, it is difficult to see the changes over time in a strict sense. Considering results among different type of schools, cross-sectional studies that correct for selection processes generally find that students attending government-funded private schools show better performance, yet these advantages become small or insignificant with longitudinal data (Lara, Mizala and Repetto, 2009; Anand, Mizala and Repetto, 2009).

Data from the 1980s signal a segregation of students, such that government-dependent private schools were better able to attract better students. Evidence suggests that schools were, in fact, sensitive to the market incentives of demand-side subsidies, but private schools responded by enhancing their ability to attract better students instead of improving productivity. Government-dependent private schools were allowed to reject students, and parents sought not necessarily the most productive schools, but those with the most advantaged student populations (Carnoy, 1998; Gauri, 1998; Raudenbush and Willms, 1995). The introduction of this shared-funding system in 1993 did not favour socio-economic equity; but the system does not seem to have exacerbated socio-economic segregation between the municipal and private sectors, either. There is no evidence, however, as to the effects of segregation within government-funded private schools (Beyer, 2008). Despite the interventions on the part of the Ministry of Education and the introduction of the shared-funding system, the essential features of the demand-side subsidies introduced in the 1980s remained unchanged for more than a quarter century (Hsieh and Urquiola, 2006; Beyer, 2008).

While there are mixed views on whether the introduction of demand-side subsidies and school choice have improved the performance of Chilean schools, there seems to be more consistent understanding regarding their impact on equity: the introduction of demand-side subsidies and school choice had no clear positive effects on equity; if anything, the reforms of the 1980s may have contributed to socio-economic segregation in the school system.

In fact, the first major modification to the demand-side subsidies was prompted by the observation that performance of Chilean students was related to their socio-economic background, among other things. The experience of providing school choice and voucher systems in other countries also attracted the attention of Chilean policy makers. The examples of the Netherlands and student-weighted funds in the United States showed that targeting resources, through vouchers and school choice, towards students with greater academic need may promote greater equity (Romaguera and Gallegos, 2010). In 2006, the *Ley General de Educación* (LGE) law eliminated selection processes based on academic achievement in the early grades of primary school, and delayed the possibility of expelling struggling students until after these students had been given the opportunity to repeat a grade.

In 2008, the government passed the *Subvención Escolar Preferencial* (SEP) law. The SEP involves new subsidies for socio-economically disadvantaged students together with greater school accountability and government oversight of schools. The value of the subsidies for disadvantaged students was increased to mitigate inequalities in learning opportunities. The accountability measures associated with the SEP impose greater conditions based on student performance in the past and greater technical and pedagogical support to struggling schools, with the aim of ensuring high-quality education for all students (Romaguera and Gallegos, 2010; BCN, 2008).

The SEP is voluntary: schools eligible to receive the extra funds must sign an Agreement of Equal Opportunities and Academic Excellence (*Convenio de Igualdad de Oportunidades y Excelencia Educativa*). This agreement allows schools to receive over 50% more funds for each "priority student" (e.g. socio-economically disadvantaged student) they enrol, and another subsidy if more than 15% of a school's total enrolment is composed by "priority students". Those resources could not be used freely: the original law established the ways in which they could be spent. In exchange, schools are obliged to formulate a plan for educational improvement, set and accomplish these goals, provide a detailed account of the use of resources, and charge no tuition fees for "priority students". The plan is developed by each school; however, those schools classified as among the poorest performers were obliged to receive technical support from the Ministry and/or some specialised and authorised private agency. Schools that fail to improve after this assistance may lose their license and access to any subsidies from the government (Romaguera and Gallegos, 2010; Fernandez, 2010; BCN, 2008). In 2011, the subsidies for most disadvantaged students were further increased and more autonomy in the use of those resources, for example, to hire teachers, was granted to the schools.

The SEP was enacted in 2008 and resulted in important changes in the Chilean school system. Although voluntary, of the around 9 000 eligible schools, some 82% took part in the agreement. Some 99% of municipal schools and 60% of government-funded private schools are actively participating and began receiving funds in 2011. This high coverage dramatically changed the relationship between schools and the Ministry of Education. Moreover, the system lost its regressive funding structure. On average, the schools that did not adhere to the SEP enrol a lower proportion of disadvantaged students and seem to have undergone a cost-benefit analysis, weighing the increased accountability and oversight required against the receipt of additional funds (Romaguera and Gallegos, 2010; CEPPE, 2010).

Although it is too soon to evaluate the programme in isolation from other aspects and its effect on performance and equity, preliminary studies suggest the SEP produced substantive changes in the schools involved.[6] Schools have welcomed the clear pedagogical goals and the provision of methodological and diagnostic tools tailored to them. Moreover, schools have signalled improvements in the learning environment thanks to higher expectations for better education. However, schools have struggled with the restriction on the use of resources and the new systems in place to report how resources are spent. Municipal and government-funded private schools account for 60% and 71%, respectively, of the resources received (MINEDUC, 2011). Better-performing schools are more likely to use the resources in technical assistance and training, while poor-performing schools are more likely to spend the extra monies on equipment for pedagogical support (CEPPE, 2010; Fernández, 2010).

In addition, the achievement goals may be too ambitious. In the past, only around 10% of schools made achievement progress similar to that proposed in the agreement, and it is likely that many schools fail to achieve these standards at the end of the first cycle of the programme (CEPPE, 2010). Initial trends and estimates of the impact of the law on student performance and equity will be available in mid-2012 when the results from the 2011 standardised assessments become publicly available.

More recently, the regulatory incentives of the SEP have been complemented by other laws that create agencies to supervise all schools and ensure the quality of the education that they provide. These laws have increased the value of the subsidy offered to disadvantaged students. A recent law promulgated in 2011 created the Agency for the Quality of Education, which is a government body that will be responsible for evaluating the educational system in order to improve the quality and equity of education opportunities in each level of education. Among other functions, the Agency will be responsible for assessing student learning and classifying schools according to different quality standards. A second new body, the Education Superintendence, is charged with monitoring compliance with the laws, regulations and instructions issued by the Superintendence. It will also monitor how subsidised schools use the resources allocated to them. Privately funded schools will be supervised by the Superintendence only if complaints have been lodged against them. The Ministry of Education may be required to appoint a temporary administrator to manage subsidised schools if they constantly show poor student outcomes. Both bodies will be independent of the Ministry and will be headed by professionals elected under the system of High Direction Service.

References

Anand, P., A. Mizala, and **A. Repetto** (2009), "Using School Scholarships to Estimate the Effect of Government Subsidized Private Education on Academic Achievement in Chile", *Documentos de Trabajo,* No. 230, Centro de Economía Aplicada, Universidad de Chile, Santiago.

Auguste, S., and **J.P. Valenzuela** (2004), *Do Students Benefit from School Competition? Evidence from Chile*, University of Michigan, Ann Arbor.

BCN (2008), Historia de la Ley No. 20.248, Establece Ley de Subvención Escolar Preferencial, Biblioteca del Congreso Nacional, Valparaíso.

Beyer, H. (2000), "Entre la Autonomía y la Intervención: Las Reformas de la Educación en Chile", in B. Felipe Larraín and M. Rodrigo Vergara (eds.), *La Transformación Económica de Chile*, Chapter 15.

Beyer, H. (2008), "Más Financiamiento en Educación y un Mejor Diseño de la Subvención", in C. Bellei, D. Contreras and J.P. Valenzuela (eds.), *La Agenda Pendiente en Educación*, Ocho Libros Editores, Santiago, pp. 183-204.

Carnoy, M. (1998), "National voucher plans in Chile and Sweden: Did privatization reforms make for better education?", *Comparative Education Review,* Vol. 42, No. 3, pp. 309-337.

CEPPE (2010), Planes de Mejoramiento SEP: Sistematización, Análisis y Aprendizajes de Política, Centro de Estudios de Políticas y Prácticas en Educación, Santiago.

Cox, C. (2003), "Las Políticas Educacionales de Chile en las Últimas Dos Décadas del Siglo XX" in C. Cox (ed.), *Políticas Educacionales en el Cambio de Siglo*, Editorial Universitaria, Santiago, pp. 19-114.

Elacqua, G. (2009), "The impact of school choice and public policy on segregation: Evidence from Chile", Centro de Politicas Comparadas de Educación, Universidad Diego Portales, Santiago, Chile

Fernandez, M. (2010), *The Preferential Subvention Law in Chile: Differences in the Use of Resources*, M.A. Thesis, Teachers College, University of Columbia, New York, New York.

Gallego, F. (2006), *Voucher-School Competition, Incentives, and Outcomes: Evidence from Chile,* Mimeo, Pontificia Universidad Católica de Chile, Santiago.

Gauri, V. (1998), *School Choice in Chile: Two Decades of Educational Reform,* University of Pittsburgh Press, Pittsburgh, Pennsylvania.

Hsieh, C.T. and **M. Urquiola** (2006), "The effects of generalized school choice on achievement and stratification: Evidence from Chile's voucher program", *Journal of Public Economics,* Vol. 90, No. 8-9, pp. 1477-1503.

Lara, B., A. Mizala, and **A. Repetto** (2009), "The Effectiveness of Private Voucher Education: Evidence from Structural School Switches", *Documentos de Trabajo,* No. 263, Centro de Economía Aplicada, Universidad de Chile, Santiago.

McEwan, P.J. and **M. Carnoy** (2000), "The effectiveness and efficiency of private schools in Chile's voucher system", *Educational Evaluation and Policy Analysis,* Vol. 22, No. 3, pp. 213-239.

OECD (2010), *PISA 2009 Results: What Makes a School Successful? Resources, Policies and Practices* (Volume IV), OECD Publishing.

OECD (2011), *Education at a Glance 2011: OECD Indicators*, OECD Publishing.

Raudenbush, S. and **J.D. Willms** (1995), "The Estimation of School Effects", *Journal of Educational and Behavioral Statistics,* Vol. 20, No. 4, pp. 307-335.

Romaguera, P. and **S. Gallegos** (2010), "Financiando la Educación de Grupos Vulnerables: La Subvención Escolar Preferencial" in O. Larrañaga and D. Contreras (eds.), *Las Nuevas Políticas de Protección Social en Chile*, PNUD, Santiago, pp. 189-236.

Notes

1. Teachers are no longer hired by the Ministry; they are hired by each municipality under the regulations of private contracts.

2. Municipal schools are those that are administered by municipalities, are part of the public system and are funded with state resources. Government-funded private schools are defined as privately managed schools mainly funded by government subsidies per student. In fact, according to official 2010 data from Chilean Ministry of Education, 40.4% of students are enrolled in municipal schools, 50.8% are in privately managed schools that receive some public funding, and 7.4% are in privately managed schools that do not receive any public funding (1.5% of students attend schools administered by private corporations and receive direct funding from the Ministry of Education).

3. This evaluation was considered in the Estatuto Docente and it took the government almost 15 years to implement it. In 1991, "Estatuto Docente" was introduced. This is a policy that aimed to regulate teachers' working conditions in the municipal schools. This policy affected teacher mobility and financing. In fact, after this policy was introduced, teachers started negotiating their salaries with the government. As a result, 80% to 90% of resources for education are spent on teachers' salaries; and less than 1% of those resources were allocated based on teachers' performance.

4. This shared financing scheme also permits the government to use certain amount of budget to focus on the low-income students.

5. The maximum amount of such fees is set and schools cannot charge more than this maximum amount.

6. According to the study by Elacqua (2009), preliminary evidence suggests that weighted subsidisations introduced in 2008 may have been linked to the decrease in segregation.

Country Box C

A brief history of public and private involvement in schools in the Netherlands

The Netherlands has by far the largest number of students enrolled in privately managed schools among all OECD countries. PISA 2009 data show that only one-third of students attend publicly managed schools, while around two-thirds of 15-year-olds attend privately managed schools. The majority of these students attend privately managed schools that receive over 90% or more of their core funding from government agencies (OECD, 2010a). In fact, there are few privately managed schools that have chosen not to receive public funding, accounting for less than 1% of primary and secondary schools (Waslander, 2010).

However, it was not until public funding was provided to privately managed schools on an equal per-student basis that privately managed schools flourished. The Constitution of 1917 ended a longstanding school dispute by enshrining the right to found schools, freedom of choice, and equal funding and treatment of publicly and privately managed schools. Together, these rights guide and limit the scope and type of policies that can be implemented. Public funding of privately managed schools helped to realise the right to choose a school. In 1917, most students attended publicly managed schools; a decade later, the trend had already reversed (Patrinos, 2010). Government-dependent private schools could only apply admissions criteria based on ideology, religion or pedagogical identity. Segregation along religious lines was not a concern at the time and little attention was paid to socio-economic stratification (Karsten, et al., 2006).

The move towards secularisation after World War II meant that admissions criteria based on religion were applied far less frequently; but socio-economic stratification among schools began to take root (Ladd and Fiske, 2011). In addition, the large migration inflows during the second half of the 20th century led to growing concern about ethnic segregation of schools, particularly from the 1980s (Karsten, et al., 2006). Populations with multiple disadvantages, such as their ethnicity and socio-economic status, were concentrated in certain geographic areas; and schools in those areas struggled to educate their students. In the 1970s, experiments that involved weighted student funding and providing additional resources to schools in disadvantaged areas were introduced in Amsterdam, Rotterdam and Utrecht (Driessen and Dekker, 1997). In 1985, the Dutch Parliament established the basis of the current funding system with the law on Educational Priority Policy (EPP). The EPP's two-pronged approach, school- and area-based, was the result of a political compromise between conservatives, who were in favour of targeting schools, and progressives, who were more inclined to area-based approaches.

The school-based component represents the largest share of the EPP budget. It introduces additional weights per student in the formula to fund schools, reflecting socio-economic disadvantage. The formula follows the student to the chosen school, creating a financial incentive for schools to attract and retain students. In particular, Dutch working-class students were assigned a factor of 1.25 and ethnic minority students 1.9. The additional weights were targeted to primary schools serving large proportions – more than 9% – of disadvantaged students; additional funding was provided depending on the percentage of students above this threshold. Funding arrangements were comparable for secondary schools, but schools were only eligible for additional funding if at least 30% of their students came from deprived neighbourhoods. The area-based component involved encouraging networks of primary and secondary schools, support centres, cultural organisations and welfare agencies to work together, at the local or regional level, to combat disadvantages.

As countries began introducing more market mechanisms into education in the 1980s and 1990s, the Dutch gave even greater autonomy to schools. Schools in the Netherlands have nearly the greatest level of autonomy among all OECD countries (OECD, 2010a). Schools have full responsibility for organising teaching personnel and materials; for resource allocation; and for the construction and use of facilities. The additional funds provided to disadvantaged schools were initially earmarked for certain types of expenditures, but since there was no requirement that funds be spent on disadvantaged students, these were mostly used to reduce class sizes (Driessen and Dekkers, 1997). Since 2006, additional funding has been provided in the form of a lump-sum grant covering total costs instead of separate budget allocations for infrastructure, personnel and running costs. Although this provides more discretion to boards for resource allocation, some boards have expressed concerns that additional funding targeted to high-weight schools have been transferred to low-weight schools. At the same time, the management of schools shifted from municipal authorities to independent boards, and the relationship between the two was re-defined. Today, three out of four publicly managed schools are operated by a foundation, and although municipal governments continue to play an important role in enhancing horizontal co-operation at the local level, area-based funding represents only around 10% of schools' budgets.

Weighted student funding was adopted by a socialist government and has been sustained through different centre-right and neo-liberal governments (Ladd and Fiske, 2011), but the specific weights have been subject to political debate and have been modified over time. In 2006, the weights were changed to reflect a modification in attitudes towards immigrants and rural support for the centre-right government. In particular, the indicator on ethnicity was withdrawn and the 1.25 weight was replaced with a 1.4 weight for students whose parents have low levels of education and 2.2 for children whose parents have very low levels of education. In addition, the threshold proportion of disadvantage students above which schools are eligible for additional funding was reduced from 9% to 6%.

There are growing concerns of stratification between schools along ethnic lines (Karsten, et al., 2006; Waslander, 2010; Ladd, Fiske and Ruijs, 2011). In primary education, socio-economic stratification is driven by parental choice and residential segregation; the situation is particularly worrying in the four major Dutch cities. Certain government-dependent private schools request contributions from parents and adopt specific teaching pedagogies to attract students from better-off backgrounds (Karsten, et al., 2006). However, there are more schools with higher concentrations of students with an immigrant background than there are schools with an over-representation of well-off native students (Karsten, et al., 2006). Indeed, most privately managed school enrolments involve religious schools, but student composition is no longer solely related to a specific religion, with the exception of Islamic and Hindu schools. Recently, Islamic schools have been at the centre of the debate since they cater almost exclusively to students of the same ethnic group (Denessen, Driessen and Sleegers, 2005; Waslander, 2010). In addition to choice and residence, in secondary education, early tracking exacerbates stratification because differences in intakes are based on prior academic achievement, which is correlated with socio-economic background. In the past decade, local governments, particularly in the larger cities, have been taking policy initiatives to create more socio-economically and ethnically diverse school populations. Current efforts to reduce stratification include strengthening the co-operation with stakeholders to establish fixed enrolment dates, promoting voluntary parental initiatives, experimenting with central subscription systems, and introducing double waiting lists (Ladd, Fiske and Ruijs, 2009).

Growing concerns about segregation have increased the role that central government plays in setting education policy (structure and attainment targets), providing funding to schools, and accountability (examinations and publicly reported inspections). The *Good Education, Good Governance* law, which was adopted in late 2009, has introduced more stringent requirements for quality assurance in publicly funded schools. If the Inspectorate judges that quality is below standards, the school is considered to be performing poorly, is placed under intensified supervision, and is required to draft and execute an improvement plan. The Ministry of Education has ultimate control over persistently poor-performing schools. Funding has rarely been denied as a means to force schools to close down. But this is changing, and some schools have been closed down over the past of couple of years.

Weighted student funding has failed to help all disadvantaged students achieve at the same level as other students, but it has provided disadvantaged schools with significantly more resources (Ladd and Fiske, 2011). Primary schools with a high proportion of weighted students have, on average, about 58% more teachers per student and also significantly more support staff (Ladd and Fiske, 2011). The most disadvantaged students in the Netherlands perform well above their peers in other countries in international assessments, and the differences between students within the Netherlands are small compared to those in other OECD countries, even after taking socio-economic background into account (OECD, 2010b). The Netherlands has high levels of school competition, autonomy and accountability, institutional features that recent research has found to be associated with high performance (Woessmann, 2007).

References

Denessen, E., G. Driessen and **P. Sleegers** (2005), "Segregation by choice? A study of group-specific reasons for school choice", *Journal of Education Policy*, Vol. 20, No. 3, pp. 347-368.

Driessen, G., and **H. Dekkers** (1997), "Educational Opportunities in the Netherlands: Policy, Students' Performance and Issues", *International Review of Education*, Vol. 43, No. 4, pp. 299-315.

Karsten, S., et al. (2006), "Choosing integration or segregation? The extent and effects of ethnic segregation in Dutch cities", *Journal of Education and Urban Society*, Vol. 38, No. 2, pp. 228-247.

Ladd, H., and **E. Fiske** (2011), "Weighted student funding in the Netherlands: A model for the U.S.?" *Journal of Policy Analysis and Management*, Vol. 30, No. 3, pp. 470-498.

Ladd, H., E. Fiske and **N. Ruijs** (2009), "Parental choice in the Netherlands: Growing concerns about segregation", paper prepared for the conference on School Choice and School Improvement: Research in State, District and Community Contexts, Vanderbilt University, 25-27 October, 2009.

OECD (2010a), *PISA 2009 Results: What Makes a School Successful? Resources, Policies and Practices* (Volume IV), OECD Publishing.

OECD (2010b), *PISA 2009 Results: Overcoming Social Background: Equity in Learning Opportunities and Outcomes* (Volume II), OECD Publishing.

Patrinos, H. (2010), "Private education provision and public finance: the Netherlands", The World Bank, Policy Research Working Paper Series, No. 5185.

Waslander, S. (2010), "Government, School Autonomy, and Legitimacy: Why the Dutch Government is Adopting an Unprecedent Level of Interference with Independent Schools", *Journal of School Choice*, Vol. 4, No. 4, pp. 398-417.

Woessmann, L. (2007), "International Evidence on School Competition, Autonomy and Accountability: A Review", *Peabody Journal of Education*, Vol. 82, No. 2-3, pp 473-497.

Annex A

TECHNICAL BACKGROUND
All tables in Annex A are available on line at *http://dx.doi.org/10.1787/9789264175006-en*

Annex A1: Construction of reading scales and indices from the student, school and parent context questionnaires

Annex A2: Technical notes on preliminary multilevel regression analysis for performance

Annex A3: Standard errors, significance tests and subgroup comparisons

ANNEX A1
CONSTRUCTION OF READING SCALES AND INDICES FROM THE STUDENT, SCHOOL AND PARENT CONTEXT QUESTIONNAIRES

How the PISA 2009 reading assessments were designed, analysed and scaled

The development of the PISA 2009 reading tasks was co-ordinated by an international consortium of educational research institutions contracted by the OECD, under the guidance of a group of reading experts from participating countries. Participating countries contributed stimulus material and questions, which were reviewed, tried out and refined iteratively over the three years leading up to the administration of the assessment in 2009. The development process involved provisions for several rounds of commentary from participating countries, as well as small-scale piloting and a formal field trial in which samples of 15-year-olds from all participating countries took part. The reading expert group recommended the final selection of tasks, which included material submitted by 21 of the participating countries. The selection was made with regard to both their technical quality, assessed on the basis of their performance in the field trial, and their cultural appropriateness and interest level for 15-year-olds, as judged by the participating countries. Another essential criterion for selecting the set of material as a whole was its fit to the framework described in *Volume 1, What Students Know and Can Do* (OECD, 2010), to maintain the balance across various categories of text, aspect and situation. Finally, it was carefully ensured that the set of questions covered a range of difficulty, allowing good measurement and description of the reading literacy of all 15-year-old students, from the least proficient to the highly able.

More than 130 print reading questions were used in PISA 2009, but each student in the sample only saw a fraction of the total pool because different sets of questions were given to different students. The reading questions selected for inclusion in PISA 2009 were organised into half-hour clusters. These, along with clusters of mathematics and science questions, were assembled into booklets containing four clusters each. Each participating student was then given a two-hour assessment. As reading was the focus of the PISA 2009 assessment, every booklet included at least one cluster of reading material. The clusters were rotated so that each cluster appeared in each of the four possible positions in the booklets, and each pair of clusters appeared in at least one of the 13 booklets that were used.

This design, similar to those used in previous PISA assessments, makes it possible to construct a single scale of reading proficiency, in which each question is associated with a particular point on the scale that indicates its difficulty, whereby each student's performance is associated with a particular point on the same scale that indicates his or her estimated proficiency. A description of the modelling technique used to construct this scale can be found in the *PISA 2009 Technical Report* (OECD, 2012).

The relative difficulty of tasks in a test is estimated by considering the proportion of test takers who answer each question correctly. The relative proficiency of students taking a particular test can be estimated by considering the proportion of test questions they answer correctly. A single continuous scale shows the relationship between the difficulty of questions and the proficiency of students. By constructing a scale that shows the difficulty of each question, it is possible to locate the level of reading literacy that the question represents. By showing the proficiency of each student on the same scale, it is possible to describe the level of reading literacy that the student possesses.

The location of student proficiency on this scale is set in relation to the particular group of questions used in the assessment. However, just as the sample of students taking PISA in 2009 is drawn to represent all the 15-year-olds in the participating countries, so the individual questions used in the assessment are designed to represent the definition of reading literacy adequately. Estimates of student proficiency reflect the kinds of tasks they would be expected to perform successfully. This means that students are likely to be able to complete questions successfully at or below the difficulty level associated with their own position on the scale (but they may not always do so). Conversely, they are unlikely to be able to successfully complete questions above the difficulty level associated with their position on the scale (but they may sometimes do so).

The further a student's proficiency is located above a given question, the more likely he or she is to successfully complete the question (and other questions of similar difficulty); the further the student's proficiency is located below a given question, the lower the probability that the student will be able to successfully complete the question, and other questions of similar difficulty.

How reading proficiency levels are defined in PISA 2009

PISA 2009 provides an overall reading literacy scale for the reading texts, drawing on all the questions in the reading assessment, as well as scales for three aspects and two text formats. The metric for the overall reading scale is based on a mean for OECD countries set at 500 in PISA 2000, with a standard deviation of 100. To help interpret what students' scores mean in substantive terms, the scale is divided into levels, based on a set of statistical principles, and then descriptions are generated, based on the tasks that are located within each level, to describe the kinds of skills and knowledge needed to successfully complete those tasks.

For PISA 2009, the range of difficulty of tasks allows for the description of seven levels of reading proficiency: Level 1b is the lowest described level, then Level 1a, Level 2, Level 3 and so on up to Level 6.

Students with a proficiency within the range of Level 1b are likely to be able to successfully complete Level 1b tasks (and others like them), but are unlikely to be able to complete tasks at higher levels. Level 6 reflects tasks that present the greatest challenge in terms of reading skills and knowledge. Students with scores in this range are likely to be able to complete reading tasks located at that level successfully, as well as all the other reading tasks in PISA.

PISA applies a standard methodology for constructing proficiency scales. Based on a student's performance on the tasks in the test, his or her score is generated and located in a specific part of the scale, thus allowing the score to be associated with a defined proficiency level. The level at which the student's score is located is the highest level for which he or she would be expected to answer correctly, most of a random selection of questions within the same level. Thus, for example, in an assessment composed of tasks spread uniformly across Level 3, students with a score located within Level 3 would be expected to complete at least 50% of the tasks successfully. Because a level covers a range of difficulty and proficiency, success rates across the band vary. Students near the bottom of the level would be likely to succeed on just over 50% of the tasks spread uniformly across the level, while students at the top of the level would be likely to succeed on well over 70% of the same tasks.

Figure I.2.12 in Volume I (OECD, 2010) provides details of the nature of reading skills, knowledge and understanding required at each level of the reading scale.

Explanation of indices

This section explains the indices derived from the student and school context questionnaires used in PISA 2009.

Several PISA measures reflect indices that summarise responses from students, their parents or school representatives (typically principals) to a series of related questions. The questions were selected from a larger pool of questions on the basis of theoretical considerations and previous research. Structural equation modelling was used to confirm the theoretically expected behaviour of the indices and to validate their comparability across countries. For this purpose, a model was estimated separately for each country and collectively for all OECD countries.

For a detailed description of other PISA indices and details on the methods, see *PISA 2009 Technical Report* (OECD, 2012).

There are two types of indices: simple indices and scale indices.

Simple indices are the variables that are constructed through the arithmetic transformation or recoding of one or more items, in exactly the same way across assessments. Here, item responses are used to calculate meaningful variables, such as the recoding of the four-digit ISCO-88 codes into "Highest parents' socio-economic index (HISEI)" or, teacher-student ratio based on information from the school questionnaire.

Scale indices are the variables constructed through the scaling of multiple items. Unless otherwise indicated, the index was scaled using a weighted maximum likelihood estimate (WLE), using a one-parameter item response model (a partial credit model was used in the case of items with more than two categories).

The scaling was done in three stages:

- The item parameters were estimated from equal-sized subsamples of students from each OECD country.
- The estimates were computed for all students and all schools by anchoring the item parameters obtained in the preceding step.
- The indices were then standardised so that the mean of the index value for the OECD student population was zero and the standard deviation was one (countries being given equal weight in the standardisation process).

Sequential codes were assigned to the different response categories of the questions in the sequence in which the latter appeared in the student, school or parent questionnaires. Where indicated in this section, these codes were inverted for the purpose of constructing indices or scales. It is important to note that negative values for an index do not necessarily imply that students responded negatively to the underlying questions. A negative value merely indicates that the respondents answered less positively than all respondents did on average across OECD countries. Likewise, a positive value on an index indicates that the respondents answered more favourably, or more positively, than respondents did, on average, in OECD countries. Terms enclosed in brackets < > in the following descriptions were replaced in the national versions of the student, school and parent questionnaires by the appropriate national equivalent. For example, the term <qualification at ISCED level 5A> was translated in the United States into "Bachelor's degree, post-graduate certificate program, Master's degree program or first professional degree program". Similarly the term <classes in the language of assessment> in Luxembourg was translated into "German classes" or "French classes" depending on whether students received the German or French version of the assessment instruments.

In addition to simple and scaled indices described in this annex, there are a number of variables from the questionnaires that correspond to single items not used to construct indices. These non-recoded variables have prefix of "ST" for the questionnaire items in the student questionnaire, "SC" for the items in the school questionnaire, and "PA" for the items in the parent questionnaire. All the context questionnaires as well as the PISA international database, including all variables, are available through *www.pisa.oecd.org*.

ANNEX A1: CONSTRUCTION OF READING SCALES AND INDICES FROM THE STUDENT, SCHOOL AND PARENT CONTEXT QUESTIONNAIRES

Student-level simple indices

Study programme

In PISA 2009, study programmes available to 15-year-old students in each country were collected both through the student tracking form and the student questionnaire (ST02). All study programmes were classified using ISCED (OECD, 1999). In the PISA international database, all national programmes are indicated in a variable (PROGN) where the first three digits are the ISO code for a country, the fourth digit the sub-national category and the last two digits the nationally specific programme code.

The following internationally comparable indices were derived from the data on study programmes:

- Programme level (ISCEDL) indicates whether students are (1) primary education level (ISCED 1); (2) lower-secondary education level; or (3) upper secondary education level.
- Programme designation (ISCEDD) indicates the designation of the study programme: (1) = "A" (general programmes designed to give access to the next programme level); (2) = "B" (programmes designed to give access to vocational studies at the next programme level); (3) = "C" (programmes designed to give direct access to the labour market); or (4) = "M" (modular programmes that combine any or all of these characteristics).
- Programme orientation (ISCEDO) indicates whether the programme's curricular content is (1) general; (2) pre-vocational; (3) vocational; or (4) modular programmes that combine any or all of these characteristics.

Occupational status of parents

Occupational data for both a student's father and a student's mother were obtained by asking open-ended questions in the student questionnaire (ST9a, ST9b, ST12, ST13a, ST13b and ST16). The responses were coded to four-digit ISCO codes (ILO, 1990) and then mapped to Ganzeboom et al.'s SEI index (1992). Higher scores of SEI indicate higher levels of occupational status. The following three indices are obtained:

- Mother's occupational status (BMMJ).
- Father's occupational status (BFMJ).
- The highest occupational level of parents (HISEI) corresponds to the higher SEI score of either parent or to the only available parent's SEI score.

Educational level of parents

The educational level of parents is classified using ISCED (OECD, 1999) based on students' responses in the student questionnaire (ST10, ST11, ST14 and ST15). Please note that the question format for school education in PISA 2009 differs from the one used in PISA 2000, 2003 and 2006 but the method used to compute parental education is the same.

As in PISA 2000, 2003 and 2006, indices were constructed by selecting the highest level for each parent and then assigning them to the following categories: (0) None, (1) ISCED 1 (primary education), (2) ISCED 2 (lower secondary), (3) ISCED Level 3B or 3C (vocational/pre-vocational upper secondary), (4) ISCED 3A (upper secondary) and/or ISCED 4 (non-tertiary post-secondary), (5) ISCED 5B (vocational tertiary), (6) ISCED 5A, 6 (theoretically oriented tertiary and post-graduate). The following three indices with these categories are developed:

- Mother's educational level (MISCED).
- Father's educational level (FISCED).
- Highest educational level of parents (HISCED) corresponds to the higher ISCED level of either parent.

Highest educational level of parents was also converted into the number of years of schooling (PARED). For the conversion of level of education into years of schooling, see Table A1.1.

Immigration and language background

Information on the country of birth of students and their parents (ST17) is collected in a similar manner as in PISA 2000, PISA 2003 and PISA 2006 by using nationally specific ISO coded variables. The ISO codes of the country of birth for students and their parents are available in the PISA international database (COBN_S, COBN_M, and COBN_F).

The index on immigrant background (IMMIG) has the following categories: (1) native students (those students born in the country of assessment, or those with at least one parent born in that country; students who were born abroad with at least one parent born in the country of assessment are also classified as 'native' students), (2) second-generation students (those born in the country of assessment but whose parents were born in another country) and (3) first-generation students (those born outside the country of assessment and whose parents were also born in another country). Students with missing responses for either the student or for both parents, or for all three questions have been given missing values for this variable.

Table A1.1 **Levels of parental education converted into years of schooling**

		Did not go to school	Completed ISCED Level 1 (primary education)	Completed ISCED Level 2 (lower secondary education)	Completed ISCED Levels 3B or 3C (upper secondary education providing direct access to the labor market or to ISCED 5B programmes)	Completed ISCED Level 3A (upper secondary education providing access to ISCED 5A and 5B programmes) and/or ISCED Level 4 (non-tertiary post-secondary)	Completed ISCED Level 5A (university level tertiary education) or ISCED Level 6 (advanced research programmes)	Completed ISCED Level 5B (non-university tertiary education)
OECD	Australia	0.0	6.0	10.0	11.0	12.0	15.0	14.0
	Austria	0.0	4.0	9.0	12.0	12.5	17.0	15.0
	Belgium	0.0	6.0	9.0	12.0	12.0	17.0	14.5
	Canada	0.0	6.0	9.0	12.0	12.0	17.0	15.0
	Chile	0.0	6.0	8.0	12.0	12.0	17.0	16.0
	Czech Republic	0.0	5.0	9.0	11.0	13.0	16.0	16.0
	Denmark	0.0	6.0	9.0	12.0	12.0	17.0	15.0
	Finland	0.0	6.0	9.0	12.0	12.0	16.5	14.5
	France	0.0	5.0	9.0	12.0	12.0	15.0	14.0
	Germany	0.0	4.0	10	13.0	13.0	18.0	15.0
	Greece	0.0	6.0	9.0	11.5	12.0	17.0	15.0
	Hungary	0.0	4.0	8.0	10.5	12.0	16.5	13.5
	Iceland	0.0	7.0	10.0	13.0	14.0	18.0	16.0
	Ireland	0.0	6.0	9.0	12.0	12.0	16.0	14.0
	Italy	0.0	5.0	8.0	12.0	13.0	17.0	16.0
	Japan	0.0	6.0	9.0	12.0	12.0	16.0	14.0
	Korea	0.0	6.0	9.0	12.0	12.0	16.0	14.0
	Luxembourg	0.0	6.0	9.0	12.0	13.0	17.0	16.0
	Mexico	0.0	6.0	9.0	12.0	12.0	16.0	14.0
	Netherlands	0.0	6.0	10.0	a	12.0	16.0	a
	New Zealand	0.0	5.5	10.0	11.0	12.0	15.0	14.0
	Norway	0.0	6.0	9.0	12.0	12.0	16.0	14.0
	Poland	0.0	a	8.0	11.0	12.0	16.0	15.0
	Portugal	0.0	6.0	9.0	12.0	12.0	17.0	15.0
	Scotland	0.0	7.0	11.0	13.0	13.0	16.0	16.0
	Slovak Republic	0.0	4.5	8.5	12.0	12.0	17.5	13.5
	Spain	0.0	5.0	8.0	10.0	12.0	16.5	13.0
	Sweden	0.0	6.0	9.0	11.5	12.0	15.5	14.0
	Switzerland	0.0	6.0	9.0	12.5	12.5	17.5	14.5
	Turkey	0.0	5.0	8.0	11.0	11.0	15.0	13.0
	United Kingdom	0.0	6.0	9.0	12.0	13.0	16.0	15.0
	United States	0.0	6.0	9.0	a	12.0	16.0	14.0
Partners	Albania	0.0	6.0	9.0	12.0	12.0	16.0	16.0
	Argentina	0.0	6.0	10.0	12.0	12.0	17.0	14.5
	Azerbaijan	0.0	4.0	9.0	11.0	11.0	17.0	14.0
	Brazil	0.0	4.0	8.0	11.0	11.0	16.0	14.5
	Bulgaria	0.0	4.0	8.0	12.0	12.0	17.5	15.0
	Colombia	0.0	5.0	9.0	11.0	11.0	15.5	14.0
	Croatia	0.0	4.0	8.0	11.0	12.0	17.0	15.0
	Dubai	0.0	5.0	9.0	12.0	12.0	16.0	15.0
	Estonia	0.0	4.0	9.0	12.0	12.0	16.0	15.0
	Hong Kong-China	0.0	6.0	9.0	11.0	13.0	16.0	14.0
	Indonesia	0.0	6.0	9.0	12.0	12.0	15.0	14.0
	Israel	0.0	6.0	9.0	12.0	12.0	15.0	15.0
	Jordan	0.0	6.0	10.0	12.0	12.0	16.0	14.5
	Kazakhstan	0.0	4.0	9.0	11.5	12.5	15.0	14.0
	Kyrgyzstan	0.0	4.0	8.0	11.0	10.0	15.0	13.0
	Latvia	0.0	3.0	8.0	11.0	11.0	16.0	16.0
	Liechtenstein	0.0	5.0	9.0	11.0	13.0	17.0	14.0
	Lithuania	0.0	3.0	8.0	11.0	11.0	16.0	15.0
	Macao-China	0.0	6.0	9.0	11.0	12.0	16.0	15.0
	Montenegro	0.0	4.0	8.0	11.0	12.0	16.0	15.0
	Panama	0.0	6.0	9.0	12.0	12.0	16.0	a
	Peru	0.0	6.0	9.0	11.0	11.0	17.0	14.0
	Qatar	0.0	6.0	9.0	12.0	12.0	16.0	15.0
	Romania	0.0	4.0	8.0	11.5	12.5	16.0	14.0
	Russian Federation	0.0	4.0	9.0	11.5	12.0	15.0	a
	Serbia	0.0	4.0	8.0	11.0	12.0	17.0	14.5
	Shanghai-China	0.0	6.0	9.0	12.0	12.0	16.0	15.0
	Singapore	0.0	6.0	8.0	10.5	10.5	12.5	12.5
	Slovenia	0.0	4.0	8.0	11.0	12.0	16.0	15.0
	Chinese Taipei	0.0	6.0	9.0	12.0	12.0	16.0	14.0
	Thailand	0.0	6.0	9.0	12.0	12.0	16.0	14.0
	Trinidad & Tobago	0.0	5.0	9.0	12.0	12.0	16.0	15.0
	Tunisia	0.0	6.0	9.0	12.0	13.0	17.0	16.0
	Uruguay	0.0	6.0	9.0	12.0	12.0	17.0	15.0

Source: OECD (2010), *PISA 2009 Results: Learning to Learn – Student Engagement, Strategies and Practices* (Volume III).

ANNEX A1: CONSTRUCTION OF READING SCALES AND INDICES FROM THE STUDENT, SCHOOL AND PARENT CONTEXT QUESTIONNAIRES

Students indicate the language they usually speak at home. The data are captured in nationally-specific language codes, which were recoded into variable ST19Q01 with the following two values: (1) language at home is the same as the language of assessment, and (2) language at home is a different language than the language of assessment.

Student-level scale indices

Family wealth

The *index of family wealth* (WEALTH) is based on the students' responses on whether they had the following at home: a room of their own, a link to the Internet, a dishwasher (treated as a country-specific item), a DVD player, and three other country-specific items (some items in ST20); and their responses on the number of cellular phones, televisions, computers, cars and the rooms with a bath or shower (ST21).

Home educational resources

The *index of home educational resources* (HEDRES) is based on the items measuring the existence of educational resources at home including a desk and a quiet place to study, a computer that students can use for schoolwork, educational software, books to help with students' school work, technical reference books and a dictionary (some items in ST20).

Cultural possessions

The *index of cultural possessions* (CULTPOSS) is based on the students' responses to whether they had the following at home: classic literature, books of poetry and works of art (some items in ST20).

Economic, social and cultural status

The *PISA index of economic, social and cultural status* (ESCS) was derived from the following three indices: highest occupational status of parents (HISEI), highest educational level of parents in years of education according to ISCED (PARED), and home possessions (HOMEPOS). The *index of home possessions* (HOMEPOS) comprises all items on the indices of WEALTH, CULTPOSS and HEDRES, as well as books in the home recoded into a four-level categorical variable (0-10 books, 11-25 or 26-100 books, 101-200 or 201-500 books, more than 500 books).

The *PISA index of economic, social and cultural status* (ESCS) was derived from a principal component analysis of standardised variables (each variable has an OECD mean of zero and a standard deviation of one), taking the factor scores for the first principal component as measures of the index of economic, social and cultural status.

Principal component analysis was also performed for each participating country to determine to what extent the components of the index operate in similar ways across countries. The analysis revealed that patterns of factor loading were very similar across countries, with all three components contributing to a similar extent to the index. For the occupational component, the average factor loading was 0.80, ranging from 0.66 to 0.87 across countries. For the educational component, the average factor loading was 0.79, ranging from 0.69 to 0.87 across countries. For the home possession component, the average factor loading was 0.73, ranging from 0.60 to 0.84 across countries. The reliability of the index ranged from 0.41 to 0.81. These results support the cross-national validity of the *PISA index of economic, social and cultural status*.

The imputation of components for students missing data on one component was done on the basis of a regression on the other two variables, with an additional random error component. The final values on the *PISA index of economic, social and cultural status* (ESCS) have an OECD mean of 0 and a standard deviation of one.

Disciplinary climate

The *index of disciplinary climate* (DISCLIMA) was derived from students' reports on how often the followings happened in their lessons of the language of instruction (ST36): *i)* students don't listen to what the teacher says; *ii)* there is noise and disorder; *iii)* the teacher has to wait a long time for the students to <quieten down>; *iv)* students cannot work well; and *v)* students don't start working for a long time after the lesson begins. As all items are inverted for scaling, higher values on this index indicate a better disciplinary climate.

School-level simple indices

School size

The *index of school size* (SCHSIZE) was derived by summing up the number of girls and boys at a school (SC06).

School-level scale indices

School responsibility for resource allocation

School principals were asked to report whether "principals", "teachers", "school governing board", "regional or local education authority" or "national education authority" has a considerable responsibility for the following tasks (SC24): *i)* selecting teachers for hire;

ii) dismissing teachers; *iii)* establishing teachers' starting salaries; *iv)* determining teachers' salaries increases; *v)* formulating the school budget; and *vi)* deciding on budget allocations within the school. *The index of school responsibility for resource allocation* (RESPRES) was derived from these six items. The ratio of the number of responsibility that "principals" and/or "teachers" have for these six items to the number of responsibility that "regional or local education authority" and/or "national education authority" have for these six items was computed. Positive values on this index indicate relatively more responsibility for schools than local, regional or national education authority. This index has an OECD mean of 0 and a standard deviation of 1.

School responsibility for curriculum and assessment

School principals were asked to report whether "principals", "teachers", "school governing board", "regional or local education authority", or "national education authority" has a considerable responsibility for the following tasks (SC24): *i)* establishing student assessment policies; *ii)* choosing which textbooks are used; *iii)* determining course content; and *iv)* deciding which courses are offered. The *index of school responsibility for curriculum and assessment* (RESPCURR) was derived from these four items. The ratio of the number of responsibility that "principals" and/or "teachers" have for these four items to the number of responsibility that "regional or local education authority" and/or "national education authority" have for these four items was computed. Positive values on this index indicate relatively more responsibility for schools than local, regional or national education authority. This index has an OECD mean of 0 and a standard deviation of 1.

Teacher shortage

The *index of teacher shortage* (TCSHORT) was derived from four items measuring school principals' perceptions of potential factors hindering instruction at their school (SC11). These factors are a lack of: *i)* qualified science teachers; *ii)* a lack of qualified mathematics teachers; *iii)* qualified <test language> teachers; and *iv)* qualified teachers of other subjects. Higher values on this index indicate school principals' reports of higher teacher shortage at a school.

School's educational resources

The *index on the school's educational resources* (SCMATEDU) was derived from seven items measuring school principals' perceptions of potential factors hindering instruction at their school (SC11). These factors are: *i)* shortage or inadequacy of science laboratory equipment; *ii)* shortage or inadequacy of instructional materials; *iii)* shortage or inadequacy of computers for instruction; *iv)* lack or inadequacy of Internet connectivity; *v)* shortage or inadequacy of computer software for instruction; *vi)* shortage or inadequacy of library materials; and *vii)* shortage or inadequacy of audio-visual resources. As all items were inverted for scaling, higher values on this index indicate better quality of educational resources.

References

Ganzeboom, H. B. G., P. M. De Graaf and **D. J. Treiman** (1992), "A Standard International Socio-economic Index of Occupational Status", Social Science Research 2, pp. 1-56.

ILO (International Labour Organization) (1990), International Standard Classification of Occupations (ISCO-88), Geneva.

OECD (2012), *PISA 2009 Technical Report,* OECD Publishing.

OECD (2010), *PISA 2009 Results: What Students Know and Can Do: Student Performance in Reading, Mathematics and Science* (Volume I), OECD Publishing.

OECD (1999), *Classifying Educational Programmes: Manual for ISCED-97 Implementation in OECD Countries,* OECD Publishing.

ANNEX A2
TECHNICAL NOTES ON PRELIMINARY MULTILEVEL REGRESSION ANALYSIS FOR PERFORMANCE

The relationship between public and private involvement in schools and countries' performance in reading is examined based on a multilevel analysis. A three-level regression analysis is conducted using HLM 6.08, with students serving as level 1, schools as level 2 and countries as level 3. The model coefficients and statistics are estimated using Maximum Likelihood method procedure. Normalised student final weights are used, so that the sum of the weights was equal to the number of students in the dataset, and each country contributed equally to the analysis. Five plausible values for performance in reading (PV1READ to PV5READ) are used.

This preliminary analysis does not show clear patterns in the relationship between public management and countries' performance in reading, while the level of public funding seems to be related negatively to performance only after accounting for background and institutional characteristics of schools (see Table A2.2). However, before developing any policy recommendations, further study is required to better understand the inter-relationship between public and private involvement in schools, background and institutional variables and countries' performance in reading. The reminder of this annex provides details of how the preliminary analysis is conducted.

Data

The data file used for the multilevel analysis includes 287 566 students from 10 591 schools in 32 OECD countries. Austria and France are excluded as data for public funding or management were not available. All indicators used at the student and school levels were from PISA 2009 student and school questionnaires. Country-level indicators are either from *Education at a Glance 2010: OECD Indicators* (OECD, 2010a) or were extracted from the PISA system-level data collection 2010. All of these country-level indicators are presented in *PISA 2009 Results, What Makes a School Successful? Policies, Practices and Resources* (Volume IV) (OECD, 2010b).

Selecting and recording variables

Two country-level variables – public funding and public management – are used to examine the relationships between these variables and student performance. These variables were collected at the school level through the PISA 2009 School Questionnaire, but were aggregated at the country level for this analysis.

Demographic and socio-economic background variables as well as institutional variables are also selected based on previous studies (Woessmann, 2006; Woessmann, 2009; OECD, 2010b). Five institutional variables at the country level are those shown to be related to performance, even after accounting for GDP per capita (OECD, 2010b). These variables are included in the net models – i.e. models accounting for background variables – in order to examine the net effects of public management and funding. The variables used in the models are:

- Student level
  - *PISA index of economic, social and cultural status* (ESCS);
  - gender;
  - language spoken at home;
  - immigrant status;
  - dummy variables for grade levels;
  - age; and
  - learning time in test language.

- School level
  - school average *PISA index of economic, social and cultural status* (ESCS);
  - school size and its squared value;
  - school location;
  - standardised test;
  - school autonomy for curriculum and assessment;
  - school autonomy for resource allocation;
  - availability of computers;
  - school's educational resources; and
  - proportion of qualified teachers.

TECHNICAL NOTES ON PRELIMINARY MULTILEVEL REGRESSION ANALYSIS FOR PERFORMANCE: ANNEX A2

- Country level
  - GDP per capita;
  - percentage of students who repeated one or more grades;
  - percentage of students in schools that group students by ability in all subjects;
  - percentage of students in schools that transfer students to other schools due to low achievement, behavioural problems or special learning needs;
  - average index of school responsibility for curriculum and assessment; and
  - teachers' salaries to GDP per capita (weighted average of upper and lower secondary school teachers).

The descriptive statistics for all variables are listed in Table A2.1. The variables with "M" in the first are missing dummies, which is explained in detail in the following section.

[Part 1/1]
Table A2.1 Descriptive statistics of explanatory and background variables

Variable description	Variable name	Mean	S.D.	Min.	Max.	Missing
SYSTEM LEVEL						
Percentage of students who attend publicly managed school (1 unit = 10 percentage-point increase)	YPUB10	8.19	2.05	3.05	9.92	no
Percentage of total funding for school for a typical school year that comes from government (1 unit = 10 percentage-point increase)	GFUND10	8.55	1.48	4.39	9.98	no
GDP per capita (1 000 USD converted using PPPs)	GDP	32.07	13.28	13.36	82.46	no
Teachers' salaries to GDP per capita (weighted average of upper and lower secondary school teachers) (ratio - 1)	ZSALARY	0.62	0.38	0.16	1.78	2 countries
Average index of school responsibility for curriculum and assessment (1 unit = one standard deviation across OECD countries)	YRESPC	-0.05	0.61	-1.25	1.06	no
Percentage of students in schools that group students by ability in all subjects (1 unit = 100 percentage-point increase)	YABG	0.13	0.12	0.00	0.49	no
Percentage of students in schools that transfer students to other schools due to low achievement, behavioural problems or special learning needs (1 unit = 100 percentage-point increase)	YTRANS	0.15	0.14	0.00	0.63	no
Percentage of students who repeated one or more grades (1 unit = 100 percentage-point increase)	YREPEA	0.12	0.11	0.00	0.37	no

	Variable name	Mean	S.D.	Min.	Max.	% missing
SCHOOL LEVEL						
School average PISA index of economic, social and cultural status (ESCS) (1 unit = one index point)	XESCS; MXESCS	0.00	0.65	-3.87	2.13	0.03
School size (100 students)	SCHSIZE; MSCHSIZE	7.50	5.82	0.02	112.68	3.71
School located in a city (with over 100 000)	CITY; MCITY	0.35	0.48	0.00	1.00	1.98
School located in a small town or village (fewer than 15 000)	RURAL	0.31	0.46	0.00	1.00	1.98
School-level index of quality of school educational resources (1 unit = one index point)	SCMATEDU; MSCHMATEDU	0.04	0.98	-3.39	1.93	2.25
School average number of computers available for students	IRATCOMP; MIRATCOMP	0.55	0.41	0.00	2.50	6.94
Proportion of teachers who have an ISCED 5A qualification	PROPQUAL; MPROPQUAL	0.74	0.37	0.00	1.00	12.32
School autonomy for curriculum and assessment (1 unit = 1 index point)	RESPCURR; MRESPCURR	-0.05	0.99	-1.37	1.36	1.90
School autonomy for resource allocation (1 unit = 1 index point)	RESPRES	-0.04	0.95	-0.84	2.45	1.90
Students are assessed using standardised test at least more than 1 time a year	XSTD_TEST; MXSTD_TEST	0.77	0.42	0.00	1.00	3.80
STUDENT LEVEL						
Student is female	GENDER; MGENDER	0.49	0.50	0.00	1.00	0.00
Student's PISA index of economic, social and cultural status (ESCS) (1 unit = one index point)	ESCS; MESCS	0.00	1.01	-6.04	3.53	1.36
Student has no immigration background	NATIVE; MNATIVE	0.90	0.30	0.00	1.00	2.09
Student speaks the test language or other national langue most of the time or always at home	SLANG; MSLANG	0.91	0.29	0.00	1.00	3.76
Student's age	AGE	15.76	0.29	15.17	16.33	0.00
Student's grade (4 = modal grade in country; 1 unit = one grade)	GRADE1; MGRADE	3.91	0.57	1.00	7.00	0.42
Learning time in test language per week (mins)	LMINS; MLMINS	217.54	84.74	0.00	1 000	7.03

1. Since the variable GRADE varies from 1 to 7, six dummy variables (i.e. GRADE-3, GRADE-2, GRADE-1, GRADE1, GRADE2 and GRADE3) are created. The reference group is the students in the modal grade in each country.
Source: OECD, *PISA 2009 Database*.

ANNEX A2: TECHNICAL NOTES ON PRELIMINARY MULTILEVEL REGRESSION ANALYSIS FOR PERFORMANCE

Treatment of missing data

The proportion of missing values for the variables considered in the analysis is presented in Table A2.1. Even though the missing rate is less than 5% for most of the variables, a list-wise deletion of observations that have a missing value of at least one variable would have reduced the sample size by 26.9%, since around 20 variables are included in the models. Therefore, missing values are imputed in order to include the maximum number of cases in the analysis.

Since the missing rates are not high for most of the variables, a simple imputation approach was used to circumvent the problem of missing data: predictors at the individual and school levels were imputed using a dummy variable adjustment (Cohen and Cohen, 1985).

It is known that this imputation method generally produces biased estimates of coefficients (Jones, 1996), and that standard errors of those variables that contain missing values are underestimated since they do not account for the uncertainty introduced through imputation. However, given that more than 5% of the data are missing on only three variables (Table A2.1), this bias is considered negligible.

As a first step of the imputation, a so-called "missing dummy" variable is created for all variables with missing values, regardless of whether a variable was continuous, categorical or dichotomous. A missing dummy variable is set to 1 if the data were missing on that variable; it was set to 0 if the data are not missing. The first letter "M" in the variable names in Table A2.1 signifies a missing dummy.

As a second step, missing values are imputed for continuous variables. Missing values are replaced by the weighted school average of the variable. If all data on the respective variable are missing in one school, such that the weighted school mean could not be computed, the weighted country mean is imputed. If all data on the respective variable are missing in a country, the weighted international mean is imputed. When a missing value is replaced by the country or school mean, the weights are proportional to the sampling probability (weighting factor W_FSTUWT from the PISA 2009 dataset). When a missing value is replaced by the international mean, equal country weights are used, i.e. each country is given an equal weight of 1 000 cases.

All 32 countries have data for all country-level variables except one variable, teachers' salaries to GDP per capita. As these data are missing in Canada and New Zealand, these missing values are replaced by the international mean without including a missing dummy.

Student weights

For the multilevel analysis, data files are weighted at the student level with "normalised student final weights", which are computed based on the student final weights (W_FSTUWT) in the PISA 2009 dataset.

The student final weights (W_FSTUWT) are normalised at the international level, including 32 of the 34 OECD countries, to *i)* make the sum of the weights across the 32 countries equal to the number of students across the 32 countries in the dataset; *ii)* maintain the same proportion of weights as in the student final weights (W_FSTUWT) within each country; and *iii)* ensure that each individual country's contribution to the analysis is equal by introducing a country factor (i.e. the sum of the weights within each country is the same for all 32 countries).

Modelling student performance

In order to examine how the country-level public management and public funding variables are related to students' performance in reading before and after accounting for background characteristics of students, schools and countries, ten models are developed. Model 1 in Table A2.2 is the simplest model that contains aggregated variables for public funding and management at the country level, without any background variables. In Model 2, an interaction effect between public management and public funding is added to Model 1. Models 1 and 2 are gross models that do not account for any background variables listed in Table A2.1. Models 3 to 8 are net models. Model 3 accounts for student-level background variables. Model 4 accounts for school-level background variables. Model 5 accounts for country-level background variables. Models 6 to 8 account for different combinations of background variables at the student, school and country levels. Model 9 accounts for background variables at student, school and country levels altogether. In Model 10, an interaction effect between public management and public funding is added to Model 9.

In all models, all the slopes are fixed and only the intercepts are randomised at all three levels. Public management and public funding variables are centred on the international mean and the interaction is computed. Six other country-level variables are also centred on the international mean. Student- and school-level variables are not centred.

As an example, the detailed specification of Model 2 is presented below.

Detailed specification of Model 2

Level 1: Reading = $P0 + E$

Level 2: $P0 = B00 + R0$

Level 3: $B00 = G000 + G001(GFUND10) + G002(YPUB10) + G003(I\_FPUB) + U00$

TECHNICAL NOTES ON PRELIMINARY MULTILEVEL REGRESSION ANALYSIS FOR PERFORMANCE: ANNEX A2

In Model 1, both the prevalence of publicly managed schools and the level of public funding for schools are not significantly related to performance. Even after including the interaction between these two variables in Model 2, no clear pattern is observed in the relationship between public and private involvement in schools and countries' performance in reading. Similarly, in Model 3, after accounting for the student-level background variables, and in Model 5, after accounting for the country-level background variables, public involvement in managing and funding schools are not related to performance. Only after accounting for school-level background variables in Models 4, 6 and 8, do countries that provide higher levels of public funding for schools tend to have lower scores than countries that provide lower levels of public funding. The prevalence of publicly managed schools is not related to performance. Similar results can be obtained from Models 9 and 10, which account for background variables at the student, school and country levels altogether. The interaction between public funding and public management in Model 10 is not significantly related to performance.

[Part 1/3]
Table A2.2 Relationship between public and private involvement in schools and performance in reading

	Variable	Model 1 Coef.	S.E.	p-value	Model 2 Coef.	S.E.	p-value	Model 3 Coef.	S.E.	p-value
Percentage of students who attend publicly managed school (1 unit = 10 percentage-point increase)	YPUB10	-0.83	(2.21)	(0.71)	-1.12	(2.80)	(0.69)	-1.48	(2.09)	(0.48)
Percentage of total funding for school for a typical school year that comes from government (1 unit = 10 percentage-point increase)	GFUND10	2.77	(5.41)	(0.61)	3.25	(4.06)	(0.43)	-2.49	(3.03)	(0.42)
Interaction between public funding and public management	I_FPUB				2.33	(2.92)	(0.43)			
Intercept	INTRCPT1	487.89	(5.24)	(0.00)	486.10	(4.36)	(0.00)	555.97	(34.19)	(0.00)

Country-level variables

GDP per capita (1 000 USD converted using PPPs)	GDP									
Teachers' salaries to GDP per capita (weighted average of upper and lower secondary school teachers)	ZSALARY									
Average index of school responsibility for curriculum and assessment (1 unit = 1 standard deviation across OECD countries)	YRESPC									
Percentage of students in schools that group students by ability in all subjects (1 unit = 100 percentage-point increase)	YABG									
Percentage of students in schools that transfer students to other schools due to low achievement, behavioural problems or special learning needs (1 unit = 100 percentage-point increase)	YTRANS									
Percentage of students who repeated one or more grades (1 unit = 100 percentage-point increase)	YREPEA									

School level variables

School average PISA index of economic, social and cultural status (ESCS) (1 unit = 1 index point)	XESCS									
School size (100 students)	SCHSIZE									
School size squared	SCHSIZE2									
School located in a city (with over 100 000 people)	CITY									
School located in a small town or village (fewer than 15 000 people)	RURAL									
School-level index of quality of school educational resources (1 unit = 1 index point)	SCMATEDU									
Proportion of teachers who have an ISCED 5A qualification	PROPQUAL									
Average number of computers available for students in the school	IRATCOMP									
School autonomy for curriculum and assessment (1 unit = 1 index point)	RESPCURR									
School autonomy for resource allocation (1 unit = 1 index point)	RESPRES									
Students are assessed using standardised tests more than once a year	XSTDT									

Student-level variables

Student is female	GENDER							30.74	(1.87)	(0.00)
Student's PISA index of economic, social and cultural status (ESCS) (1 unit = 1 index point)	ESCS							17.48	(1.46)	(0.00)
Student has no immigration background	NATIVE							10.25	(2.81)	(0.00)
Student speaks the test language or other national language most of the time or always at home	SLANG							13.57	(3.29)	(0.00)
Student's age	AGE							-5.79	(2.14)	(0.01)
Student's grade	GRADE-3							-113.62	(7.04)	(0.00)
	GRADE-2							-94.12	(4.90)	(0.00)
	GRADE-1							-45.36	(2.66)	(0.00)
	GRADE1							33.73	(2.58)	(0.00)
	GRADE2							29.19	(7.88)	(0.00)
	GRADE3							91.09	(33.13)	(0.02)
Learning time in test language per week (mins)	LMINS							0.00	(0.01)	(0.94)

Note: Values that are statistically significant are indicated in bold at the 5% level (p<0.05); at the 10% level (p>0.10) they are indicated in italic.
Source: OECD, PISA 2009 Database.

ANNEX A2: TECHNICAL NOTES ON PRELIMINARY MULTILEVEL REGRESSION ANALYSIS FOR PERFORMANCE

[Part 2/3]

Table A2.2 Relationship between public and private involvement in schools and performance in reading

	Variable	Model 4 Coef.	Model 4 S.E.	Model 4 p-value	Model 5 Coef.	Model 5 S.E.	Model 5 p-value	Model 6 Coef.	Model 6 S.E.	Model 6 p-value
Percentage of students who attend publicly managed school (1 unit = 10 percentage-point increase)	YPUB10	1.04	(1.46)	(0.48)	1.39	(2.27)	(0.55)	-0.39	(1.66)	(0.82)
Percentage of total funding for school for a typical school year that comes from government (1 unit = 10 percentage-point increase)	GFUND10	**-9.23**	(3.25)	(0.01)	-1.66	(2.97)	(0.58)	**-8.30**	(2.57)	(0.00)
Interaction between public funding and public management	I_FPUB									
Intercept	INTRCPT1	**464.90**	(8.98)	(0.00)	**488.22**	(2.71)	(0.00)	**529.87**	(9.23)	(0.00)
Country-level variables										
GDP per capita (1 000 USD converted using PPPs)	GDP				**1.00**	(0.24)	(0.00)			
Teachers' salaries to GDP per capita (weighted average of upper and lower secondary school teachers)	ZSALARY				7.28	(10.47)	(0.49)			
Average index of school responsibility for curriculum and assessment (1 unit = 1 standard deviation across OECD countries)	YRESPC				*13.23*	*(7.21)*	*(0.08)*			
Percentage of students in schools that group students by ability in all subjects (1 unit = 100 percentage-point increase)	YABG				-44.54	(38.75)	(0.26)			
Percentage of students in schools that transfer students to other schools due to low achievement, behavioural problems or special learning needs (1 unit = 100 percentage-point increase)	YTRANS				**-72.94**	(27.89)	(0.02)			
Percentage of students who repeated one or more grades (1 unit = 100 percentage-point increase)	YREPEA				7.92	(30.75)	(0.80)			
School level variables										
School average PISA index of economic, social and cultural status (ESCS) (1 unit = 1 index point)	XESCS	**76.07**	(5.76)	(0.00)				**43.70**	(0.85)	(0.00)
School size (100 students)	SCHSIZE	**1.94**	(0.44)	(0.00)				**1.33**	(0.12)	(0.00)
School size squared	SCHSIZE2	**-0.02**	(0.01)	(0.01)				**-0.01**	(0.00)	(0.00)
School located in a city (with over 100 000 people)	CITY	**-5.43**	(1.89)	(0.01)				-0.71	(1.00)	(0.48)
School located in a small town or village (fewer than 15 000 people)	RURAL	**5.40**	(2.22)	(0.02)				**6.94**	(0.97)	(0.00)
School-level index of quality of school educational resources (1 unit = 1 index point)	SCMATEDU	0.92	(0.91)	(0.31)				0.58	(0.42)	(0.16)
Proportion of teachers who have an ISCED 5A qualification	PROPQUAL	**27.21**	(7.96)	(0.00)				**18.33**	(1.85)	(0.00)
Average number of computers available for students in the school	IRATCOMP	-1.90	(2.52)	(0.45)				-1.09	(1.06)	(0.30)
School autonomy for curriculum and assessment (1 unit = 1 index point)	RESPCURR	0.51	(1.22)	(0.67)				0.42	(0.49)	(0.38)
School autonomy for resource allocation (1 unit = 1 index point)	RESPRES	-0.87	(0.95)	(0.36)				*-1.00*	*(0.51)*	*(0.05)*
Students are assessed using standardised tests more than once a year	XSTDT	-2.77	(1.74)	(0.11)				1.07	(0.98)	(0.27)
Student-level variables										
Student is female	GENDER							**30.65**	(0.28)	(0.00)
Student's PISA index of economic, social and cultural status (ESCS) (1 unit = 1 index point)	ESCS							**15.76**	(0.19)	(0.00)
Student has no immigration background	NATIVE							**10.45**	(0.73)	(0.00)
Student speaks the test language or other national language most of the time or always at home	SLANG							**13.11**	(0.70)	(0.00)
Student's age	AGE							**-5.56**	(0.53)	(0.00)
Student's grade	GRADE-3							**-102.95**	(3.01)	(0.00)
	GRADE-2							**-87.09**	(1.30)	(0.00)
	GRADE-1							**-43.29**	(0.54)	(0.00)
	GRADE1							**33.02**	(0.67)	(0.00)
	GRADE2							**28.88**	(2.80)	(0.00)
	GRADE3							**88.59**	(38.29)	(0.03)
Learning time in test language per week (mins)	LMINS							0.00	(0.00)	(0.79)

Note: Values that are statistically significant are indicated in bold at the 5% level (p<0.05); at the 10% level (p>0.10) they are indicated in italic.
Source: OECD, PISA 2009 Database.

[Part 3/3]
Table A2.2 Relationship between public and private involvement in schools and performance in reading

	Variable	Model 7 Coef.	Model 7 S.E.	Model 7 p-value	Model 8 Coef.	Model 8 S.E.	Model 8 p-value	Model 9 Coef.	Model 9 S.E.	Model 9 p-value	Model 10 Coef.	Model 10 S.E.	Model 10 p-value
Percentage of students who attend publicly managed school (1 unit = 10 percentage-point increase)	YPUB10	0.70	(2.58)	(0.79)	0.97	(1.72)	(0.58)	0.52	(1.83)	(0.78)	0.70	(1.78)	(0.70)
Percentage of total funding for school for a typical school year that comes from government (1 unit = 10 percentage-point increase)	GFUND10	-4.48	(2.66)	(0.11)	-7.80	(3.88)	(0.06)	**-7.41**	(2.99)	(0.02)	**-6.99**	(2.91)	(0.03)
Interaction between public funding and public management	I_FPUB										-1.85	(1.29)	(0.17)
Intercept	INTRCPT1	**556.86**	(34.29)	(0.00)	**465.20**	(8.35)	(0.00)	**530.95**	(9.05)	(0.00)	**532.13**	(9.06)	(0.00)
Country-level variables													
GDP per capita (1 000 USD converted using PPPs)	GDP	0.14	(0.23)	(0.54)	-0.56	(0.31)	(0.09)	**-0.67**	(0.23)	(0.01)	**-0.64**	(0.23)	(0.01)
Teachers' salaries to GDP per capita (weighted average of upper and lower secondary school teachers)	ZSALARY	0.62	(9.23)	(0.95)	-0.02	(15.18)	(1.00)	-4.52	(10.82)	(0.68)	1.32	(11.24)	(0.91)
Average index of school responsibility for curriculum and assessment (1 unit = 1 standard deviation across OECD countries)	YRESPC	7.58	(8.40)	(0.38)	0.23	(5.78)	(0.97)	1.31	(6.74)	(0.85)	0.76	(6.54)	(0.91)
Percentage of students in schools that group students by ability in all subjects (1 unit = 100 percentage-point increase)	YABG	-19.89	(38.85)	(0.61)	-4.44	(42.09)	(0.92)	0.10	(35.17)	(1.00)	-7.56	(34.51)	(0.83)
Percentage of students in schools that transfer students to other schools due to low achievement, behavioural problems or special learning needs (1 unit = 100 percentage-point increase)	YTRANS	-50.36	(30.99)	(0.12)	*-43.75*	(21.25)	(0.05)	-33.70	(25.80)	(0.21)	-35.12	(25.02)	(0.17)
Percentage of students who repeated one or more grades (1 unit = 100 percentage-point increase)	YREPEA	**71.98**	(31.40)	(0.03)	33.82	(38.16)	(0.39)	*84.49*	(41.92)	(0.06)	*75.20*	(41.12)	(0.08)
School level variables													
School average PISA index of economic, social and cultural status (ESCS) (1 unit = 1 index point)	XESCS				**76.11**	(5.78)	(0.00)	**43.80**	(0.85)	(0.00)	**43.81**	(0.85)	(0.00)
School size (100 students)	SCHSIZE				**1.95**	(0.44)	(0.00)	**1.33**	(0.12)	(0.00)	**1.33**	(0.12)	(0.00)
School size squared	SCHSIZE2				**-0.02**	(0.01)	(0.01)	**-0.01**	(0.00)	(0.00)	**-0.01**	(0.00)	(0.00)
School located in a city (with over 100 000 people)	CITY				**-5.48**	(1.90)	(0.00)	-0.73	(1.00)	(0.47)	-0.72	(1.00)	(0.47)
School located in a small town or village (fewer than 15 000 people)	RURAL				**5.38**	(2.21)	(0.02)	**6.95**	(0.97)	(0.00)	**6.95**	(0.97)	(0.00)
School-level index of quality of school educational resources (1 unit = 1 index point)	SCMATEDU				0.92	(0.91)	(0.31)	0.59	(0.42)	(0.16)	0.59	(0.42)	(0.16)
Proportion of teachers who have an ISCED 5A qualification	PROPQUAL				**27.00**	(7.92)	(0.00)	**18.12**	(1.84)	(0.00)	**18.07**	(1.84)	(0.00)
Average number of computers available for students in the school	IRATCOMP				-1.88	(2.55)	(0.46)	-1.06	(1.06)	(0.32)	-1.06	(1.06)	(0.32)
School autonomy for curriculum and assessment (1 unit = 1 index point)	RESPCURR				0.47	(1.23)	(0.70)	0.42	(0.49)	(0.39)	0.42	(0.49)	(0.39)
School autonomy for resource allocation (1 unit = 1 index point)	RESPRES				-0.90	(0.95)	(0.35)	**-1.04**	(0.51)	(0.04)	**-1.04**	(0.51)	(0.04)
Students are assessed using standardised tests more than once a year	XSTDT				-2.75	(1.74)	(0.11)	1.11	(0.98)	(0.26)	1.12	(0.98)	(0.25)
Student-level variables													
Student is female	GENDER	**30.74**	(1.87)	(0.00)				**30.65**	(0.28)	(0.00)	**30.65**	(0.28)	(0.00)
Student's PISA index of economic, social and cultural status (ESCS) (1 unit = 1 index point)	ESCS	**17.48**	(1.46)	(0.00)				**15.76**	(0.19)	(0.00)	**15.76**	(0.19)	(0.00)
Student has no immigration background	NATIVE	**10.25**	(2.80)	(0.00)				**10.45**	(0.73)	(0.00)	**10.45**	(0.73)	(0.00)
Student speaks the test language or other national language most of the time or always at home	SLANG	**13.56**	(3.30)	(0.00)				**13.09**	(0.70)	(0.00)	**13.08**	(0.70)	(0.00)
Student's age	AGE	**-5.78**	(2.14)	(0.01)				**-5.56**	(0.53)	(0.00)	**-5.55**	(0.53)	(0.00)
Student's grade	GRADE-3	**-113.60**	(7.06)	(0.00)				**-102.97**	(3.01)	(0.00)	**-102.96**	(3.01)	(0.00)
	GRADE-2	**-94.10**	(4.90)	(0.00)				**-87.11**	(1.30)	(0.00)	**-87.10**	(1.30)	(0.00)
	GRADE-1	**-45.35**	(2.66)	(0.00)				**-43.30**	(0.54)	(0.00)	**-43.30**	(0.54)	(0.00)
	GRADE1	**33.72**	(2.59)	(0.00)				**33.01**	(0.67)	(0.00)	**33.01**	(0.67)	(0.00)
	GRADE2	**29.17**	(7.87)	(0.00)				**28.88**	(2.80)	(0.00)	**28.87**	(2.80)	(0.00)
	GRADE3	**91.07**	(33.13)	(0.02)				**88.58**	(38.29)	(0.03)	**88.57**	(38.29)	(0.03)
Learning time in test language per week (mins)	LMINS	0.00	(0.01)	(0.93)				0.00	(0.00)	(0.77)	0.00	(0.00)	(0.78)

Note: Values that are statistically significant are indicated in bold at the 5% level (p<0.05); at the 10% level (p>0.10) they are indicated in italic.
Source: OECD, PISA 2009 Database.

References

OECD (2010a), *Education at a Glance 2010: OECD Indicators*, OECD Publishing.

OECD (2010b), *PISA 2009 Results, What Makes a School Successful? Policies, Practices and Resources* (Volume IV), OECD Publishing.

Woessmann, L. (2006), "Public-private partnerships and schooling outcomes across countries", Cesifo Working Paper, No. 1662, Center for Economic Studies, Institute for Economic Research, Munich.

Woessmann, L., et al. (2009), *School Accountability, Autonomy, and Choice around the World*, Edward Elgar, Cheltenham.

ANNEX A3
STANDARD ERRORS, SIGNIFICANCE TESTS AND SUBGROUP COMPARISONS

The statistics in this report represent estimates of national performance based on samples of students, rather than values that could be calculated if every student in every country had answered every question. Consequently, it is important to measure the degree of uncertainty of the estimates. In PISA, each estimate has an associated degree of uncertainty, which is expressed through a standard error. The use of confidence intervals provides a way to make inferences about the population means and proportions in a manner that reflects the uncertainty associated with the sample estimates. From an observed sample statistic and assuming a normal distribution, it can be inferred that the corresponding population result would lie within the confidence interval in 95 out of 100 replications of the measurement on different samples drawn from the same population.

In many cases, readers are primarily interested in whether a given value in a particular country is different from a second value in the same or another country, e.g. whether females in a country perform better than males in the same country. In the tables and charts used in this report, differences are labelled as statistically significant when a difference of that size, smaller or larger, would be observed less than 5% of the time, if there were actually no difference in corresponding population values. Similarly, the risk of reporting a correlation as significant if there is, in fact, no correlation between two measures, is contained at 5%.

Throughout the report, significance tests were undertaken to assess the statistical significance of the comparisons made.

Change in the *PISA index of economic, social and cultural status* performance per unit of the independent variable

For many tables, the difference in *PISA index of economic, social and cultural status* per unit of the independent variable shown was calculated. Figures in bold indicate that the differences are statistically significantly different from zero at the 95% confidence level.

Difference in various characteristics between publicly and privately managed schools

Differences in various characteristics (e.g. *PISA index of economic, social and cultural status* and reading performance) between publicly and privately schools were tested for statistical significance. For this purpose, government-dependent and government-independent private schools were jointly considered as privately managed schools. Positive differences represent higher scores for private schools while negative differences represent higher scores for public schools. Figures in bold in data tables presented in Annex B of this report indicate statistically significant different scores at the 95% confidence level.

Annex B

DATA TABLES

Additional material is available at: *www.pisa.oecd.org*

ANNEX B: DATA TABLES

[Part 1/1]
Table B1.1 Public and private involvement in managing schools

	Publicly managed schools		Privately managed schools	
	Schools that are directly or indirectly managed by a public education authority, government agency, or governing board appointed by government or elected by public franchise		Schools that are directly or indirectly managed by a non-government organisation, such as a church, trade union, business, or other private institution	
	Percentage of students	S.E.	Percentage of students	S.E.

OECD

Country	% public	S.E.	% private	S.E.
Australia	59.7	(0.8)	40.3	(0.8)
Austria	87.4	(2.4)	12.6	(2.4)
Belgium	30.5	(0.7)	69.5	(0.7)
Canada	92.5	(0.7)	7.5	(0.7)
Chile	42.0	(1.7)	58.0	(1.7)
Czech Republic	96.4	(1.0)	3.6	(1.0)
Denmark	77.2	(2.8)	22.8	(2.8)
Estonia	96.7	(1.2)	3.3	(1.2)
Finland	96.1	(1.2)	3.9	(1.2)
France	w	w	w	w
Germany	94.9	(1.5)	5.1	(1.5)
Greece	94.8	(0.8)	5.2	(0.8)
Hungary	87.0	(2.5)	13.0	(2.5)
Iceland	99.1	(0.1)	0.9	(0.1)
Ireland	38.5	(0.4)	61.5	(0.4)
Israel	82.1	(2.6)	17.9	(2.6)
Italy	94.1	(0.6)	5.9	(0.6)
Japan	70.7	(1.3)	29.3	(1.3)
Korea	62.6	(4.3)	37.4	(4.3)
Luxembourg	85.2	(0.1)	14.8	(0.1)
Mexico	88.5	(1.1)	11.5	(1.1)
Netherlands	34.0	(3.9)	66.0	(3.9)
New Zealand	94.3	(0.4)	5.7	(0.4)
Norway	98.6	(0.4)	1.4	(0.4)
Poland	97.9	(0.1)	2.1	(0.1)
Portugal	85.5	(2.7)	14.5	(2.7)
Slovak Republic	91.0	(2.4)	9.0	(2.4)
Slovenia	97.3	(0.1)	2.7	(0.1)
Spain	65.9	(0.9)	34.1	(0.9)
Sweden	90.0	(0.8)	10.0	(0.8)
Switzerland	93.6	(1.6)	6.4	(1.6)
Turkey	99.2	(0.6)	0.8	(0.6)
United Kingdom	93.7	(1.1)	6.3	(1.1)
United States	91.2	(1.4)	8.8	(1.4)
OECD average	**82.1**	**(0.3)**	**17.9**	**(0.3)**

Partners

Country	% public	S.E.	% private	S.E.
Albania	88.9	(2.1)	11.1	(2.1)
Argentina	63.9	(2.1)	36.1	(2.1)
Azerbaijan	99.6	(0.1)	0.4	(0.1)
Brazil	87.7	(0.6)	12.3	(0.6)
Bulgaria	98.1	(0.8)	1.9	(0.8)
Colombia	80.5	(2.4)	19.5	(2.4)
Croatia	98.1	(1.1)	1.9	(1.1)
Dubai (UAE)	21.4	(0.0)	78.6	(0.0)
Hong Kong-China	7.4	(0.2)	92.6	(0.2)
Indonesia	57.2	(2.8)	42.8	(2.8)
Jordan	81.4	(0.7)	18.6	(0.7)
Kazakhstan	96.8	(1.4)	3.2	(1.4)
Kyrgyzstan	97.1	(1.2)	2.9	(1.2)
Latvia	99.2	(0.5)	0.8	(0.5)
Liechtenstein	94.4	(0.0)	5.6	(0.0)
Lithuania	99.0	(0.7)	1.0	(0.7)
Macao-China	4.0	(0.0)	96.0	(0.0)
Montenegro	99.5	(0.0)	0.5	(0.0)
Panama	76.7	(2.6)	23.3	(2.6)
Peru	77.9	(2.3)	22.1	(2.3)
Qatar	68.9	(0.1)	31.1	(0.1)
Romania	99.5	(0.5)	0.5	(0.5)
Russian Federation	99.9	(0.1)	0.1	(0.1)
Serbia	98.8	(0.9)	1.2	(0.9)
Shanghai-China	89.7	(0.6)	10.3	(0.6)
Singapore	98.2	(0.9)	1.8	(0.9)
Chinese Taipei	63.7	(1.1)	36.3	(1.1)
Thailand	82.9	(0.7)	17.1	(0.7)
Trinidad and Tobago	89.2	(0.1)	10.8	(0.1)
Tunisia	98.3	(0.4)	1.7	(0.4)
Uruguay	82.1	(0.8)	17.9	(0.8)

Source: OECD, *PISA 2009 Database*.

DATA TABLES: ANNEX B

[Part 1/3]
Table B1.2 **School autonomy, resources, climate and performance, by publicly and privately managed schools**

		\multicolumn{6}{c}{Index of school responsibility for curriculum and assessment}	\multicolumn{6}{c}{Index of school responsibility for resource allocation}
		\multicolumn{2}{c}{Publicly managed schools}	\multicolumn{2}{c}{Privately managed schools}	\multicolumn{2}{c}{Difference (private – public)}	\multicolumn{2}{c}{Publicly managed schools}	\multicolumn{2}{c}{Privately managed schools}	\multicolumn{2}{c}{Difference (private – public)}
		Mean index	S.E.	Mean index	S.E.	Dif.	S.E.	Mean index	S.E.	Mean index	S.E.	Dif.	S.E.
OECD	Australia	0.04	(0.07)	0.36	(0.08)	**0.32**	(0.11)	-0.50	(0.01)	0.57	(0.08)	**1.06**	(0.09)
	Austria	-0.33	(0.06)	-0.27	(0.15)	0.07	(0.17)	-0.64	(0.01)	-0.41	(0.13)	0.24	(0.13)
	Belgium	-0.36	(0.07)	-0.09	(0.06)	**0.27**	(0.09)	-0.46	(0.03)	-0.32	(0.01)	**0.14**	(0.03)
	Canada	-0.73	(0.02)	0.23	(0.16)	**0.96**	(0.16)	-0.49	(0.01)	0.87	(0.18)	**1.37**	(0.18)
	Chile	-0.50	(0.10)	0.24	(0.12)	**0.75**	(0.16)	-0.66	(0.03)	1.25	(0.10)	**1.91**	(0.11)
	Czech Republic	0.91	(0.06)	1.07	(0.21)	0.15	(0.21)	1.11	(0.08)	1.66	(0.41)	0.55	(0.42)
	Denmark	-0.08	(0.08)	0.50	(0.14)	**0.57**	(0.17)	-0.04	(0.05)	0.93	(0.19)	**0.96**	(0.19)
	Estonia	0.23	(0.07)	-0.26	(0.24)	-0.50	(0.26)	-0.07	(0.04)	0.87	(0.45)	**0.94**	(0.45)
	Finland	-0.17	(0.06)	0.38	(0.42)	0.56	(0.42)	-0.44	(0.03)	0.93	(0.55)	**1.37**	(0.56)
	France	w	w	w	w	w	w	w	w	w	w	w	w
	Germany	-0.27	(0.05)	0.13	(0.25)	0.41	(0.26)	-0.60	(0.02)	0.77	(0.39)	**1.36**	(0.39)
	Greece	-1.27	(0.01)	-0.83	(0.20)	**0.45**	(0.20)	-0.78	(0.01)	-0.65	(0.04)	**0.13**	(0.04)
	Hungary	0.03	(0.08)	0.64	(0.21)	**0.61**	(0.22)	0.72	(0.10)	1.54	(0.24)	**0.82**	(0.27)
	Iceland	0.23	(0.00)	c	c	c	c	-0.08	(0.00)	c	c	c	c
	Ireland	0.01	(0.13)	0.01	(0.09)	0.00	(0.15)	-0.60	(0.03)	-0.32	(0.02)	**0.28**	(0.03)
	Israel	-0.10	(0.08)	0.34	(0.19)	**0.44**	(0.20)	-0.43	(0.04)	0.58	(0.22)	**1.01**	(0.22)
	Italy	0.21	(0.04)	0.05	(0.11)	-0.16	(0.13)	-0.76	(0.01)	0.93	(0.23)	**1.69**	(0.23)
	Japan	0.98	(0.07)	1.26	(0.05)	**0.28**	(0.08)	-0.67	(0.03)	0.99	(0.18)	**1.66**	(0.18)
	Korea	0.74	(0.10)	0.87	(0.11)	0.13	(0.14)	-0.73	(0.01)	0.06	(0.15)	**0.80**	(0.15)
	Luxembourg	-0.93	(0.00)	-0.44	(0.00)	**0.49**	(0.00)	-0.60	(0.00)	1.59	(0.00)	**2.18**	(0.00)
	Mexico	-0.97	(0.02)	-0.53	(0.10)	**0.44**	(0.10)	-0.59	(0.01)	1.29	(0.12)	**1.88**	(0.12)
	Netherlands	1.04	(0.09)	1.04	(0.07)	-0.01	(0.11)	1.26	(0.14)	1.32	(0.14)	0.06	(0.20)
	New Zealand	0.81	(0.05)	0.92	(0.06)	0.12	(0.08)	0.01	(0.04)	1.88	(0.33)	**1.86**	(0.33)
	Norway	-0.57	(0.05)	c	c	c	c	-0.25	(0.04)	c	c	c	c
	Poland	0.30	(0.06)	0.67	(0.18)	0.36	(0.19)	-0.41	(0.02)	1.58	(0.25)	**1.99**	(0.25)
	Portugal	-1.05	(0.01)	-0.21	(0.12)	**0.84**	(0.12)	-0.65	(0.01)	0.80	(0.31)	**1.46**	(0.31)
	Slovak Republic	0.11	(0.08)	-0.18	(0.25)	-0.29	(0.25)	0.45	(0.09)	0.99	(0.34)	0.54	(0.36)
	Slovenia	-0.38	(0.01)	-0.38	(0.01)	-0.01	(0.01)	-0.14	(0.01)	0.18	(0.01)	**0.33**	(0.02)
	Spain	-0.67	(0.04)	-0.11	(0.07)	**0.56**	(0.08)	-0.74	(0.01)	0.06	(0.07)	**0.80**	(0.07)
	Sweden	0.17	(0.07)	0.53	(0.19)	0.35	(0.20)	0.65	(0.08)	2.28	(0.07)	**1.63**	(0.11)
	Switzerland	-0.68	(0.05)	0.34	(0.28)	**1.02**	(0.28)	-0.31	(0.03)	1.13	(0.33)	**1.44**	(0.33)
	Turkey	-1.05	(0.03)	c	c	c	c	-0.75	(0.01)	c	c	c	c
	United Kingdom	0.80	(0.05)	1.34	(0.02)	**0.55**	(0.05)	0.75	(0.08)	2.08	(0.12)	**1.33**	(0.15)
	United States	-0.29	(0.06)	0.68	(0.40)	**0.97**	(0.41)	0.34	(0.06)	1.09	(0.29)	**0.75**	(0.29)
	OECD average	-0.12	(0.01)	0.28	(0.03)	**0.36**	(0.04)	-0.22	(0.01)	0.88	(0.04)	**1.08**	(0.05)
Partners	Albania	-0.50	(0.07)	0.21	(0.16)	**0.71**	(0.18)	-0.73	(0.01)	0.49	(0.26)	**1.22**	(0.26)
	Argentina	-0.69	(0.05)	-0.37	(0.09)	**0.32**	(0.11)	-0.71	(0.01)	-0.28	(0.10)	**0.43**	(0.10)
	Azerbaijan	-0.63	(0.08)	c	c	c	c	-0.55	(0.02)	c	c	c	c
	Brazil	-0.72	(0.03)	0.63	(0.11)	**1.35**	(0.11)	-0.78	(0.01)	1.33	(0.15)	**2.11**	(0.15)
	Bulgaria	-0.91	(0.04)	c	c	c	c	1.36	(0.09)	c	c	c	c
	Colombia	-0.33	(0.08)	0.35	(0.12)	**0.68**	(0.14)	-0.71	(0.03)	1.48	(0.22)	**2.20**	(0.22)
	Croatia	-0.95	(0.02)	c	c	c	c	-0.43	(0.01)	c	c	c	c
	Dubai (UAE)	-1.19	(0.00)	0.51	(0.00)	**1.70**	(0.00)	-0.71	(0.00)	1.23	(0.00)	**1.94**	(0.00)
	Hong Kong-China	0.38	(0.15)	0.96	(0.06)	**0.58**	(0.16)	-0.53	(0.05)	0.26	(0.06)	**0.79**	(0.08)
	Indonesia	-0.10	(0.11)	0.44	(0.12)	**0.53**	(0.17)	-0.60	(0.02)	0.90	(0.11)	**1.51**	(0.11)
	Jordan	-1.28	(0.01)	-0.86	(0.17)	**0.42**	(0.17)	-0.73	(0.01)	-0.19	(0.14)	**0.55**	(0.14)
	Kazakhstan	-0.98	(0.04)	-0.96	(0.13)	0.02	(0.14)	-0.42	(0.04)	1.62	(0.53)	**2.04**	(0.53)
	Kyrgyzstan	-0.27	(0.08)	0.51	(0.38)	**0.78**	(0.39)	-0.50	(0.03)	1.96	(0.34)	**2.46**	(0.33)
	Latvia	-0.54	(0.05)	c	c	c	c	0.05	(0.05)	c	c	c	c
	Liechtenstein	-0.14	(0.01)	c	c	c	c	0.07	(0.01)	c	c	c	c
	Lithuania	0.13	(0.06)	c	c	c	c	-0.28	(0.03)	c	c	c	c
	Macao-China	c	c	0.93	(0.00)	c	c	c	c	1.70	(0.00)	c	c
	Montenegro	-0.97	(0.00)	c	c	c	c	-0.39	(0.00)	c	c	c	c
	Panama	-0.68	(0.09)	-0.25	(0.18)	**0.43**	(0.20)	-0.71	(0.02)	0.97	(0.21)	**1.68**	(0.21)
	Peru	-0.44	(0.07)	0.72	(0.15)	**1.16**	(0.15)	-0.56	(0.04)	2.07	(0.12)	**2.63**	(0.13)
	Qatar	-0.88	(0.00)	0.04	(0.01)	**0.91**	(0.01)	0.07	(0.00)	0.54	(0.01)	**0.47**	(0.01)
	Romania	-0.36	(0.06)	c	c	c	c	-0.75	(0.01)	c	c	c	c
	Russian Federation	-0.36	(0.06)	c	c	c	c	-0.08	(0.05)	c	c	c	c
	Serbia	-1.03	(0.02)	c	c	c	c	-0.40	(0.02)	c	c	c	c
	Shanghai-China	-0.14	(0.08)	0.39	(0.28)	0.53	(0.29)	0.69	(0.07)	1.99	(0.16)	**1.30**	(0.18)
	Singapore	-0.12	(0.00)	c	c	c	c	-0.44	(0.00)	c	c	c	c
	Chinese Taipei	0.24	(0.11)	0.62	(0.12)	**0.38**	(0.16)	-0.49	(0.02)	1.00	(0.16)	**1.49**	(0.16)
	Thailand	0.73	(0.07)	0.90	(0.17)	0.17	(0.18)	-0.02	(0.07)	1.73	(0.21)	**1.75**	(0.23)
	Trinidad and Tobago	-0.67	(0.01)	-0.13	(0.01)	**0.54**	(0.01)	-0.63	(0.00)	0.54	(0.01)	**1.17**	(0.01)
	Tunisia	-1.30	(0.01)	-1.08	(0.06)	**0.21**	(0.06)	-0.74	(0.01)	1.19	(0.64)	**1.93**	(0.64)
	Uruguay	-1.10	(0.02)	-0.49	(0.12)	**0.61**	(0.12)	-0.76	(0.00)	0.61	(0.17)	**1.37**	(0.17)

Note: Values that are statistically significant are indicated in bold (see Annex A3).
Source: OECD, *PISA 2009 Database*.

ANNEX B: DATA TABLES

[Part 2/3]
Table B1.2 **School autonomy, resources, climate and performance, by publicly and privately managed schools**

| | | Index of the school's educational resources |||||| Index of teacher shortage ||||||
| | | Publicly managed schools || Privately managed schools || Difference (private – public) || Publicly managed schools || Privately managed schools || Difference (private – public) ||
		Mean index	S.E.	Mean index	S.E.	Dif.	S.E.	Mean index	S.E.	Mean index	S.E.	Dif.	S.E.
OECD	Australia	0.17	(0.08)	0.84	(0.08)	**0.66**	(0.11)	0.29	(0.08)	-0.09	(0.08)	**-0.38**	(0.11)
	Austria	0.27	(0.07)	0.18	(0.19)	-0.09	(0.21)	-0.26	(0.07)	-0.92	(0.05)	**-0.66**	(0.09)
	Belgium	0.12	(0.11)	0.10	(0.08)	-0.02	(0.13)	0.60	(0.07)	0.47	(0.07)	-0.13	(0.10)
	Canada	0.32	(0.04)	1.23	(0.12)	**0.90**	(0.14)	-0.24	(0.03)	-0.18	(0.14)	0.06	(0.15)
	Chile	-1.00	(0.16)	-0.01	(0.10)	**0.99**	(0.19)	0.54	(0.15)	0.12	(0.12)	**-0.41**	(0.19)
	Czech Republic	-0.13	(0.05)	0.27	(0.17)	**0.40**	(0.18)	-0.01	(0.04)	-0.24	(0.25)	-0.22	(0.26)
	Denmark	0.10	(0.05)	0.27	(0.11)	0.16	(0.11)	-0.06	(0.05)	-0.32	(0.08)	**-0.26**	(0.09)
	Estonia	0.03	(0.05)	0.35	(0.31)	0.32	(0.32)	-0.11	(0.05)	-0.15	(0.21)	-0.04	(0.21)
	Finland	-0.21	(0.07)	0.48	(0.37)	0.69	(0.37)	-0.43	(0.04)	-0.12	(0.33)	0.31	(0.33)
	France	w	w	w	w	w	w	w	w	w	w	w	w
	Germany	-0.01	(0.07)	0.01	(0.21)	0.01	(0.23)	0.55	(0.06)	0.28	(0.36)	-0.26	(0.37)
	Greece	-0.14	(0.07)	0.79	(0.37)	**0.93**	(0.38)	-0.44	(0.07)	-0.93	(0.06)	**-0.49**	(0.09)
	Hungary	0.23	(0.07)	0.46	(0.19)	0.23	(0.21)	-0.56	(0.06)	-0.50	(0.15)	0.06	(0.16)
	Iceland	0.43	(0.00)	c	c	c	c	-0.24	(0.00)	c	c	c	c
	Ireland	-0.29	(0.16)	-0.37	(0.13)	-0.08	(0.20)	-0.16	(0.11)	-0.36	(0.09)	-0.20	(0.14)
	Israel	-0.01	(0.08)	-0.14	(0.25)	-0.12	(0.27)	0.31	(0.08)	-0.36	(0.17)	**-0.67**	(0.18)
	Italy	-0.12	(0.03)	0.47	(0.16)	**0.60**	(0.16)	0.15	(0.04)	-0.32	(0.11)	**-0.48**	(0.12)
	Japan	0.38	(0.09)	0.82	(0.13)	**0.44**	(0.16)	-0.58	(0.05)	-0.41	(0.12)	0.17	(0.13)
	Korea	0.08	(0.10)	0.03	(0.09)	-0.05	(0.13)	-0.18	(0.10)	0.25	(0.14)	**0.42**	(0.16)
	Luxembourg	0.16	(0.00)	1.27	(0.01)	**1.10**	(0.01)	1.32	(0.00)	0.04	(0.01)	**-1.28**	(0.01)
	Mexico	-1.00	(0.03)	0.53	(0.12)	**1.53**	(0.12)	0.55	(0.03)	-0.26	(0.10)	**-0.81**	(0.11)
	Netherlands	0.14	(0.12)	0.41	(0.09)	0.27	(0.15)	0.53	(0.10)	0.50	(0.08)	-0.03	(0.13)
	New Zealand	0.13	(0.06)	1.51	(0.23)	**1.38**	(0.23)	0.10	(0.05)	-0.53	(0.20)	**-0.63**	(0.21)
	Norway	-0.24	(0.05)	c	c	c	c	0.31	(0.06)	c	c	c	c
	Poland	0.28	(0.06)	0.52	(0.17)	0.24	(0.18)	-0.77	(0.04)	-0.94	(0.05)	**-0.17**	(0.06)
	Portugal	-0.34	(0.06)	0.78	(0.17)	**1.11**	(0.18)	-0.79	(0.04)	-0.86	(0.08)	-0.07	(0.08)
	Slovak Republic	-0.48	(0.05)	-0.25	(0.37)	0.23	(0.37)	-0.31	(0.05)	-0.18	(0.21)	0.13	(0.22)
	Slovenia	0.48	(0.01)	0.78	(0.01)	**0.30**	(0.01)	-0.72	(0.00)	-0.62	(0.01)	**0.10**	(0.01)
	Spain	-0.05	(0.05)	0.12	(0.09)	0.17	(0.10)	-0.78	(0.03)	-0.78	(0.04)	0.01	(0.05)
	Sweden	-0.04	(0.06)	0.39	(0.23)	0.43	(0.25)	-0.34	(0.05)	-0.34	(0.12)	-0.01	(0.14)
	Switzerland	0.54	(0.07)	0.48	(0.19)	-0.06	(0.21)	-0.04	(0.05)	-0.67	(0.12)	**-0.63**	(0.14)
	Turkey	-1.35	(0.06)	c	c	c	c	2.04	(0.10)	c	c	c	c
	United Kingdom	0.44	(0.07)	0.60	(0.28)	0.16	(0.28)	-0.03	(0.06)	-0.86	(0.09)	**-0.83**	(0.12)
	United States	0.50	(0.09)	0.63	(0.32)	0.13	(0.35)	-0.46	(0.06)	-0.34	(0.38)	0.12	(0.38)
	OECD average	**-0.02**	**(0.01)**	**0.45**	**(0.04)**	**0.43**	**(0.04)**	**-0.01**	**(0.01)**	**-0.32**	**(0.03)**	**-0.24**	**(0.03)**
Partners	Albania	-0.92	(0.05)	0.69	(0.17)	**1.61**	(0.18)	0.04	(0.07)	-0.83	(0.05)	**-0.88**	(0.08)
	Argentina	-0.86	(0.10)	-0.23	(0.23)	**0.63**	(0.26)	0.03	(0.08)	-0.52	(0.10)	**-0.55**	(0.13)
	Azerbaijan	-0.59	(0.07)	c	c	c	c	-0.02	(0.09)	c	c	c	c
	Brazil	-0.95	(0.04)	0.89	(0.17)	**1.84**	(0.17)	0.25	(0.05)	-0.74	(0.08)	**-0.99**	(0.09)
	Bulgaria	-0.12	(0.07)	c	c	c	c	-0.64	(0.05)	c	c	c	c
	Colombia	-1.49	(0.10)	0.40	(0.21)	**1.89**	(0.25)	0.37	(0.11)	-0.63	(0.12)	**-1.00**	(0.16)
	Croatia	-0.21	(0.07)	c	c	c	c	-0.19	(0.06)	c	c	c	c
	Dubai (UAE)	-0.01	(0.00)	1.11	(0.00)	**1.11**	(0.00)	0.28	(0.00)	-0.61	(0.00)	**-0.89**	(0.00)
	Hong Kong-China	0.92	(0.23)	0.82	(0.08)	-0.10	(0.24)	-0.42	(0.26)	-0.51	(0.07)	-0.09	(0.27)
	Indonesia	-1.08	(0.13)	-1.35	(0.13)	-0.27	(0.18)	0.10	(0.09)	0.55	(0.13)	**0.45**	(0.16)
	Jordan	-0.38	(0.08)	-0.12	(0.25)	0.26	(0.27)	0.81	(0.11)	0.55	(0.26)	-0.26	(0.28)
	Kazakhstan	-0.79	(0.08)	0.20	(0.44)	**0.99**	(0.45)	0.49	(0.09)	-0.18	(0.32)	**-0.67**	(0.32)
	Kyrgyzstan	-1.76	(0.07)	-0.44	(0.43)	**1.32**	(0.44)	0.91	(0.09)	1.26	(0.38)	0.34	(0.38)
	Latvia	-0.11	(0.05)	c	c	c	c	-0.42	(0.06)	c	c	c	c
	Liechtenstein	1.05	(0.01)	c	c	c	c	-0.08	(0.01)	c	c	c	c
	Lithuania	-0.18	(0.04)	c	c	c	c	-0.36	(0.05)	c	c	c	c
	Macao-China	c	c	0.06	(0.00)	c	c	c	c	0.32	(0.00)	c	c
	Montenegro	-0.79	(0.00)	c	c	c	c	-0.36	(0.01)	c	c	c	c
	Panama	-1.36	(0.11)	0.93	(0.17)	**2.29**	(0.20)	0.01	(0.11)	-0.56	(0.14)	**-0.57**	(0.18)
	Peru	-1.37	(0.09)	-0.07	(0.22)	**1.30**	(0.26)	0.52	(0.07)	-0.20	(0.13)	**-0.73**	(0.15)
	Qatar	0.40	(0.00)	0.86	(0.01)	**0.46**	(0.01)	-0.11	(0.00)	-0.52	(0.00)	**-0.41**	(0.01)
	Romania	0.08	(0.06)	c	c	c	c	-0.74	(0.03)	c	c	c	c
	Russian Federation	-0.63	(0.07)	c	c	c	c	0.13	(0.08)	c	c	c	c
	Serbia	-0.39	(0.07)	c	c	c	c	-0.64	(0.05)	c	c	c	c
	Shanghai-China	0.16	(0.10)	0.11	(0.34)	-0.05	(0.36)	0.60	(0.11)	0.09	(0.29)	-0.51	(0.31)
	Singapore	1.07	(0.00)	c	c	c	c	0.08	(0.00)	c	c	c	c
	Chinese Taipei	0.20	(0.11)	0.38	(0.16)	0.18	(0.19)	-0.09	(0.12)	-0.10	(0.19)	-0.01	(0.22)
	Thailand	-0.59	(0.07)	0.23	(0.21)	**0.82**	(0.22)	0.89	(0.08)	0.32	(0.22)	**-0.57**	(0.24)
	Trinidad and Tobago	-0.71	(0.01)	-0.17	(0.01)	**0.54**	(0.01)	0.58	(0.01)	-0.26	(0.01)	**-0.84**	(0.01)
	Tunisia	-0.48	(0.07)	-0.94	(0.41)	-0.46	(0.42)	-0.61	(0.04)	-0.37	(0.27)	0.24	(0.27)
	Uruguay	-0.05	(0.07)	0.99	(0.15)	**1.04**	(0.17)	0.25	(0.05)	-0.51	(0.13)	**-0.76**	(0.14)

Note: Values that are statistically significant are indicated in bold (see Annex A3).
Source: OECD, *PISA 2009 Database*.

[Part 3/3]

Table B1.2 **School autonomy, resources, climate and performance, by publicly and privately managed schools**

		Index of disciplinary climate					Performance in reading				
		Publicly managed schools		Privately managed schools		Difference (private – public)		Publicly managed schools		Privately managed schools		Difference (private – public)	
		Mean index	S.E.	Mean index	S.E.	Dif.	S.E.	Mean index	S.E.	Mean index	S.E.	Dif.	S.E.
OECD	Australia	-0.18	(0.03)	0.08	(0.03)	**0.27**	(0.04)	497	(3.9)	542	(3.0)	**45**	(5.4)
	Austria	0.08	(0.04)	0.27	(0.10)	0.20	(0.11)	465	(3.5)	497	(13.7)	**31**	(15.0)
	Belgium	-0.14	(0.04)	-0.04	(0.03)	**0.10**	(0.05)	w	w	w	w	w	w
	Canada	-0.10	(0.01)	0.17	(0.06)	**0.27**	(0.06)	521	(1.5)	566	(7.1)	**45**	(7.4)
	Chile	-0.19	(0.04)	-0.05	(0.04)	**0.14**	(0.06)	423	(5.2)	469	(3.9)	**46**	(6.2)
	Czech Republic	-0.18	(0.04)	-0.09	(0.19)	0.09	(0.19)	477	(3.0)	509	(19.8)	32	(20.1)
	Denmark	0.00	(0.03)	0.05	(0.06)	0.05	(0.07)	491	(2.2)	508	(5.7)	**17**	(6.3)
	Estonia	0.05	(0.03)	0.01	(0.14)	-0.04	(0.15)	501	(2.7)	510	(18.9)	9	(19.2)
	Finland	-0.29	(0.02)	-0.41	(0.13)	-0.12	(0.14)	536	(2.2)	542	(18.7)	7	(18.7)
	France	w	w	w	w	w	w	w	w	w	w	w	w
	Germany	0.25	(0.03)	0.39	(0.07)	**0.14**	(0.07)	497	(3.2)	513	(19.6)	17	(20.7)
	Greece	-0.42	(0.03)	-0.14	(0.06)	**0.28**	(0.07)	480	(4.5)	542	(16.3)	**62**	(17.2)
	Hungary	-0.02	(0.04)	-0.04	(0.08)	-0.02	(0.09)	492	(3.7)	507	(12.4)	15	(14.0)
	Iceland	-0.07	(0.01)	c	c	c	c	498	(1.5)	c	c	c	c
	Ireland	-0.10	(0.06)	0.01	(0.03)	0.11	(0.07)	474	(4.9)	509	(3.7)	**35**	(6.2)
	Israel	0.01	(0.03)	0.42	(0.06)	**0.41**	(0.08)	470	(4.5)	498	(13.0)	28	(14.9)
	Italy	0.05	(0.02)	-0.23	(0.10)	**-0.28**	(0.10)	489	(1.6)	448	(9.0)	**-41**	(9.3)
	Japan	0.80	(0.03)	0.64	(0.05)	**-0.17**	(0.06)	522	(4.0)	514	(8.1)	-8	(9.5)
	Korea	0.30	(0.03)	0.51	(0.04)	**0.20**	(0.05)	533	(5.2)	549	(5.4)	15	(8.6)
	Luxembourg	-0.22	(0.02)	-0.12	(0.04)	**0.10**	(0.05)	472	(1.3)	473	(2.7)	1	(2.7)
	Mexico	0.11	(0.01)	0.10	(0.04)	-0.01	(0.04)	420	(2.1)	468	(4.4)	**48**	(5.1)
	Netherlands	-0.32	(0.03)	-0.26	(0.03)	0.07	(0.04)	515	(9.6)	504	(8.1)	-11	(14.4)
	New Zealand	-0.14	(0.02)	0.29	(0.06)	**0.43**	(0.07)	517	(2.3)	586	(10.6)	**69**	(10.8)
	Norway	-0.24	(0.02)	c	c	c	c	503	(2.6)	c	c	c	c
	Poland	0.07	(0.03)	0.15	(0.14)	0.08	(0.14)	499	(2.7)	554	(11.7)	**55**	(12.2)
	Portugal	0.16	(0.02)	0.35	(0.10)	0.20	(0.10)	485	(3.3)	516	(9.2)	**31**	(9.7)
	Slovak Republic	-0.04	(0.03)	0.21	(0.12)	**0.26**	(0.13)	475	(3.0)	499	(14.3)	24	(15.8)
	Slovenia	-0.12	(0.02)	0.43	(0.08)	**0.55**	(0.08)	481	(1.0)	561	(6.0)	**80**	(6.2)
	Spain	0.03	(0.02)	0.20	(0.04)	**0.17**	(0.05)	469	(2.3)	505	(3.8)	**36**	(4.2)
	Sweden	-0.07	(0.03)	0.25	(0.06)	**0.31**	(0.07)	494	(2.8)	529	(11.1)	**35**	(11.3)
	Switzerland	0.09	(0.03)	0.17	(0.10)	0.08	(0.10)	500	(2.6)	518	(9.6)	18	(10.5)
	Turkey	0.03	(0.02)	c	c	c	c	464	(3.6)	c	c	c	c
	United Kingdom	0.08	(0.03)	0.65	(0.08)	**0.57**	(0.08)	492	(2.5)	553	(5.4)	**62**	(6.0)
	United States	0.12	(0.02)	0.55	(0.09)	**0.43**	(0.09)	494	(3.4)	565	(15.3)	**72**	(15.6)
	OECD average	-0.02	(0.01)	0.15	(0.02)	**0.16**	(0.02)	489	(0.6)	519	(2.1)	**30**	(2.3)
Partners	Albania	0.50	(0.02)	0.75	(0.15)	0.25	(0.15)	378	(4.2)	442	(10.9)	**65**	(11.7)
	Argentina	-0.22	(0.03)	-0.33	(0.06)	-0.11	(0.07)	367	(5.6)	453	(8.4)	**86**	(10.5)
	Azerbaijan	0.57	(0.03)	c	c	c	c	361	(3.3)	c	c	c	c
	Brazil	-0.19	(0.02)	-0.01	(0.05)	**0.18**	(0.05)	398	(3.2)	516	(6.7)	**117**	(7.5)
	Bulgaria	0.01	(0.04)	c	c	c	c	428	(6.8)	c	c	c	c
	Colombia	0.17	(0.02)	0.26	(0.07)	0.09	(0.08)	400	(4.0)	468	(6.7)	**69**	(7.7)
	Croatia	-0.14	(0.03)	c	c	c	c	475	(3.1)	c	c	c	c
	Dubai (UAE)	-0.13	(0.03)	0.20	(0.01)	**0.33**	(0.03)	386	(1.9)	480	(1.3)	**94**	(2.1)
	Hong Kong-China	0.37	(0.07)	0.38	(0.02)	0.01	(0.07)	553	(10.1)	531	(2.2)	-22	(10.4)
	Indonesia	0.26	(0.03)	0.26	(0.03)	0.00	(0.04)	409	(5.0)	391	(5.1)	-18	(7.2)
	Jordan	0.22	(0.03)	0.28	(0.07)	0.06	(0.07)	401	(3.6)	424	(8.8)	23	(9.5)
	Kazakhstan	0.77	(0.03)	0.88	(0.18)	0.11	(0.18)	389	(3.2)	439	(24.4)	50	(25.1)
	Kyrgyzstan	0.35	(0.02)	0.51	(0.06)	**0.16**	(0.07)	310	(3.2)	439	(16.0)	**129**	(16.7)
	Latvia	0.24	(0.03)	c	c	c	c	484	(2.9)	c	c	c	c
	Liechtenstein	0.11	(0.05)	c	c	c	c	498	(2.9)	c	c	c	c
	Lithuania	0.30	(0.03)	c	c	c	c	468	(2.4)	c	c	c	c
	Macao-China	c	c	0.11	(0.01)	c	c	c	c	488	(0.9)	c	c
	Montenegro	0.28	(0.01)	c	c	c	c	408	(1.7)	c	c	c	c
	Panama	0.07	(0.04)	-0.04	(0.07)	-0.12	(0.08)	343	(6.6)	463	(13.7)	**119**	(15.2)
	Peru	0.18	(0.02)	0.22	(0.04)	0.04	(0.04)	350	(3.5)	439	(10.2)	**89**	(10.5)
	Qatar	-0.08	(0.02)	0.16	(0.02)	**0.24**	(0.03)	339	(1.0)	460	(1.8)	**121**	(2.2)
	Romania	0.43	(0.03)	c	c	c	c	425	(4.1)	c	c	c	c
	Russian Federation	0.44	(0.02)	c	c	c	c	459	(3.3)	c	c	c	c
	Serbia	-0.03	(0.03)	c	c	c	c	441	(2.6)	c	c	c	c
	Shanghai-China	0.45	(0.02)	0.46	(0.09)	0.02	(0.09)	554	(2.4)	574	(11.7)	20	(11.9)
	Singapore	0.12	(0.01)	c	c	c	c	527	(1.0)	c	c	c	c
	Chinese Taipei	0.15	(0.02)	-0.01	(0.03)	**-0.16**	(0.04)	510	(3.4)	470	(3.8)	**-40**	(5.1)
	Thailand	0.32	(0.02)	0.34	(0.04)	0.02	(0.04)	423	(2.9)	416	(6.9)	-7	(7.6)
	Trinidad and Tobago	-0.01	(0.02)	-0.10	(0.04)	-0.09	(0.05)	417	(1.4)	436	(3.3)	**19**	(3.7)
	Tunisia	-0.19	(0.02)	-0.23	(0.14)	-0.03	(0.14)	405	(2.9)	326	(6.0)	**-79**	(6.7)
	Uruguay	-0.03	(0.02)	0.06	(0.06)	0.10	(0.06)	409	(2.7)	504	(5.3)	**95**	(5.9)

Note: Values that are statistically significant are indicated in bold (see Annex A3).
Source: OECD, *PISA 2009 Database*.

ANNEX B: DATA TABLES

[Part 1/1]
Table B1.3 **Public and private involvement in funding schools**

Percentage of total school funding for a typical school year comes from:

		Government, including departments, local, regional state and national authorities		Student fees or school charges paid by parents		Benefactors, donations, bequests, sponsorships, parents' fundraising		Other	
		%	S.E.	%	S.E.	%	S.E.	%	S.E.
OECD	Australia	71.5	(1.0)	24.5	(0.9)	2.5	(0.2)	1.5	(0.2)
	Austria	m	m	m	m	m	m	m	m
	Belgium	87.0	(1.0)	9.5	(0.9)	1.2	(0.2)	2.3	(0.3)
	Canada	89.7	(0.8)	8.2	(0.7)	1.4	(0.1)	0.7	(0.1)
	Chile	71.6	(2.0)	26.1	(1.9)	1.4	(0.4)	0.9	(0.5)
	Czech Republic	95.9	(0.6)	1.4	(0.4)	0.5	(0.1)	2.2	(0.5)
	Denmark	92.0	(0.9)	7.6	(0.8)	0.2	(0.1)	0.2	(0.1)
	Estonia	98.0	(0.5)	1.1	(0.5)	0.3	(0.1)	0.5	(0.1)
	Finland	99.8	(0.1)	0.1	(0.1)	0.1	(0.0)	0.1	(0.0)
	France	w	w	w	w	w	w	w	w
	Germany	97.2	(0.5)	0.6	(0.2)	1.8	(0.3)	0.4	(0.1)
	Greece	80.8	(1.0)	5.0	(0.8)	0.8	(0.2)	13.4	(0.8)
	Hungary	91.8	(0.7)	0.3	(0.2)	2.4	(0.4)	5.6	(0.7)
	Iceland	99.6	(0.0)	0.2	(0.0)	0.1	(0.0)	0.0	(0.0)
	Ireland	87.5	(1.9)	8.8	(1.8)	3.1	(0.5)	0.6	(0.2)
	Israel	76.2	(2.4)	17.8	(1.9)	2.7	(0.6)	3.3	(1.2)
	Italy	69.2	(1.1)	21.9	(0.8)	1.9	(0.2)	7.0	(0.8)
	Japan	72.8	(1.2)	22.1	(1.0)	2.4	(0.5)	2.8	(0.4)
	Korea	47.6	(2.2)	47.5	(2.2)	0.6	(0.1)	4.3	(1.0)
	Luxembourg	95.3	(0.0)	2.6	(0.0)	0.2	(0.0)	1.9	(0.0)
	Mexico	43.9	(1.3)	46.4	(1.3)	6.1	(0.7)	3.6	(0.5)
	Netherlands	96.5	(0.4)	2.4	(0.4)	0.1	(0.0)	1.0	(0.2)
	New Zealand	77.2	(1.0)	16.8	(0.9)	2.5	(0.3)	3.5	(0.4)
	Norway	99.7	(0.1)	0.2	(0.1)	0.1	(0.0)	0.0	(0.0)
	Poland	96.9	(0.5)	2.1	(0.4)	0.6	(0.1)	0.3	(0.1)
	Portugal	83.0	(1.4)	10.5	(1.3)	0.7	(0.2)	5.8	(0.8)
	Slovak Republic	96.5	(0.5)	0.7	(0.4)	1.3	(0.1)	1.6	(0.3)
	Slovenia	94.7	(0.1)	1.9	(0.1)	0.9	(0.0)	2.5	(0.0)
	Spain	86.1	(1.2)	7.6	(0.9)	2.7	(0.4)	3.6	(1.1)
	Sweden	99.8	(0.1)	0.0	(0.0)	0.0	(0.0)	0.1	(0.1)
	Switzerland	95.1	(1.4)	4.4	(1.4)	0.3	(0.1)	0.3	(0.1)
	Turkey	60.4	(2.3)	16.7	(1.7)	19.0	(1.5)	3.9	(0.8)
	United Kingdom	92.6	(1.2)	6.9	(1.2)	0.3	(0.1)	0.2	(0.1)
	United States	89.3	(1.8)	7.5	(1.4)	2.0	(0.7)	1.2	(0.6)
	OECD average	**85.5**	**(0.2)**	**10.3**	**(0.2)**	**1.9**	**(0.1)**	**2.4**	**(0.1)**
Partners	Albania	76.9	(2.5)	14.4	(2.0)	5.9	(1.4)	2.7	(1.0)
	Argentina	57.6	(2.6)	26.8	(2.6)	13.1	(3.0)	2.4	(0.7)
	Azerbaijan	98.7	(0.3)	0.5	(0.2)	0.2	(0.1)	0.5	(0.3)
	Brazil	83.5	(1.0)	11.7	(1.0)	2.6	(0.4)	2.2	(0.6)
	Bulgaria	96.7	(0.8)	1.9	(0.8)	0.6	(0.1)	0.8	(0.2)
	Colombia	62.1	(3.0)	31.5	(2.8)	2.5	(0.5)	3.8	(1.0)
	Croatia	93.7	(1.1)	2.9	(1.1)	1.0	(0.2)	2.3	(0.3)
	Dubai (UAE)	14.0	(0.0)	82.2	(0.0)	1.0	(0.0)	2.8	(0.0)
	Hong Kong-China	91.8	(1.1)	6.9	(1.1)	0.7	(0.2)	0.6	(0.1)
	Indonesia	58.6	(2.6)	30.0	(2.4)	8.3	(1.7)	2.9	(0.7)
	Jordan	77.9	(1.4)	12.3	(1.2)	1.5	(0.7)	8.2	(1.2)
	Kazakhstan	94.4	(1.5)	4.0	(1.3)	1.5	(0.7)	0.1	(0.1)
	Kyrgyzstan	87.1	(1.8)	7.0	(1.3)	4.7	(0.8)	1.2	(0.5)
	Latvia	96.6	(0.6)	0.6	(0.2)	0.6	(0.1)	2.2	(0.6)
	Liechtenstein	95.0	(0.0)	4.6	(0.0)	0.4	(0.0)	0.0	(0.0)
	Lithuania	98.5	(0.3)	0.0	(0.0)	1.0	(0.2)	0.4	(0.1)
	Macao-China	84.3	(0.0)	12.5	(0.0)	0.5	(0.0)	2.7	(0.0)
	Montenegro	91.1	(0.2)	3.0	(0.1)	0.5	(0.0)	5.4	(0.1)
	Panama	66.0	(2.7)	27.7	(2.7)	3.9	(1.0)	2.4	(0.7)
	Peru	40.5	(3.3)	39.4	(2.6)	6.2	(1.1)	13.9	(2.1)
	Qatar	65.9	(0.1)	29.7	(0.1)	1.3	(0.0)	3.0	(0.0)
	Romania	94.3	(0.8)	0.8	(0.5)	1.6	(0.3)	3.2	(0.5)
	Russian Federation	96.3	(0.5)	0.9	(0.3)	2.5	(0.6)	0.3	(0.1)
	Serbia	93.6	(0.9)	0.9	(0.3)	2.4	(0.4)	3.0	(0.8)
	Shanghai-China	77.1	(1.3)	21.1	(1.3)	0.3	(0.1)	1.5	(0.4)
	Singapore	79.7	(0.8)	16.1	(0.2)	3.5	(0.5)	0.7	(0.1)
	Chinese Taipei	64.0	(1.6)	31.0	(1.5)	1.3	(0.5)	3.7	(0.5)
	Thailand	81.3	(1.3)	11.0	(1.2)	5.8	(0.9)	1.9	(0.4)
	Trinidad and Tobago	86.1	(0.1)	4.4	(0.0)	7.6	(0.0)	1.9	(0.0)
	Tunisia	79.9	(0.8)	18.5	(0.8)	0.4	(0.2)	1.2	(0.4)
	Uruguay	76.9	(1.0)	19.2	(1.0)	2.9	(0.5)	1.0	(0.2)

Source: OECD, *PISA 2009 Database*.

[Part 1/1]

Table B1.4 **Public and private involvement in funding schools, by publicly and privately managed schools**

Percentage of total school funding for a typical school year comes from:

		Government, including departments, local, regional state and national authorities				Student fees or school charges paid by parents				Benefactors, donations, bequests, sponsorships, parents' fundraising				Other			
		Publicly managed schools		Privately managed schools		Publicly managed schools		Privately managed schools		Publicly managed schools		Privately managed schools		Publicly managed schools		Privately managed schools	
		%	S.E.	%	S.E.	%	S.E.	%	S.E.	%	S.E.	%	S.E.	%	S.E.	%	S.E.
OECD	Australia	82.8	(1.4)	54.7	(1.6)	13.2	(1.2)	41.2	(1.5)	2.7	(0.3)	2.1	(0.4)	1.3	(0.3)	1.9	(0.3)
	Belgium	92.3	(1.5)	84.7	(1.2)	6.2	(1.4)	10.9	(1.1)	0.5	(0.1)	1.5	(0.3)	1.1	(0.5)	2.9	(0.4)
	Canada	93.5	(0.5)	42.1	(4.1)	4.7	(0.4)	52.1	(4.5)	1.2	(0.1)	3.7	(1.0)	0.6	(0.1)	2.1	(0.8)
	Chile	74.6	(4.4)	68.5	(2.0)	21.0	(4.1)	30.4	(2.0)	2.3	(0.8)	1.0	(0.3)	2.2	(1.2)	0.1	(0.1)
	Czech Republic	96.9	(0.5)	70.5	(4.8)	0.7	(0.2)	19.3	(6.0)	0.5	(0.1)	1.0	(0.6)	1.9	(0.5)	9.1	(6.4)
	Denmark	99.3	(0.3)	67.3	(1.8)	0.6	(0.3)	31.1	(2.0)	0.0	(0.0)	0.6	(0.5)	0.0	(0.0)	1.0	(0.5)
	Estonia	98.9	(0.2)	74.0	(10.6)	0.4	(0.2)	23.1	(10.1)	0.2	(0.1)	2.1	(1.8)	0.5	(0.1)	0.9	(0.8)
	Finland	99.9	(0.0)	97.4	(1.5)	0.0	(0.0)	1.9	(1.5)	0.0	(0.0)	0.5	(0.4)	0.1	(0.0)	0.3	(0.1)
	Germany	97.7	(0.5)	85.7	(3.6)	0.2	(0.1)	9.6	(3.7)	1.9	(0.4)	0.2	(0.1)	0.2	(0.1)	4.5	(1.5)
	Greece	85.4	(0.8)	0.0	(0.0)	0.1	(0.0)	93.0	(3.9)	0.5	(0.1)	5.7	(3.5)	14.1	(0.8)	1.3	(1.1)
	Hungary	93.5	(0.7)	80.7	(3.8)	0.1	(0.0)	1.6	(1.6)	1.7	(0.3)	7.4	(2.5)	4.9	(0.6)	10.4	(4.1)
	Ireland	96.6	(0.9)	81.8	(3.0)	1.1	(0.3)	13.6	(2.9)	1.5	(0.7)	4.1	(0.7)	0.8	(0.5)	0.5	(0.2)
	Israel	78.3	(2.6)	65.0	(5.5)	17.3	(2.2)	20.8	(4.2)	1.0	(0.2)	11.2	(3.3)	3.4	(1.4)	2.9	(2.2)
	Italy	71.2	(1.1)	36.2	(6.4)	19.7	(0.8)	58.4	(6.1)	1.9	(0.2)	1.4	(0.6)	7.2	(0.8)	4.0	(1.8)
	Japan	87.4	(1.5)	36.8	(1.3)	8.6	(1.3)	55.2	(1.1)	2.7	(0.7)	1.6	(0.3)	1.4	(0.5)	6.4	(1.0)
	Korea	46.3	(2.9)	50.0	(2.7)	48.4	(3.0)	45.8	(3.0)	0.7	(0.2)	0.3	(0.1)	4.6	(1.3)	3.9	(1.1)
	Luxembourg	97.1	(0.0)	82.9	(0.1)	0.6	(0.0)	16.2	(0.1)	0.2	(0.0)	0.0	(0.0)	2.1	(0.0)	0.9	(0.0)
	Mexico	49.4	(1.3)	0.9	(0.5)	40.7	(1.4)	91.1	(2.6)	6.2	(0.7)	5.0	(2.5)	3.7	(0.6)	3.1	(1.1)
	Netherlands	96.5	(0.4)	96.4	(0.6)	2.3	(0.4)	2.5	(0.5)	0.1	(0.0)	0.1	(0.1)	1.1	(0.3)	0.9	(0.2)
	New Zealand	81.0	(0.9)	9.6	(1.0)	12.9	(0.8)	86.9	(0.8)	2.5	(0.3)	2.1	(0.6)	3.6	(0.5)	1.4	(0.6)
	Poland	98.0	(0.5)	46.0	(4.6)	1.1	(0.4)	48.1	(4.0)	0.6	(0.1)	2.8	(1.1)	0.2	(0.1)	3.1	(1.8)
	Portugal	88.2	(1.1)	52.6	(7.0)	4.5	(0.8)	45.4	(6.9)	0.8	(0.2)	0.2	(0.1)	6.5	(0.9)	1.8	(1.3)
	Slovak Republic	96.9	(0.4)	91.9	(3.1)	0.0	(0.0)	7.0	(3.0)	1.4	(0.1)	0.6	(0.2)	1.7	(0.4)	0.4	(0.2)
	Slovenia	94.9	(0.1)	86.6	(0.2)	1.8	(0.1)	5.9	(0.1)	0.9	(0.0)	2.1	(0.0)	2.4	(0.0)	5.4	(0.1)
	Spain	95.3	(1.3)	67.6	(1.8)	1.9	(0.5)	19.1	(2.7)	0.7	(0.2)	6.7	(1.3)	2.1	(1.2)	6.5	(1.3)
	Sweden	99.8	(0.1)	99.6	(0.3)	0.0	(0.0)	0.3	(0.3)	0.0	(0.0)	0.1	(0.0)	0.1	(0.1)	0.0	(0.0)
	Switzerland	98.6	(0.3)	39.6	(13.1)	1.0	(0.2)	57.9	(13.0)	0.1	(0.1)	2.3	(0.7)	0.3	(0.1)	0.2	(0.2)
	United Kingdom	99.6	(0.1)	0.0	(0.0)	0.0	(0.0)	97.6	(0.8)	0.2	(0.0)	2.0	(0.8)	0.2	(0.1)	0.4	(0.4)
	United States	97.3	(0.7)	0.0	(0.0)	0.9	(0.3)	81.1	(7.2)	0.6	(0.2)	17.8	(6.9)	1.2	(0.6)	1.1	(0.8)
	OECD average	**89.2**	**(0.2)**	**57.6**	**(0.8)**	**7.2**	**(0.2)**	**36.8**	**(0.8)**	**1.2**	**(0.1)**	**3.0**	**(0.3)**	**2.4**	**(0.1)**	**2.7**	**(0.3)**
Partners	Albania	86.6	(1.8)	0.0	(0.0)	7.1	(1.3)	73.3	(8.1)	4.7	(1.4)	15.8	(5.8)	1.7	(0.6)	10.9	(7.0)
	Argentina	65.3	(3.3)	45.7	(4.0)	18.3	(2.5)	40.1	(5.6)	12.9	(2.7)	13.5	(6.5)	3.5	(1.1)	0.7	(0.3)
	Brazil	95.1	(0.8)	1.9	(1.1)	0.8	(0.6)	88.3	(4.8)	2.4	(0.4)	3.2	(1.4)	1.6	(0.4)	6.6	(4.4)
	Colombia	71.9	(3.3)	20.4	(4.8)	21.5	(3.0)	74.4	(5.7)	2.6	(0.5)	2.2	(1.6)	4.0	(1.2)	3.0	(1.4)
	Dubai (UAE)	80.1	(0.0)	0.2	(0.0)	5.4	(0.1)	98.3	(0.0)	3.4	(0.0)	0.5	(0.0)	11.1	(0.1)	1.1	(0.0)
	Hong Kong-China	98.4	(1.1)	91.3	(1.2)	1.2	(0.7)	7.3	(1.2)	0.1	(0.1)	0.8	(0.2)	0.4	(0.4)	0.6	(0.1)
	Indonesia	72.3	(3.6)	40.2	(3.7)	16.3	(2.5)	48.6	(4.1)	9.8	(2.6)	6.3	(1.7)	1.5	(0.4)	4.9	(1.4)
	Jordan	95.5	(1.5)	0.9	(0.3)	2.5	(1.2)	55.6	(4.7)	1.1	(0.6)	3.5	(2.3)	1.0	(0.8)	40.0	(4.7)
	Kazakhstan	97.4	(0.8)	3.6	(3.2)	1.6	(0.7)	75.4	(17.8)	0.9	(0.3)	19.9	(18.1)	0.1	(0.0)	1.1	(0.8)
	Kyrgyzstan	89.7	(1.6)	0.0	(0.0)	5.1	(1.2)	68.6	(11.5)	3.9	(0.7)	31.4	(11.5)	1.3	(0.5)	0.0	(0.0)
	Panama	82.8	(2.2)	1.5	(0.7)	9.8	(1.6)	96.0	(1.4)	4.4	(1.2)	2.2	(1.2)	3.0	(0.9)	0.2	(0.1)
	Peru	52.9	(4.0)	2.8	(1.8)	21.3	(2.4)	94.6	(2.3)	7.9	(1.5)	0.9	(0.4)	17.9	(2.7)	1.6	(1.0)
	Qatar	94.3	(0.0)	0.6	(0.0)	1.9	(0.0)	93.3	(0.1)	1.0	(0.0)	2.3	(0.0)	2.7	(0.0)	3.8	(0.1)
	Shanghai-China	85.0	(1.0)	3.4	(3.2)	13.0	(0.9)	96.5	(3.2)	0.3	(0.1)	0.1	(0.1)	1.6	(0.4)	0.1	(0.1)
	Chinese Taipei	93.4	(0.7)	8.8	(2.3)	4.9	(0.6)	79.9	(2.9)	1.0	(0.3)	1.9	(1.2)	0.8	(0.2)	9.3	(1.4)
	Thailand	84.8	(1.2)	64.4	(5.5)	7.3	(0.9)	28.8	(5.1)	6.0	(0.8)	4.9	(3.1)	1.9	(0.4)	2.0	(1.2)
	Trinidad and Tobago	89.7	(0.1)	55.1	(0.3)	2.0	(0.0)	25.1	(0.3)	6.7	(0.0)	14.2	(0.2)	1.5	(0.0)	5.6	(0.1)
	Tunisia	81.2	(0.8)	0.0	(0.0)	17.1	(0.8)	100.0	(0.0)	0.4	(0.2)	0.0	(0.0)	1.2	(0.4)	0.0	(0.0)
	Uruguay	93.3	(0.8)	0.0	(0.0)	2.7	(0.5)	96.6	(1.4)	2.9	(0.5)	2.5	(1.2)	1.0	(0.2)	0.9	(0.4)

Source: OECD, *PISA 2009 Database*.

ANNEX B: DATA TABLES

[Part 1/1]

Table B2.1 Socio-economic stratification between students who attend publicly and privately managed schools

		PISA index of economic, social and cultural status (ESCS)					Proportion of students who attend privately managed schools, by national quarters of the PISA index of economic, social and cultural status (ESCS)							
		Publicly managed schools — Schools that are directly or indirectly managed by a public education authority, government agency, or governing board appointed by government or elected by public franchise		Privately managed schools — Schools that are directly or indirectly managed by a non-government organisation, such as a church, trade union, business, or other private institution		Difference (private – public)		Bottom quarter		Second quarter		Third quarter		Top quarter	
		Mean index	S.E.	Mean index	S.E.	Dif.	S.E.	%	S.E.	%	S.E.	%	S.E.	%	S.E.
OECD	Australia	0.15	(0.02)	0.62	(0.02)	**0.47**	(0.03)	21.6	(1.3)	35.1	(1.2)	46.0	(1.2)	60.6	(1.8)
	Austria	0.01	(0.03)	0.36	(0.09)	**0.34**	(0.10)	6.4	(1.4)	11.1	(2.2)	14.2	(3.1)	17.3	(4.5)
	Belgium	-0.03	(0.03)	0.29	(0.02)	**0.32**	(0.04)	60.5	(1.7)	67.2	(1.1)	70.7	(1.2)	80.4	(1.4)
	Canada	0.46	(0.02)	1.00	(0.06)	**0.54**	(0.06)	3.1	(0.5)	4.1	(0.4)	8.8	(0.9)	14.3	(1.8)
	Chile	-1.01	(0.06)	-0.22	(0.06)	**0.79**	(0.08)	37.8	(3.2)	51.7	(2.7)	63.5	(2.1)	79.6	(2.2)
	Czech Republic	-0.10	(0.01)	0.19	(0.09)	**0.29**	(0.10)	2.1	(0.8)	2.9	(1.2)	3.6	(1.2)	5.6	(1.2)
	Denmark	0.25	(0.03)	0.47	(0.05)	**0.22**	(0.06)	16.4	(2.5)	21.5	(2.9)	25.5	(3.3)	28.2	(3.9)
	Estonia	0.14	(0.02)	0.45	(0.16)	0.31	(0.16)	2.4	(1.3)	1.9	(0.7)	3.5	(1.5)	5.2	(2.1)
	Finland	0.36	(0.02)	0.52	(0.16)	0.16	(0.16)	2.8	(1.1)	4.0	(1.6)	4.0	(1.3)	4.9	(1.9)
	France	w	w	w	w	w	w	w	w	w	w	w	w	w	w
	Germany	0.17	(0.03)	0.46	(0.14)	**0.29**	(0.15)	2.7	(1.1)	4.4	(1.4)	5.5	(1.9)	6.9	(2.4)
	Greece	-0.08	(0.03)	0.98	(0.17)	**1.05**	(0.17)	1.3	(1.1)	1.2	(0.4)	4.0	(0.9)	14.6	(2.1)
	Hungary	-0.24	(0.03)	0.12	(0.12)	**0.36**	(0.14)	8.0	(2.2)	10.7	(2.5)	14.4	(3.0)	19.0	(5.0)
	Iceland	0.71	(0.02)	c	c	c	c	0.2	(0.2)	0.3	(0.2)	0.8	(0.4)	2.2	(0.5)
	Ireland	-0.14	(0.03)	0.16	(0.04)	**0.30**	(0.05)	52.1	(2.3)	60.0	(1.7)	63.4	(1.5)	74.6	(2.0)
	Israel	-0.03	(0.03)	0.09	(0.08)	0.12	(0.09)	15.3	(2.6)	17.5	(2.8)	20.0	(3.3)	19.5	(4.2)
	Italy	-0.13	(0.01)	0.10	(0.10)	**0.24**	(0.10)	5.5	(1.0)	4.8	(0.8)	4.6	(0.6)	8.5	(0.8)
	Japan	-0.07	(0.02)	0.15	(0.03)	**0.22**	(0.03)	20.4	(1.6)	26.8	(1.7)	33.0	(1.8)	37.4	(2.2)
	Korea	-0.17	(0.04)	-0.13	(0.06)	0.03	(0.08)	37.0	(6.0)	36.6	(4.4)	37.2	(4.7)	38.6	(5.0)
	Luxembourg	0.20	(0.02)	0.11	(0.04)	**-0.09**	(0.04)	17.8	(1.0)	14.7	(0.9)	11.9	(0.8)	15.1	(0.7)
	Mexico	-1.38	(0.02)	0.05	(0.10)	**1.43**	(0.10)	2.5	(0.7)	4.1	(0.6)	9.8	(1.1)	29.6	(2.9)
	Netherlands	0.32	(0.07)	0.24	(0.04)	-0.08	(0.09)	69.2	(4.8)	66.8	(4.3)	65.9	(4.0)	63.1	(5.1)
	New Zealand	0.04	(0.01)	0.81	(0.06)	**0.77**	(0.06)	0.3	(0.2)	2.9	(0.5)	6.2	(1.0)	13.7	(1.7)
	Norway	0.47	(0.02)	c	c	c	c	1.6	(1.0)	1.5	(0.6)	0.8	(0.2)	1.4	(0.9)
	Poland	-0.30	(0.02)	0.75	(0.10)	**1.06**	(0.11)	0.6	(0.2)	0.7	(0.3)	1.0	(0.3)	6.2	(0.5)
	Portugal	-0.39	(0.04)	0.09	(0.14)	**0.48**	(0.14)	11.5	(3.0)	10.7	(2.8)	12.7	(3.1)	23.2	(3.3)
	Slovak Republic	-0.11	(0.02)	0.07	(0.10)	0.18	(0.10)	7.6	(2.2)	7.3	(2.2)	10.3	(3.1)	10.9	(3.2)
	Slovenia	0.06	(0.01)	0.69	(0.06)	**0.63**	(0.06)	0.5	(0.2)	2.1	(0.4)	2.7	(0.4)	5.3	(0.5)
	Spain	-0.55	(0.03)	0.13	(0.06)	**0.68**	(0.06)	17.7	(1.4)	27.3	(1.4)	38.1	(1.4)	53.5	(2.3)
	Sweden	0.29	(0.02)	0.71	(0.08)	**0.43**	(0.08)	5.6	(1.2)	7.1	(1.0)	10.4	(1.0)	17.2	(2.3)
	Switzerland	0.06	(0.03)	0.43	(0.14)	**0.37**	(0.15)	4.2	(1.1)	4.4	(1.3)	6.3	(1.5)	10.6	(4.0)
	Turkey	-1.19	(0.05)	c	c	c	c	0.0	(0.0)	0.0	(0.0)	0.0	(0.0)	3.2	(2.2)
	United Kingdom	0.16	(0.02)	0.92	(0.05)	**0.76**	(0.05)	0.6	(0.2)	2.9	(0.7)	6.6	(1.5)	15.6	(2.5)
	United States	0.09	(0.04)	1.01	(0.14)	**0.92**	(0.15)	1.0	(0.8)	3.9	(1.3)	8.7	(2.0)	21.9	(3.9)
	OECD average	**-0.06**	**(0.01)**	**0.39**	**(0.02)**	**0.45**	**(0.02)**	**13.2**	**(0.3)**	**15.7**	**(0.3)**	**18.6**	**(0.4)**	**24.5**	**(0.5)**
Partners	Albania	-1.05	(0.04)	-0.21	(0.10)	**0.84**	(0.11)	3.2	(1.2)	5.7	(1.8)	13.4	(3.1)	22.4	(3.7)
	Argentina	-0.95	(0.05)	-0.02	(0.12)	**0.93**	(0.13)	17.4	(4.0)	24.9	(3.0)	37.8	(2.9)	64.5	(3.4)
	Azerbaijan	-0.65	(0.03)	c	c	c	c	0.0	(0.0)	0.1	(0.1)	0.2	(0.1)	1.2	(0.4)
	Brazil	-1.35	(0.03)	0.27	(0.09)	**1.62**	(0.09)	1.2	(0.4)	2.9	(0.5)	9.2	(1.2)	36.0	(1.9)
	Bulgaria	-0.13	(0.04)	c	c	c	c	0.2	(0.2)	0.5	(0.3)	2.0	(1.2)	5.0	(1.6)
	Colombia	-1.43	(0.04)	-0.03	(0.10)	**1.40**	(0.11)	2.3	(0.6)	8.8	(1.7)	20.6	(3.9)	46.6	(4.1)
	Croatia	-0.20	(0.02)	c	c	c	c	0.2	(0.2)	0.2	(0.2)	1.3	(0.9)	5.8	(3.3)
	Dubai (UAE)	-0.13	(0.02)	0.57	(0.01)	**0.71**	(0.03)	54.6	(1.1)	83.4	(0.9)	88.1	(0.8)	88.5	(0.9)
	Hong Kong-China	-0.89	(0.17)	-0.81	(0.04)	0.09	(0.18)	91.2	(1.9)	93.4	(0.5)	93.8	(1.1)	91.8	(1.6)
	Indonesia	-1.49	(0.08)	-1.63	(0.08)	-0.14	(0.12)	45.1	(3.8)	46.3	(3.4)	42.3	(3.7)	37.6	(5.0)
	Jordan	-0.66	(0.03)	-0.14	(0.09)	**0.52**	(0.10)	12.7	(2.1)	13.4	(0.8)	18.3	(1.7)	30.2	(2.5)
	Kazakhstan	-0.53	(0.03)	0.01	(0.21)	**0.54**	(0.21)	1.3	(0.8)	1.6	(1.1)	4.0	(1.7)	6.1	(2.7)
	Kyrgyzstan	-0.68	(0.03)	0.48	(0.24)	**1.17**	(0.25)	0.5	(0.4)	1.2	(0.8)	1.2	(0.5)	8.7	(3.9)
	Latvia	-0.13	(0.03)	c	c	c	c	0.7	(0.6)	0.4	(0.3)	0.5	(0.3)	1.4	(1.0)
	Liechtenstein	0.07	(0.05)	c	c	c	c	1.3	(1.2)	5.1	(2.5)	11.4	(2.3)	5.1	(2.4)
	Lithuania	-0.05	(0.02)	c	c	c	c	0.7	(0.6)	1.2	(0.9)	0.8	(0.7)	1.2	(1.1)
	Macao-China	c	c	-0.69	(0.01)	c	c	93.4	(0.5)	95.6	(0.5)	97.0	(0.4)	98.1	(0.3)
	Montenegro	-0.25	(0.02)	c	c	c	c	0.1	(0.1)	0.6	(0.2)	0.5	(0.2)	0.9	(0.2)
	Panama	-1.20	(0.07)	0.53	(0.13)	**1.73**	(0.14)	1.5	(0.8)	6.3	(1.7)	23.5	(3.4)	68.1	(5.3)
	Peru	-1.62	(0.04)	-0.25	(0.11)	**1.36**	(0.13)	2.5	(0.5)	11.8	(2.4)	24.9	(3.1)	49.5	(4.6)
	Qatar	0.38	(0.01)	0.78	(0.01)	**0.41**	(0.01)	13.5	(0.5)	34.2	(1.0)	41.0	(1.0)	35.7	(0.8)
	Romania	-0.35	(0.03)	c	c	c	c	0.1	(0.1)	0.4	(0.4)	0.2	(0.2)	1.1	(1.1)
	Russian Federation	-0.21	(0.02)	c	c	c	c	0.1	(0.1)	0.0	(0.0)	0.1	(0.1)	0.2	(0.2)
	Serbia	0.06	(0.02)	c	c	c	c	1.1	(0.9)	1.8	(1.4)	1.1	(0.7)	0.9	(0.6)
	Shanghai-China	-0.53	(0.03)	-0.18	(0.19)	0.35	(0.19)	6.9	(2.7)	8.4	(1.6)	10.4	(1.1)	15.3	(1.5)
	Singapore	-0.43	(0.01)	c	c	c	c	1.3	(1.1)	2.2	(1.7)	2.0	(0.7)	1.9	(0.6)
	Chinese Taipei	-0.29	(0.03)	-0.40	(0.04)	**-0.11**	(0.05)	40.7	(2.4)	37.1	(1.6)	36.4	(2.2)	30.9	(2.0)
	Thailand	-1.36	(0.04)	-1.09	(0.12)	**0.27**	(0.13)	11.8	(2.3)	15.1	(1.8)	20.2	(2.1)	20.9	(2.3)
	Trinidad and Tobago	-0.59	(0.02)	-0.36	(0.03)	**0.23**	(0.03)	7.6	(0.5)	10.2	(0.7)	10.9	(0.8)	14.5	(0.8)
	Tunisia	-1.21	(0.05)	-0.67	(0.07)	**0.54**	(0.09)	0.2	(0.1)	1.5	(0.4)	3.3	(0.9)	1.6	(0.4)
	Uruguay	-0.99	(0.03)	0.63	(0.07)	**1.62**	(0.08)	0.9	(0.3)	4.7	(0.9)	18.4	(1.7)	48.3	(2.3)

Note: Values that are statistically significant are indicated in bold (see Annex A3). The percentage of students who attend privately managed schools in each quarter is calculated over the student population in each quarter.
Source: OECD, PISA 2009 Database.

[Part 1/1]

Table B2.2 **Socio-economic stratification, by lower and upper secondary education**

		\multicolumn{6}{c	}{Lower secondary education (ISCED 2)}	\multicolumn{6}{c}{Upper secondary education (ISCED 3)}
		\multicolumn{2}{c	}{Percentage of 15-year-old students enrolled in lower secondary education}	\multicolumn{4}{c	}{Management}	Socio-economic stratification	\multicolumn{2}{c	}{Percentage of 15-year-old students enrolled in upper secondary education}	\multicolumn{4}{c	}{Management}	Socio-economic stratification
				\multicolumn{2}{c	}{Publicly managed schools}	\multicolumn{2}{c	}{Privately managed schools}				\multicolumn{2}{c	}{Publicly managed schools}	\multicolumn{2}{c	}{Privately managed schools}	
		%	S.E.	%	S.E.	%	S.E.	Dif. in index (priv. – pub.)	S.E.	%	S.E.	%	S.E.	%	S.E.	Dif. in index (priv. – pub.)	S.E.

OECD

Country	%	S.E.	%	S.E.	%	S.E.	Dif.	S.E.	%	S.E.	%	S.E.	%	S.E.	Dif.	S.E.
Australia	81.4	(0.7)	58.1	(1.1)	41.9	(1.1)	**0.48**	(0.03)	18.6	(0.7)	63.6	(2.1)	36.4	(2.1)	**0.45**	(0.05)
Austria	6.8	(1.1)	97.6	(1.3)	2.4	(1.3)	c	c	93.2	(1.1)	86.6	(2.5)	13.4	(2.5)	**0.28**	(0.10)
Belgium	8.9	(0.6)	41.6	(3.3)	58.4	(3.3)	-0.03	(0.08)	91.1	(0.6)	29.4	(0.7)	70.6	(0.7)	**0.32**	(0.04)
Canada	14.8	(0.5)	90.0	(1.1)	10.0	(1.1)	**0.66**	(0.08)	85.2	(0.5)	93.0	(0.7)	7.0	(0.7)	**0.53**	(0.06)
Chile	4.9	(0.6)	64.3	(5.5)	35.7	(5.5)	**0.67**	(0.24)	95.1	(0.6)	40.9	(1.7)	59.1	(1.7)	**0.77**	(0.09)
Czech Republic	53.8	(1.1)	98.5	(0.5)	1.5	(0.5)	**0.70**	(0.14)	46.2	(1.1)	94.0	(2.2)	6.0	(2.2)	0.11	(0.11)
Denmark	99.1	(0.5)	77.0	(2.8)	23.0	(2.8)	0.23	(0.06)	0.9	(0.5)	100.0	(0.0)	0.0	c	c	c
Estonia	98.1	(0.2)	96.9	(1.1)	3.1	(1.1)	0.29	(0.16)	1.9	(0.2)	86.7	(8.2)	13.3	(8.2)	c	c
Finland	99.6	(0.1)	96.1	(1.2)	3.9	(1.2)	0.15	(0.16)	0.4	(0.1)	89.3	(8.0)	10.7	(8.0)	c	c
Germany	96.6	(0.4)	94.8	(1.6)	5.2	(1.6)	0.29	(0.15)	3.4	(0.4)	100.0	(0.0)	0.0	c	c	c
Greece	7.3	(1.0)	100.0	(0.0)	0.0	c	c	c	92.7	(1.0)	94.3	(0.9)	5.7	(0.9)	**1.00**	(0.18)
Hungary	10.4	(1.6)	96.3	(2.7)	3.7	(2.7)	c	c	89.6	(1.6)	86.0	(2.8)	14.0	(2.8)	**0.28**	(0.14)
Ireland	61.6	(1.0)	39.8	(0.9)	60.2	(0.9)	**0.26**	(0.05)	38.4	(1.0)	36.4	(1.4)	63.6	(1.4)	**0.36**	(0.07)
Israel	14.4	(1.1)	96.5	(1.8)	3.5	(1.8)	c	c	85.6	(1.1)	79.7	(2.8)	20.3	(2.8)	0.08	(0.10)
Italy	1.5	(0.3)	98.0	(2.0)	2.0	(2.0)	c	c	98.5	(0.3)	94.1	(0.6)	5.9	(0.6)	0.23	(0.10)
Japan	0.0	c	c	c	c	c	c	c	100.0	(0.0)	70.7	(1.3)	29.3	(1.3)	**0.22**	(0.03)
Korea	4.2	(0.9)	95.7	(2.9)	4.3	(2.9)	c	c	95.8	(0.9)	61.2	(4.5)	38.8	(4.5)	0.05	(0.08)
Luxembourg	61.8	(0.2)	86.0	(0.1)	14.0	(0.1)	**-0.26**	(0.05)	38.2	(0.2)	84.0	(0.2)	16.0	(0.2)	0.11	(0.05)
Mexico	43.5	(1.0)	91.2	(2.0)	8.8	(2.0)	**1.85**	(0.22)	56.5	(1.0)	86.4	(1.2)	13.6	(1.2)	**1.13**	(0.11)
Netherlands	74.5	(1.9)	31.6	(4.5)	68.4	(4.5)	-0.01	(0.08)	25.5	(1.9)	41.1	(6.5)	58.9	(6.5)	-0.10	(0.09)
New Zealand	5.9	(0.4)	94.9	(1.0)	5.1	(1.0)	c	c	94.1	(0.4)	94.3	(0.5)	5.7	(0.5)	**0.78**	(0.06)
Poland	99.1	(0.3)	97.9	(0.1)	2.1	(0.1)	1.06	(0.11)	0.9	(0.3)	100.0	(0.0)	0.0	c	c	c
Portugal	43.6	(2.1)	89.9	(2.1)	10.1	(2.1)	**0.37**	(0.14)	56.4	(2.1)	82.2	(3.5)	17.8	(3.5)	**0.38**	(0.17)
Slovak Republic	38.7	(1.4)	96.2	(1.8)	3.8	(1.8)	0.07	(0.16)	61.3	(1.4)	87.7	(3.7)	12.3	(3.7)	0.14	(0.11)
Slovenia	3.1	(0.8)	100.0	(0.0)	0.0	c	c	c	96.9	(0.8)	97.3	(0.1)	2.7	(0.1)	**0.62**	(0.06)
Spain	100.0	(0.0)	65.9	(0.9)	34.1	(0.9)	**0.68**	(0.06)	0.0	(0.0)	62.0	(23.8)	38.0	(23.8)	c	c
Sweden	98.4	(0.5)	90.1	(0.8)	9.9	(0.8)	**0.41**	(0.08)	1.6	(0.5)	79.5	(12.5)	20.5	(12.5)	c	c
Switzerland	79.3	(1.1)	95.4	(0.7)	4.6	(0.7)	**0.31**	(0.12)	20.7	(1.1)	87.0	(7.0)	13.0	(7.0)	0.26	(0.27)
United Kingdom	0.1	(0.1)	79.0	(18.9)	21.0	(18.9)	c	c	99.9	(0.1)	93.5	(1.1)	6.5	(1.1)	**0.77**	(0.05)
United States	11.0	(0.8)	96.6	(1.0)	3.4	(1.0)	c	c	89.0	(0.8)	90.5	(1.5)	9.5	(1.5)	**0.89**	(0.14)
OECD average	**44.1**	**(0.2)**	**84.7**	**(0.8)**	**15.3**	**(0.8)**	**0.43**	**(0.03)**	**55.9**	**(0.2)**	**79.7**	**(1.1)**	**20.3**	**(1.2)**	**0.42**	**(0.02)**

Partners

Country	%	S.E.	%	S.E.	%	S.E.	Dif.	S.E.	%	S.E.	%	S.E.	%	S.E.	Dif.	S.E.
Albania	53.4	(2.0)	90.3	(2.7)	9.7	(2.7)	1.09	(0.16)	46.6	(2.0)	87.3	(3.5)	12.7	(3.5)	**0.60**	(0.12)
Argentina	38.7	(2.1)	82.6	(2.4)	17.4	(2.4)	0.79	(0.24)	61.3	(2.1)	52.1	(2.8)	47.9	(2.8)	**0.85**	(0.15)
Brazil	24.8	(0.9)	96.5	(0.7)	3.5	(0.7)	1.12	(0.14)	75.2	(0.9)	85.0	(0.8)	15.0	(0.8)	**1.60**	(0.09)
Colombia	36.8	(1.4)	85.0	(1.8)	15.0	(1.8)	1.54	(0.16)	63.2	(1.4)	77.9	(2.9)	22.1	(2.9)	**1.26**	(0.11)
Dubai (UAE)	19.3	(0.4)	29.7	(0.6)	70.3	(0.6)	**0.78**	(0.05)	80.7	(0.4)	19.4	(0.1)	80.6	(0.1)	**0.64**	(0.03)
Hong Kong-China	34.0	(0.9)	6.1	(0.6)	93.9	(0.6)	0.23	(0.20)	66.0	(0.9)	8.1	(0.2)	91.9	(0.2)	0.07	(0.16)
Indonesia	54.0	(3.5)	59.7	(3.6)	40.3	(3.6)	-0.01	(0.10)	46.0	(3.5)	54.2	(5.7)	45.8	(5.7)	-0.37	(0.17)
Jordan	100.0	(0.0)	81.4	(0.7)	18.6	(0.7)	0.52	(0.10)	0.0	c					c	c
Kazakhstan	80.2	(2.1)	99.1	(0.6)	0.9	(0.6)	c	c	19.8	(2.1)	87.2	(5.5)	12.8	(5.5)	**0.38**	(0.19)
Kyrgyzstan	79.5	(1.5)	98.1	(0.9)	1.9	(0.9)	c	c	20.5	(1.5)	93.3	(2.7)	6.7	(2.7)	**1.17**	(0.20)
Panama	44.1	(4.6)	86.9	(3.1)	13.1	(3.1)	1.65	(0.19)	55.9	(4.6)	68.7	(5.1)	31.3	(5.1)	**1.69**	(0.16)
Peru	30.3	(1.4)	91.7	(2.0)	8.3	(2.0)	1.13	(0.14)	69.7	(1.4)	71.9	(3.1)	28.1	(3.1)	**1.21**	(0.13)
Qatar	18.8	(0.1)	71.6	(0.5)	28.4	(0.5)	**0.62**	(0.05)	81.2	(0.1)	68.3	(0.1)	31.7	(0.1)	**0.34**	(0.02)
Shanghai-China	42.2	(0.8)	81.8	(1.5)	18.2	(1.5)	0.41	(0.27)	57.8	(0.8)	95.5	(0.6)	4.5	(0.6)	0.33	(0.17)
Chinese Taipei	34.5	(0.9)	92.9	(0.9)	7.1	(0.9)	0.52	(0.10)	65.5	(0.9)	48.3	(1.3)	51.7	(1.3)	**-0.28**	(0.05)
Thailand	23.8	(1.1)	88.9	(3.1)	11.1	(3.1)	0.72	(0.38)	76.2	(1.1)	81.1	(0.6)	18.9	(0.6)	0.10	(0.13)
Trinidad and Tobago	36.2	(0.3)	89.4	(0.2)	10.6	(0.2)	0.08	(0.05)	63.8	(0.3)	89.1	(0.1)	10.9	(0.1)	**0.31**	(0.04)
Tunisia	43.7	(1.4)	96.2	(0.9)	3.8	(0.9)	0.96	(0.09)	56.3	(1.4)	100.0	(0.0)	0.0	(0.0)	c	c
Uruguay	39.2	(1.2)	95.6	(0.5)	4.4	(0.5)	1.51	(0.14)	60.8	(1.2)	73.4	(1.2)	26.6	(1.2)	**1.35**	(0.08)

Notes: Values that are statistically significant are indicated in bold (see Annex A3). The percentage of students in lower secondary education who attend publicly or privately managed schools is calculated over the total student population in lower secondary education. The percentage of students in upper secondary education who attend publicly or privately managed schools is calculated over the total student population in upper secondary education.
Source: OECD, *PISA 2009 Database*.

ANNEX B: DATA TABLES

[Part 1/1]
Table B2.3 Summary of stratification and countries' socio-economic and education characteristics

| | | Difference in socio-economic background between students in privately and publicly managed schools || Public funding for privately managed schools || Student socio-economic background (the PISA index of economic, social and cultural status [ESCS]) |||| Students in privately managed schools || Students in schools competing with at least one other school for enrolment || Performance in reading ||
| | | | | | | Standard deviation || Mean || | | | | | |
		Index dif.	S.E.	%	S.E.	S.D.	S.E.	Mean index	S.E.	%	S.E.	%	S.E.	Mean score	S.E.
OECD	Australia	0.47	(0.03)	54.7	(1.6)	0.75	(0.01)	0.34	(0.01)	40.3	(0.8)	95.7	(1.1)	515	(2.3)
	Austria	0.34	(0.10)	m	m	0.84	(0.01)	0.06	(0.02)	12.6	(2.4)	57.2	(3.8)	470	(2.9)
	Belgium	0.32	(0.04)	84.7	(1.2)	0.93	(0.01)	0.20	(0.02)	69.5	(0.7)	94.7	(1.4)	506	(2.3)
	Canada	0.54	(0.06)	42.1	(4.1)	0.83	(0.01)	0.50	(0.02)	7.5	(0.7)	84.6	(1.0)	524	(1.5)
	Chile	0.79	(0.08)	68.5	(2.0)	1.14	(0.02)	-0.57	(0.04)	58.0	(1.7)	79.0	(3.2)	449	(3.1)
	Czech Republic	0.29	(0.10)	70.5	(4.8)	0.71	(0.01)	-0.09	(0.01)	3.6	(1.0)	83.6	(2.6)	478	(2.9)
	Denmark	0.22	(0.06)	67.3	(1.8)	0.87	(0.01)	0.30	(0.02)	22.8	(2.8)	77.8	(2.7)	495	(2.1)
	Estonia	0.31	(0.16)	74.0	(10.6)	0.80	(0.01)	0.15	(0.02)	3.3	(1.2)	81.1	(2.4)	501	(2.6)
	Finland	0.16	(0.16)	97.4	(1.5)	0.78	(0.01)	0.37	(0.02)	3.9	(1.2)	57.5	(3.2)	536	(2.3)
	Germany	0.29	(0.15)	85.7	(3.6)	0.90	(0.01)	0.18	(0.02)	5.1	(1.5)	81.3	(2.5)	497	(2.7)
	Greece	1.05	(0.17)	0.0	(0.0)	0.99	(0.01)	-0.02	(0.03)	5.2	(0.8)	59.8	(3.8)	483	(4.3)
	Hungary	0.36	(0.14)	80.7	(3.8)	0.97	(0.02)	-0.20	(0.03)	13.0	(2.5)	80.0	(3.4)	494	(3.2)
	Ireland	0.30	(0.05)	81.8	(3.0)	0.85	(0.01)	0.05	(0.03)	61.5	(0.4)	81.9	(3.6)	496	(3.0)
	Israel	0.12	(0.09)	65.0	(5.5)	0.89	(0.02)	-0.02	(0.03)	17.9	(2.6)	80.2	(2.7)	474	(3.6)
	Italy	0.24	(0.10)	36.2	(6.4)	1.02	(0.01)	-0.12	(0.01)	5.9	(0.6)	88.1	(1.2)	486	(1.6)
	Japan	0.22	(0.03)	36.8	(1.3)	0.72	(0.01)	-0.01	(0.01)	29.3	(1.3)	90.8	(1.8)	520	(3.5)
	Korea	0.03	(0.08)	50.0	(2.7)	0.82	(0.01)	-0.15	(0.03)	37.4	(4.3)	86.7	(2.6)	539	(3.5)
	Luxembourg	-0.09	(0.04)	82.9	(0.1)	1.10	(0.01)	0.19	(0.01)	14.8	(0.1)	76.6	(0.1)	472	(1.3)
	Mexico	1.43	(0.10)	0.9	(0.5)	1.30	(0.01)	-1.22	(0.03)	11.5	(1.1)	86.2	(1.1)	425	(2.0)
	Netherlands	-0.08	(0.09)	96.4	(0.6)	0.86	(0.02)	0.27	(0.03)	66.0	(3.9)	97.1	(1.1)	508	(5.1)
	New Zealand	0.77	(0.06)	9.6	(1.0)	0.79	(0.01)	0.09	(0.02)	5.7	(0.4)	86.6	(2.2)	521	(2.4)
	Poland	1.06	(0.11)	46.0	(4.6)	0.88	(0.01)	-0.28	(0.02)	2.1	(0.1)	67.7	(3.4)	500	(2.6)
	Portugal	0.48	(0.14)	52.6	(7.0)	1.18	(0.02)	-0.32	(0.04)	14.5	(2.7)	79.4	(2.9)	489	(3.1)
	Slovak Republic	0.18	(0.10)	91.9	(3.1)	0.84	(0.01)	-0.09	(0.02)	9.0	(2.4)	93.5	(1.8)	477	(2.5)
	Slovenia	0.63	(0.06)	86.6	(0.2)	0.88	(0.01)	0.07	(0.01)	2.7	(0.1)	48.8	(0.4)	483	(1.0)
	Spain	0.68	(0.06)	67.6	(1.8)	1.09	(0.01)	-0.31	(0.03)	34.1	(0.9)	79.5	(2.3)	481	(2.0)
	Sweden	0.43	(0.08)	99.6	(0.3)	0.81	(0.01)	0.33	(0.02)	10.0	(0.8)	69.3	(3.5)	497	(2.9)
	Switzerland	0.37	(0.15)	39.6	(13.1)	0.88	(0.01)	0.08	(0.02)	6.4	(1.6)	37.9	(3.2)	501	(2.4)
	United Kingdom	0.76	(0.05)	0.0	(0.0)	0.79	(0.01)	0.20	(0.02)	6.3	(1.1)	88.8	(1.8)	494	(2.3)
	United States	0.92	(0.15)	0.0	(0.0)	0.93	(0.02)	0.17	(0.04)	8.8	(1.4)	78.6	(3.3)	500	(3.7)
	OECD average	**0.45**	**(0.02)**	**57.6**	**(0.8)**	**0.90**	**(0.00)**	**0.01**	**(0.00)**	**19.6**	**(0.3)**	**78.3**	**(0.5)**	**494**	**(0.5)**
Partners	Albania	0.84	(0.11)	0.0	(0.0)	1.04	(0.02)	-0.95	(0.04)	11.1	(2.1)	68.4	(3.1)	385	(4.0)
	Argentina	0.93	(0.13)	45.7	(4.0)	1.19	(0.03)	-0.62	(0.05)	36.1	(2.1)	85.1	(3.2)	398	(4.6)
	Brazil	1.62	(0.09)	1.9	(1.1)	1.21	(0.01)	-1.16	(0.03)	12.3	(0.6)	82.2	(2.2)	412	(2.7)
	Colombia	1.40	(0.11)	20.4	(4.8)	1.27	(0.02)	-1.15	(0.05)	19.5	(2.4)	86.5	(3.1)	413	(3.7)
	Dubai (UAE)	0.71	(0.03)	0.2	(0.0)	0.79	(0.01)	0.42	(0.01)	78.6	(0.0)	89.9	(0.0)	459	(1.1)
	Hong Kong-China	0.09	(0.18)	91.3	(1.2)	1.02	(0.02)	-0.80	(0.04)	92.6	(0.2)	98.0	(1.2)	533	(2.1)
	Indonesia	-0.14	(0.12)	40.2	(3.7)	1.10	(0.02)	-1.55	(0.06)	42.8	(2.8)	96.7	(1.2)	402	(3.7)
	Jordan	0.52	(0.10)	0.9	(0.3)	1.05	(0.02)	-0.57	(0.03)	18.6	(0.7)	70.6	(3.6)	405	(3.3)
	Kazakhstan	0.54	(0.21)	3.6	(3.2)	0.83	(0.01)	-0.51	(0.03)	3.2	(1.4)	75.1	(3.5)	390	(3.1)
	Kyrgyzstan	1.17	(0.25)	0.0	(0.0)	0.93	(0.01)	-0.65	(0.03)	2.9	(1.2)	67.2	(3.7)	314	(3.2)
	Panama	1.73	(0.14)	1.5	(0.7)	1.33	(0.04)	-0.81	(0.08)	23.3	(2.6)	70.7	(4.8)	371	(6.5)
	Peru	1.36	(0.13)	2.8	(1.8)	1.25	(0.03)	-1.31	(0.05)	22.1	(2.3)	77.8	(2.6)	370	(4.0)
	Qatar	0.41	(0.01)	0.6	(0.0)	0.91	(0.01)	0.51	(0.01)	31.1	(0.1)	64.2	(0.1)	372	(0.8)
	Shanghai-China	0.35	(0.19)	3.4	(3.2)	1.04	(0.02)	-0.49	(0.04)	10.3	(0.6)	84.9	(3.1)	556	(2.4)
	Chinese Taipei	-0.11	(0.05)	8.8	(2.3)	0.83	(0.01)	-0.33	(0.02)	36.3	(1.1)	95.2	(1.7)	495	(2.6)
	Thailand	0.27	(0.13)	64.4	(5.5)	1.19	(0.02)	-1.31	(0.04)	17.1	(0.7)	89.1	(1.8)	421	(2.6)
	Trinidad and Tobago	0.23	(0.03)	55.1	(0.3)	0.93	(0.01)	-0.58	(0.02)	10.8	(0.1)	89.8	(0.2)	416	(1.2)
	Tunisia	0.54	(0.09)	0.0	(0.0)	1.31	(0.02)	-1.20	(0.05)	1.7	(0.4)	65.6	(3.5)	404	(2.9)
	Uruguay	1.62	(0.08)	0.0	(0.0)	1.22	(0.02)	-0.70	(0.03)	17.9	(0.8)	54.9	(2.9)	426	(2.6)

Source: OECD, *PISA 2009 Database*.

[Part 1/1]
Table B2.4 Correlation between stratification and various system characteristics

	Correlation between "difference in socio-economic background between students in private and public schools" and…														
	Percentage of total funding for private school for a typical school year that comes from :														
	Government, including departments, local, regional state and national authorities		Student fees or school charges paid by parents		Benefactors, donations, bequests, sponsorships, parents' fundraising		Other		Standard deviation of student socio-economic background		Mean of student socio-economic background		Percentage of students in private schools		Percentage of students in schools competing with at least one other school for enrolment	
	Corr.	p-value	Corr.	p-value	Corr.	p-value	Corr.	p-value	Corr.	p-value	Corr.	p-value	Corr.	p-value	Corr.	p-value
Across OECD countries	**-0.67**	(0.000)	**0.65**	(0.000)	**0.38**	(0.045)	-0.03	(0.860)	**0.41**	(0.026)	**-0.53**	(0.003)	-0.25	(0.179)	-0.16	(0.404)
Across all countries	**-0.59**	(0.000)	**0.60**	(0.000)	0.21	(0.143)	-0.07	(0.644)	**0.55**	(0.000)	**-0.41**	(0.003)	-0.22	(0.125)	**-0.30**	(0.039)

Note: Values that are statistically significant are indicated in bold (see Annex A3).
Source: OECD, *PISA 2009 Database*.

DATA TABLES: ANNEX B

[Part 1/1]
Table B2.5 Relationships between stratification and various system characteristics

	Variable	Model 1 Coef.	Model 1 S.E.	Model 1 p-value	Model 2 Coef.	Model 2 S.E.	Model 2 p-value	Model 3 Coef.	Model 3 S.E.	Model 3 p-value	Model 4 Coef.	Model 4 S.E.	Model 4 p-value
Privately managed school (1=private; 0=public)	PRIVATE	**0.429**	(0.067)	(0.000)	**0.435**	(0.064)	(0.000)	**0.456**	(0.050)	(0.000)	**0.436**	(0.064)	(0.000)
x Percentage of students in privately managed schools (1 unit=10 percentage-point increase)	PRIVATE*PRIV10				-0.046	(0.031)	(0.145)						
x Percentage of total funding for privately managed school for a typical school year that comes from government (1 unit=10 percentage-point increase)	PRIVATE*GFUNDP10							**-0.072**	(0.014)	(0.000)			
x Country mean of student socio-economic background (1 unit = one standard deviation increase)	PRIVATE*YESCS										**-0.437**	(0.181)	0.023
x Standard deviation of student socio-economic background within a country (1 unit=one standard deviation increase)	PRIVATE*ESSTD												
x Percentage of students in schools competing with at least one other school for enrolment (one unit = 10 percentage-point increase)	PRIVATE*COMP10												
Intercept		-0.093	(0.063)	(0.155)	-0.092	(0.062)	(0.147)	-0.101	(0.061)	(0.109)	**-0.120**	(0.021)	(0.000)
Percentage of students in privately managed schools (1 unit=10 percentage-point increase)	PRIV10				-0.033	(0.043)	(0.448)						
Percentage of total funding for privately managed school for a typical school year that comes from government (one unit=10 percentage-point increase)	GFUNDP10							0.018	(0.016)	(0.258)			
Country mean of student socio-economic background (1 unit=one standard deviation increase)	YESCS										**1.274**	(0.121)	(0.000)
Standard deviation of student socio-economic background within a country (1 unit=one standard deviation increase)	ESSTD												
Percentage of students in schools competing with at least one other school for enrolment (1 unit = 10 percentage-point increase)	COMP10												

	Variance component	p-value
Privately managed school (1=private; 0=public)	**0.099**	0.000

	Variable	Model 5 Coef.	Model 5 S.E.	Model 5 p-value	Model 6 Coef.	Model 6 S.E.	Model 6 p-value	Model 7 Coef.	Model 7 S.E.	Model 7 p-value	Model 8 Coef.	Model 8 S.E.	Model 8 p-value
Privately managed school (1=private; 0=public)	PRIVATE	**0.442**	(0.065)	(0.000)	**0.428**	(0.058)	(0.000)	**0.460**	(0.050)	(0.000)	**0.462**	(0.043)	(0.000)
x Percentage of students in privately managed schools (one unit=10 percentage-point increase)	PRIVATE * PRIV10							-0.017	(0.026)	(0.516)	-0.004	(0.020)	(0.828)
x Percentage of total funding for privately managed school for a typical school year that comes from government (one unit=10 percentage-point increase)	PRIVATE * GFUNDP10							**-0.068**	(0.015)	(0.000)	**-0.063**	(0.011)	(0.000)
x Country mean of student socio-economic background (one unit=one standard deviation increase)	PRIVATE * YESCS										-0.123	(0.171)	(0.479)
x Standard deviation of student socio-economic background within a country (1 unit=one standard deviation increase)	PRIVATE * ESSTD	*0.886*	*(0.469)*	*(0.069)*							0.551	(0.442)	(0.226)
x Percentage of students in schools competing with at least one other school for enrolment (one unit=10 percentage-point increase)	PRIVATE * COMP10				*-0.101*	*(0.058)*	*(0.092)*				-0.064	(0.049)	(0.202)
Intercept		*-0.117*	*(0.058)*	*(0.053)*	-0.093	(0.063)	(0.153)	-0.104	(0.061)	(0.097)	**-0.125**	(0.018)	(0.000)
Percentage of students in privately managed schools (one unit=10 percentage-point increase)	PRIV10							-0.043	(0.042)	(0.311)	*-0.024*	*(0.012)*	*(0.054)*
Percentage of total funding for privately managed school for a typical school year that comes from government (one unit=10 percentage-point increase)	GFUNDP10							0.026	(0.016)	(0.114)	0.002	(0.004)	(0.569)
Country mean of student socio-economic background (one unit=one standard deviation increase)	YESCS										**1.182**	(0.095)	(0.000)
Standard deviation of student socio-economic background within a country (1 unit=one standard deviation increase)	ESSTD	**-1.652**	(0.641)	(0.016)							-0.240	(0.172)	(0.176)
Percentage of students in schools competing with at least one other school for enrolment (one unit=10 percentage-point increase)	COMP10				*-0.010*	*(0.034)*	*(0.773)*				0.013	(0.011)	(0.280)

Notes: Models 1 to 8 are three-level regression models (i.e. student, school and system levels) with the variable ESCS (*PISA index of economic, social and cultural status* of students) as a dependent variable. A three-level regression analysis is conducted using HLM 6.08. Some 29 OECD countries are included in the analysis. All countries are weighted equally. These are random-intercept and random-slope models: the slope of the variable PRIVATE is randomised at the system level. Models 2 to 8 are cross-level interaction models, which estimate the slope of PRIVATE (school-level variable) by various system-level variables. The variables GFUNDP10. PRIV10, YESCS, ESSTD and COMP10 are grand mean centred (i.e. the means of these variables across 29 OECD countries are set to zero), and all other variables are uncentred.

Values that are statistically significant at the 5% level (p<0.05) are indicated in bold; at the 10% level (p<0.10) they are indicated in italic.
Source: OECD, *PISA 2009 Database*.

ANNEX B: DATA TABLES

[Part 1/1]
Table B2.6 Socio-economic stratification, by the proportion of public and private funding for schools

Change in the *PISA index of economic, social and cultural status* (ESCS) associated with a 10% increase in the percentage of total school funding for a typical school year that comes from:

		Government, including departments, local, regional state and national authorities		Student fees or school charges paid by parents	
		Change in index point	S.E.	Change in index point	S.E.
OECD	Australia	**-0.11**	(0.01)	**0.13**	(0.01)
	Belgium	**-0.07**	(0.02)	**0.06**	(0.02)
	Canada	**-0.06**	(0.01)	**0.07**	(0.01)
	Chile	**-0.15**	(0.02)	**0.17**	(0.02)
	Czech Republic	**-0.04**	(0.02)	**0.07**	(0.04)
	Denmark	**-0.04**	(0.02)	**0.05**	(0.02)
	Estonia	**-0.11**	(0.04)	**0.11**	(0.04)
	Finland	-0.10	(0.17)	-0.03	(0.03)
	Germany	**-0.17**	(0.05)	**0.22**	(0.05)
	Greece	**-0.12**	(0.02)	**0.11**	(0.02)
	Hungary	0.01	(0.04)	**0.16**	(0.05)
	Iceland	**-0.12**	(0.05)	**0.25**	(0.06)
	Ireland	**-0.11**	(0.01)	**0.11**	(0.01)
	Israel	-0.02	(0.01)	**0.03**	(0.01)
	Italy	**-0.07**	(0.01)	**0.11**	(0.02)
	Japan	**-0.05**	(0.01)	**0.05**	(0.01)
	Korea	**-0.07**	(0.01)	**0.07**	(0.01)
	Luxembourg	**-0.17**	(0.01)	**0.21**	(0.01)
	Mexico	**-0.03**	(0.01)	**0.05**	(0.01)
	Netherlands	0.07	(0.08)	-0.02	(0.09)
	New Zealand	**-0.10**	(0.01)	**0.11**	(0.01)
	Norway	0.02	(0.06)	0.03	(0.08)
	Poland	**-0.17**	(0.03)	**0.19**	(0.03)
	Portugal	**-0.12**	(0.02)	**0.14**	(0.02)
	Slovak Republic	**-0.08**	(0.04)	**0.12**	(0.03)
	Slovenia	0.01	(0.01)	**0.29**	(0.05)
	Spain	**-0.11**	(0.02)	**0.14**	(0.02)
	Sweden	-0.22	(0.16)	**0.38**	(0.01)
	Switzerland	**-0.08**	(0.01)	**0.08**	(0.01)
	Turkey	-0.02	(0.02)	**0.06**	(0.03)
	United Kingdom	**-0.08**	(0.01)	**0.08**	(0.01)
	United States	**-0.08**	(0.01)	**0.11**	(0.01)
	OECD average	**-0.08**	(0.01)	**0.12**	(0.01)
Partners	Albania	**-0.06**	(0.01)	**0.07**	(0.02)
	Argentina	**-0.05**	(0.02)	**0.13**	(0.02)
	Azerbaijan	-0.05	(0.06)	**0.12**	(0.04)
	Brazil	**-0.16**	(0.01)	**0.18**	(0.01)
	Bulgaria	**-0.10**	(0.01)	**0.10**	(0.01)
	Colombia	**-0.14**	(0.02)	**0.15**	(0.02)
	Croatia	**-0.11**	(0.02)	**0.14**	(0.02)
	Dubai (UAE)	**-0.08**	(0.00)	**0.07**	(0.00)
	Hong Kong-China	**-0.19**	(0.01)	**0.20**	(0.01)
	Indonesia	**-0.08**	(0.01)	**0.08**	(0.02)
	Jordan	**-0.05**	(0.01)	**0.11**	(0.01)
	Kazakhstan	**-0.06**	(0.02)	**0.05**	(0.02)
	Kyrgyzstan	**-0.08**	(0.02)	**0.12**	(0.02)
	Latvia	**-0.11**	(0.05)	**0.15**	(0.04)
	Liechtenstein	-0.03	(0.02)	0.03	(0.02)
	Lithuania	-0.13	(0.09)	-0.97	(2.35)
	Macao-China	**-0.09**	(0.00)	**0.10**	(0.00)
	Montenegro	**0.06**	(0.01)	**-0.04**	(0.01)
	Panama	**-0.18**	(0.02)	**0.17**	(0.02)
	Peru	**-0.07**	(0.01)	**0.12**	(0.01)
	Qatar	**-0.02**	(0.00)	**0.03**	(0.00)
	Romania	-0.04	(0.04)	0.06	(0.02)
	Russian Federation	**-0.14**	(0.03)	0.09	(0.05)
	Serbia	0.03	(0.03)	0.04	(0.04)
	Shanghai-China	-0.02	(0.02)	0.02	(0.02)
	Singapore	-0.03	(0.02)	**0.03**	(0.01)
	Chinese Taipei	0.01	(0.01)	-0.01	(0.01)
	Thailand	**-0.19**	(0.02)	**0.16**	(0.03)
	Trinidad and Tobago	**-0.11**	(0.01)	**0.09**	(0.01)
	Tunisia	0.04	(0.04)	-0.05	(0.04)
	Uruguay	**-0.16**	(0.01)	**0.17**	(0.01)

Note: Values that are statistically significant are indicated in bold (see Annex A3).
Source: OECD, *PISA 2009 Database*.

[Part 1/1]

Table B2.7 Socio-economic stratification, after accounting for school funding

Difference in the *PISA index of economic, social and cultural status* (ESCS) between privately and publicly managed schools

	After accounting for the percentage of total school funding that comes from government		After accounting for the percentage of total school funding that comes from student fees or school charges paid by parents	
	Dif. in index point (private – public)	S.E.	Dif. in index point (private – public)	S.E.
OECD				
Australia	**0.22**	(0.03)	**0.19**	(0.03)
Belgium	**0.30**	(0.04)	**0.32**	(0.04)
Canada	**0.48**	(0.07)	**0.44**	(0.08)
Chile	**0.67**	(0.11)	**0.61**	(0.11)
Czech Republic	**0.29**	(0.13)	**0.27**	(0.13)
Denmark	**0.35**	(0.11)	**0.25**	(0.11)
Estonia	0.05	(0.15)	0.06	(0.14)
Finland	0.16	(0.19)	0.19	(0.19)
Germany	0.08	(0.17)	0.09	(0.21)
Greece	0.31	(0.35)	**1.80**	(0.37)
Hungary	**0.39**	(0.16)	**0.31**	(0.14)
Ireland	0.13	(0.06)	0.15	(0.05)
Israel	0.15	(0.10)	0.17	(0.09)
Italy	-0.02	(0.10)	**-0.21**	(0.09)
Japan	-0.04	(0.07)	-0.04	(0.08)
Korea	0.06	(0.08)	0.05	(0.08)
Luxembourg	**-0.24**	(0.05)	**-0.41**	(0.05)
Mexico	**1.43**	(0.11)	**1.34**	(0.12)
Netherlands	-0.15	(0.08)	-0.15	(0.08)
New Zealand	0.05	(0.12)	-0.15	(0.12)
Poland	**0.35**	(0.22)	0.36	(0.26)
Portugal	0.07	(0.13)	-0.14	(0.17)
Slovak Republic	0.14	(0.11)	0.14	(0.14)
Slovenia	**0.66**	(0.07)	**0.54**	(0.07)
Spain	**0.52**	(0.08)	**0.54**	(0.07)
Sweden	**0.42**	(0.08)	**0.42**	(0.08)
Switzerland	-0.08	(0.10)	-0.05	(0.09)
United Kingdom	0.89	(2.31)	0.16	(1.37)
United States	0.45	(0.36)	-0.76	(0.34)
OECD average	**0.28**	(0.08)	**0.22**	(0.05)
Partners				
Albania	**0.76**	(0.20)	**0.79**	(0.15)
Argentina	**0.90**	(0.11)	**0.74**	(0.12)
Brazil	**0.74**	(0.23)	**0.44**	(0.20)
Colombia	**1.04**	(0.14)	**0.97**	(0.15)
Dubai (UAE)	**0.28**	(0.10)	**0.27**	(0.06)
Hong Kong-China	-0.16	(0.10)	-0.15	(0.10)
Indonesia	**-0.49**	(0.10)	**-0.49**	(0.11)
Jordan	0.13	(0.19)	-0.15	(0.10)
Kazakhstan	-0.05	(0.26)	0.37	(0.32)
Kyrgyzstan	**0.77**	(0.29)	**0.63**	(0.28)
Panama	**1.86**	(0.43)	**2.19**	(0.45)
Peru	**1.28**	(0.16)	**1.06**	(0.18)
Qatar	**1.10**	(0.06)	**0.39**	(0.05)
Shanghai-China	0.40	(0.34)	0.53	(0.37)
Chinese Taipei	**-0.43**	(0.18)	**-0.31**	(0.20)
Thailand	-0.13	(0.12)	-0.10	(0.13)
Trinidad and Tobago	**-0.18**	(0.04)	0.04	(0.04)
Tunisia	**1.64**	(0.55)	**1.89**	(0.59)
Uruguay	**1.11**	(0.40)	0.27	(0.38)

Note: Values that are statistically significant are indicated in bold (see Annex A3).
Source: OECD, *PISA 2009 Database*.

ANNEX B: DATA TABLES

[Part 1/1]

Table B3.1 Financial incentives for parents to choose their child's school (2009)

	\multicolumn{6}{c}{Lower secondary level}	\multicolumn{6}{c}{Upper secondary level}	\multicolumn{3}{c}{Voucher systems}
	\multicolumn{3}{c}{School vouchers (also referred to as scholarships) are available and applicable}	\multicolumn{3}{c}{Tuition tax credits are available to help families offset costs of private schooling}	\multicolumn{3}{c}{School vouchers (also referred to as scholarships) are available and applicable}	\multicolumn{3}{c}{Tuition tax credits are available to help families offset costs of private schooling}	Lower secondary level: Summary of columns (1) to (6)	Upper secondary level: Summary of columns (7) to (12)	Secondary level: Summary of columns (13) and (14)
	Public schools	Government-dependent private schools	Independent private schools	Government-dependent private schools	Independent private schools	Homeschooling	Public schools	Government-dependent private schools	Independent private schools	Government-dependent private schools	Independent private schools	Homeschooling	(1 = voucher system; 0 = non-voucher system)	(1 = voucher system; 0 = non-voucher system)	(1 = voucher system; 0 = non-voucher system)
	(1)	(2)	(3)	(4)	(5)	(6)	(7)	(8)	(9)	(10)	(11)	(12)	(13)	(14)	(15)
OECD															
Belgium (Fl.)[1]	Yes	Yes	No	No	m	No	Yes	Yes	No	No	m	No	1	1	1
Belgium (Fr.)[1]	Yes	Yes	No	No	a	No	Yes	Yes	No	No	a	No	1	1	1
Chile	Yes	Yes	a	No	No	a	Yes	Yes	a	No	No	a	1	1	1
Czech Republic	No	No	a	No	a	a	No	No	a	No	a	a	0	0	0
Denmark[2]	No	No	No	No	No	No	No	No	No	No	No	No	0	1	0
England	a	a	No	No	No	No	a	a	No	No	No	No	0	0	0
Estonia	Yes	Yes	a	Yes	a	Yes	Yes	Yes	a	Yes	a	Yes	1	1	1
Finland	a	a	a	No	a	No	a	a	a	No	a	No	0	0	0
Germany	Yes	Yes	a	Yes	a	a	Yes	Yes	a	Yes	a	a	1	1	1
Greece	No	a	No	a	No	a	No	a	No	a	No	a	0	0	0
Hungary	No	No	a	No	a	No	No	No	a	No	a	No	0	0	0
Ireland[3]	No	a	No	a	No	No	No	a	No	a	No	No	0	0	0
Israel	Yes	Yes	a	No	No	No	Yes	Yes	a	No	No	No	1	1	1
Italy	Yes	a	No	a	Yes	m	Yes	a	No	a	Yes	m	0	0	0
Japan	No	a	No	a	No	a	No	a	No	a	No	a	0	0	0
Korea	No	No	a	No	a	a	No	No	No	No	No	a	0	0	0
Luxembourg	No	No	No	No	No	No	No	No	No	No	No	No	0	0	0
Netherlands	No	No	No	No	No	No	No	No	No	No	No	No	0	0	0
New Zealand[4]	No	No	No	No	No	No	m	m	m	m	m	m	0	m	0
Poland	Yes	Yes	Yes	No	No	No	Yes	Yes	Yes	No	No	No	1	1	1
Portugal	a	a	a	Yes	Yes	No	a	a	a	Yes	Yes	No	1	1	1
Slovak Republic	Yes	Yes	a	No	a	a	Yes	Yes	a	No	a	a	1	1	1
Spain	Yes	Yes	a	No	No	a	Yes	Yes	a	No	No	a	1	1	1
Sweden	No	No	a	No	a	No	No	No	a	No	a	a	0	0	0
Switzerland[5]	No	No	No	No	No	No	m	m	m	m	m	m	0	m	0

Notes: Columns (1) through (12) are based on Tables D5.5, D5.14 and D5.16 in *Education at a Glance 2011: OECD Indicators* (OECD, 2011). Federal states or countries with highly decentralised school systems may experience regulatory differences between states, provinces or regions. Refer to Annex 3 for additional information (www.oecd.org/edu/eag2011).
a: Data are not applicable because the category does not apply.
m: Data is not available.
1. Independent private schools are free to arrange education but have no permission to hand out legitimate diplomas.
2. In Denmark, 99.1% of 15-year-old students are in lower secondary education and 0.9 of them are in upper secondary education.
3. The classification of schools used here is based on the system employed by the Irish Department of Education and Skills, as published in *Education at a Glance*, which differs somewhat from the PISA classification.
4. New Zealand is considered as a non-voucher system in this report, as only 0.3% or fewer of secondary students are eligible to receive public funding for attending privately managed schools under a special scheme.
5. Year of reference 2008.
Source: *Education at a Glance 2011: OECD Indicators*, OECD Publishing.

[Part 1/1]
Table B3.2 **School vouchers only available for students from socio-economically disadvantaged backgrounds (2009)**

	Lower secondary level			Upper secondary level			Secondary level
	Vouchers are only available for socio-economically disadvantaged students			Vouchers are only available for socio-economically disadvantaged students			Vouchers are only available for socio-economically disadvantaged students
	Public schools	Government-dependent private schools	Independent private schools	Public schools	Government-dependent private schools	Independent private schools	Summary of columns (1) to (6): If YES for both public and private (gov-dependent and/or gov-independent), the value is 1. If either lower- or upper-secondary data are missing, use available data (1 = yes; 0 = no)
	(1)	(2)	(3)	(4)	(5)	(6)	(7)
Belgium (Fl.)[1]	Yes	Yes	a	Yes	Yes	a	1
Belgium (Fr.)[1]	Yes	Yes	a	Yes	Yes	a	1
Chile	No	No	a	No	No	a	0
Czech Republic	a	a	a	a	a	a	0
Denmark	a	a	a	a	a	a	0
England	a	a	a	a	a	a	0
Estonia	No	No	a	No	No	a	0
Finland	a	a	a	a	a	a	0
Germany	Yes	Yes	a	Yes	Yes	a	1
Greece	a	a	a	a	a	a	0
Hungary[2]	a	a	a	a	a	a	0
Ireland	a	a	a	a	a	a	0
Israel	Yes	Yes	a	Yes	Yes	a	1
Italy	Yes	a	a	Yes	a	a	0
Japan	a	a	a	a	a	a	0
Korea	a	a	a	a	a	a	0
Luxembourg	a	a	a	a	a	a	0
Netherlands	a	a	a	a	a	a	0
New Zealand[3]	a	a	a	m	m	m	0
Poland	No	No	No	No	No	No	0
Portugal	a	a	a	a	a	a	0
Slovak Republic	Yes	Yes	a	Yes	Yes	a	1
Spain	No	No	a	No	No	a	0
Sweden	a	a	a	a	a	a	0
Switzerland[4]	a	a	a	m	m	m	0

Note: Columns (1) through (6) are based on Table D5.14 in *Education at a Glance 2011: OECD Indicators* (OECD, 2011). Federal states or countries with highly decentralised school systems may experience regulatory differences between states, provinces or regions. Refer to Annex 3 for additional information (www.oecd.org/edu/eag2011).

a: Data are not applicable because the category does not apply or because vouchers are not used at this level.
m: Data is not available.
1. Independent private schools are free to arrange education but have no permission to hand out legitimate diplomas.
2. The classification of schools used here is based on the system employed by the Irish Department of Education and Skills, as published in *Education at a Glance*, which differs somewhat from the PISA classification.
3. New Zealand is considered as a non-voucher system in this report, as only 0.3% or fewer of secondary students are eligible to receive public funding for attending privately managed schools under a special scheme.
4. Year of reference 2008.

Source: *Education at a Glance 2011: OECD Indicators*, OECD Publishing.

ANNEX B: DATA TABLES

[Part 1/2]
Table B3.3 Relationships between stratification and various voucher systems

	Variable	Model 1 Coef. S.E. p-value	Model 2 Coef. S.E. p-value	Model 3 Coef. S.E. p-value	Model 4 Coef. S.E. p-value
Privately managed school (1=private; 0=public)	PRIVATE	**0.384** (0.061) (0.000)	**0.393** (0.048) (0.000)	**0.336** (0.058) (0.000)	**0.338** (0.057) (0.000)
x Percentage of total funding for privately managed school for a typical school year that comes from government (one unit=10 percentage-point increase)	PRIVATE * GFUNDP10		**-0.065** (0.016) (0.001)	**-0.072** (0.017) (0.001)	**-0.064** (0.019) (0.003)
x Voucher system (1=voucher system; 0 = non-voucher system)	PRIVATE * VOU			0.141 (0.095) (0.152)	**0.289** (0.125) (0.032)
x Vouchers only available for socio-economically disadvantaged students (1=yes; 0=no)	PRIVATE * DISES				**-0.266** (0.129) (0.050)
x Standard deviation of student socio-economic background (1 unit=one standard deviation increase)	PRIVATE * ESSTD				
x Percentage of total funding for privately managed school for a typical school year that comes from government (one unit=10 percentage-point increase) x Voucher system (1=voucher system; 0=non-voucher system)	PRIVATE * GFUNDP10 * VOU				
x Percentage of total funding for privately managed school for a typical school year that comes from government (one unit=10 percentage-point increase) x Vouchers only available for socio-economically disadvantaged students (1=yes; 0=no)	PRIVATE * GFUNDP10 * DISES				
Intercept		-0.090 (0.062) (0.161)	-0.090 (0.061) (0.151)	0.013 (0.070) (0.850)	0.008 (0.070) (0.912)
Percentage of total funding for privately managed school for a typical school year that comes from government (one unit=10 percentage-point increase)	GFUNDP10		0.013 (0.017) (0.469)	0.024 (0.017) (0.155)	0.016 (0.017) (0.377)
Voucher system (1=voucher system; 0=non-voucher system)	VOU			*-0.254* (0.132) (0.066)	*-0.431* (0.221) (0.064)
Vouchers only available for socio-economically disadvantaged students (1=yes; 0=no)	DISES				0.338 (0.227) (0.152)
Standard deviation of student socio-economic background (1 unit=one standard deviation increase)	ESSTD				
Percentage of total funding for privately managed school for a typical school year that comes from government (one unit=10 percentage-point increase) x Voucher system (1=voucher system; 0=non-voucher system)	GFUNDP10 * VOU				
Percentage of total funding for privately managed school for a typical school year that comes from government (one unit=10 percentage-point increase) x Vouchers only available for socio-economically disadvantaged students (1=yes; 0=no)	GFUNDP10 * DISES				

	Variance component	p-value
Privately managed school (1=private; 0=public)	0.075	(0.000)

Notes: Models 1 to 8 are three-level regression models (i.e. student, school and system levels) with the variable ESCS (*PISA index of economic, social and cultural status* of students) as a dependent variable. A three-level regression analysis is conducted using HLM 6.08. Twenty-five school systems listed in Table 13 are included in the analysis. All systems are weighted equally. These are random-intercept and random-slope models: the slope of the variable PRIVATE is randomised at the system level. Models 2 to 8 are cross-level interaction models, which estimate the slope of PRIVATE (school-level variable) by various system-level variables. The variables GFUNDP10 and ESSTD are grand mean centred (i.e. the mean of GFUNDP10 across 25 school systems is set to zero), and all other variables are uncentred.
Values that are statistically significant at the 5% level (p<0.05) are indicated in bold; at the 10% level (p<0.10) they are indicated in italic.
Source: OECD, *PISA 2009 Database*.

[Part 2/2]
Table B3.3 Relationships between stratification and various voucher systems

Variable description	Variable	Model 5 Coef.	Model 5 S.E.	Model 5 p-value	Model 6 Coef.	Model 6 S.E.	Model 6 p-value	Model 7 Coef.	Model 7 S.E.	Model 7 p-value	Model 8 Coef.	Model 8 S.E.	Model 8 p-value
Privately managed school (1=private; 0=public)	PRIVATE	**0.374**	(0.087)	(0.000)	**0.357**	(0.059)	(0.000)	**0.338**	(0.058)	(0.000)	**0.336**	(0.057)	(0.000)
x Percentage of total funding for privately managed school for a typical school year that comes from government (one unit=10 percentage-point increase)	PRIVATE*GFUNDP10				**-0.065**	(0.018)	(0.002)	**-0.068**	(0.019)	(0.002)	**-0.067**	(0.019)	(0.003)
x Voucher system (1=voucher system; 0=non-voucher system)	PRIVATE*VOU	*0.259*	(0.143)	(0.083)	*0.231*	(0.119)	(0.066)	0.380	(0.417)	(0.373)	0.133	(0.701)	(0.852)
x Vouchers only available for socio-economically disadvantaged students (1=yes; 0=no)	PRIVATE*DISES	**-0.406**	(0.119)	(0.003)	*-0.228*	(0.124)	(0.080)				-0.939	(0.734)	(0.217)
x Standard deviation of student socio-economic background (1 unit=one standard deviation increase)	PRIVATE*ESSTD				0.404	(0.408)	(0.335)						
x Percentage of total funding for privately managed school for a typical school year that comes from government (one unit=10 percentage-point increase) x Voucher system (1=voucher system; 0=non-voucher system)	PRIVATE*GFUNDP10*VOU							-0.033	(0.049)	(0.512)	0.025	(0.103)	(0.808)
x Percentage of total funding for privately managed school for a typical school year that comes from government (one unit=10 percentage-point increase) x Vouchers only available for socio-economically disadvantaged students (1=yes; 0=no)	PRIVATE*GFUNDP10*DISES										0.075	(0.106)	(0.489)
Intercept		-0.003	(0.068)	(0.970)	-0.042	(0.077)	(0.590)	0.009	(0.070)	(0.905)	0.009	(0.070)	(0.905)
Percentage of total funding for privately managed school for a typical school year that comes from government (one unit=10 percentage-point increase)	GFUNDP10				0.017	(0.013)	(0.222)	0.017	(0.018)	(0.359)	0.017	(0.018)	(0.364)
Voucher system (1=voucher system; 0=non-voucher system)	VOU	*-0.423*	(0.224)	(0.071)	*-0.286*	(0.160)	(0.089)	**-0.784**	(0.355)	(0.039)	-0.350	(0.799)	(0.666)
Vouchers only available for socio-economically disadvantaged students (1=yes; 0=no)	DISES	0.372	(0.218)	(0.101)	0.243	(0.150)	(0.122)				0.441	(0.830)	(0.601)
Standard deviation of student socio-economic background (1 unit=one standard deviation increase)	ESSTD				*-1.156*	(0.568)	(0.055)						
Percentage of total funding for privately managed school for a typical school year that comes from government (one unit=10 percentage-point increase) x Voucher system (1=voucher system; 0=non-voucher system)	GFUNDP10*VOU							*0.073*	(0.042)	(0.094)	-0.013	(0.159)	(0.936)
Percentage of total funding for privately managed school for a typical school year that comes from government (one unit=10 percentage-point increase) x Vouchers only available for socio-economically disadvantaged students (1=yes; 0=no)	GFUNDP10*DISES										-0.009	(0.162)	(0.956)

Notes: Models 1 to 8 are three-level regression models (i.e. student, school and system levels) with the variable ESCS (*PISA index of economic, social and cultural status* of students) as a dependent variable. A three-level regression analysis is conducted using HLM 6.08. Twenty-five school systems listed in Table 13 are included in the analysis. All systems are weighted equally. These are random-intercept and random-slope models: the slope of the variable PRIVATE is randomised at the system level. Models 2 to 8 are cross-level interaction models, which estimate the slope of PRIVATE (school-level variable) by various system-level variables. The variables GFUNDP10 and ESSTD are grand mean centred (i.e. the mean of GFUNDP10 across 25 school systems is set to zero), and all other variables are uncentred.
Values that are statistically significant at the 5% level (p<0.05) are indicated in bold; at the 10% level (p<0.10) they are indicated in italic.
Source: OECD, *PISA 2009 Database*.

ANNEX B: DATA TABLES

[Part 1/2]

Table B4.1 Student socio-economic background, by schools with various school-admittance criteria

Average *PISA index of economic, social and cultural status* (ESCS) in schools whose principal reported that the following factors are "never or sometimes" or "always" considered for admittance to school

		Student's record of academic performance, including placement test, and/or recommendation of feeder schools						Parents' endorsement of the instructional or religious philosophy of the school					
		Never or sometimes		Always		Difference (always – never or sometimes)		Never or sometimes		Always		Difference (always – never or sometimes)	
		Mean index	S.E.	Mean index	S.E.	Dif.	S.E.	Mean index	S.E.	Mean index	S.E.	Dif.	S.E.
OECD	Australia	0.36	(0.02)	0.30	(0.04)	-0.06	(0.05)	0.26	(0.02)	0.53	(0.03)	**0.27**	(0.04)
	Austria	-0.23	(0.04)	0.26	(0.03)	**0.48**	(0.05)	0.06	(0.02)	0.23	(0.13)	0.17	(0.13)
	Belgium	0.21	(0.02)	0.17	(0.05)	-0.04	(0.06)	0.17	(0.03)	0.26	(0.05)	0.09	(0.07)
	Canada	0.46	(0.02)	0.61	(0.03)	**0.15**	(0.03)	0.47	(0.02)	0.66	(0.05)	**0.18**	(0.05)
	Chile	-0.85	(0.06)	-0.16	(0.08)	**0.69**	(0.11)	-0.74	(0.05)	0.27	(0.11)	**1.01**	(0.13)
	Czech Republic	-0.20	(0.02)	0.03	(0.02)	**0.23**	(0.04)	-0.07	(0.02)	-0.11	(0.04)	-0.03	(0.05)
	Denmark	0.31	(0.03)	0.20	(0.15)	-0.11	(0.15)	0.28	(0.03)	0.42	(0.07)	0.14	(0.08)
	Estonia	0.10	(0.02)	0.27	(0.05)	**0.17**	(0.05)	0.15	(0.02)	0.16	(0.06)	0.01	(0.07)
	Finland	0.37	(0.02)	0.43	(0.13)	0.06	(0.13)	0.37	(0.02)	0.35	(0.03)	-0.02	(0.04)
	Germany	0.00	(0.05)	0.25	(0.03)	**0.26**	(0.06)	0.18	(0.03)	0.29	(0.10)	0.11	(0.10)
	Greece	-0.05	(0.03)	0.41	(0.19)	**0.46**	(0.21)	-0.04	(0.04)	0.19	(0.20)	0.24	(0.21)
	Hungary	-0.97	(0.09)	-0.07	(0.03)	**0.90**	(0.10)	-0.21	(0.04)	-0.10	(0.09)	0.11	(0.12)
	Ireland	0.06	(0.04)	-0.05	(0.05)	-0.12	(0.07)	-0.02	(0.04)	0.19	(0.08)	**0.22**	(0.09)
	Israel	-0.05	(0.05)	0.01	(0.04)	0.06	(0.07)	0.00	(0.04)	-0.05	(0.07)	-0.05	(0.08)
	Italy	-0.10	(0.02)	-0.14	(0.03)	-0.04	(0.05)	-0.15	(0.02)	-0.08	(0.03)	0.07	(0.05)
	Japan	0.11	(0.07)	-0.03	(0.02)	-0.14	(0.08)	-0.02	(0.02)	0.11	(0.07)	0.13	(0.07)
	Korea	-0.04	(0.04)	-0.26	(0.05)	**-0.22**	(0.07)	-0.14	(0.03)	-0.46	(0.16)	**-0.33**	(0.17)
	Luxembourg	0.27	(0.02)	0.08	(0.02)	**-0.19**	(0.03)	0.17	(0.02)	0.27	(0.04)	**0.11**	(0.04)
	Mexico	-1.43	(0.03)	-0.92	(0.06)	**0.50**	(0.06)	-1.32	(0.03)	-0.64	(0.11)	**0.68**	(0.11)
	Netherlands	0.15	(0.03)	0.28	(0.04)	**0.13**	(0.06)	0.29	(0.03)	0.17	(0.08)	-0.12	(0.09)
	New Zealand	0.06	(0.02)	0.11	(0.04)	0.05	(0.06)	0.00	(0.02)	0.36	(0.06)	**0.36**	(0.07)
	Poland	-0.36	(0.02)	0.13	(0.06)	**0.50**	(0.07)	-0.29	(0.02)	-0.01	(0.23)	0.29	(0.23)
	Portugal	-0.32	(0.04)	-0.39	(0.26)	-0.07	(0.27)	-0.41	(0.04)	0.00	(0.08)	**0.41**	(0.09)
	Slovak Republic	-0.24	(0.04)	-0.01	(0.03)	**0.23**	(0.05)	-0.12	(0.03)	0.00	(0.09)	0.12	(0.11)
	Slovenia	-0.03	(0.02)	0.32	(0.03)	**0.35**	(0.03)	0.06	(0.01)	0.17	(0.05)	**0.10**	(0.05)
	Spain	-0.32	(0.03)	0.12	(0.24)	0.43	(0.24)	-0.37	(0.04)	0.25	(0.10)	**0.63**	(0.11)
	Sweden	0.32	(0.02)	0.52	(0.10)	0.20	(0.10)	0.32	(0.02)	0.50	(0.06)	**0.18**	(0.07)
	Switzerland	0.03	(0.03)	0.11	(0.03)	0.07	(0.04)	0.08	(0.03)	0.15	(0.15)	0.07	(0.15)
	United Kingdom	0.15	(0.03)	0.47	(0.07)	**0.32**	(0.08)	0.20	(0.03)	0.29	(0.08)	0.10	(0.09)
	United States	0.07	(0.04)	0.43	(0.07)	**0.36**	(0.08)	0.11	(0.04)	0.81	(0.16)	**0.70**	(0.16)
	OECD average	**-0.07**	**(0.01)**	**0.12**	**(0.02)**	**0.19**	**(0.02)**	**-0.02**	**(0.01)**	**0.17**	**(0.02)**	**0.20**	**(0.02)**
Partners	Albania	-0.97	(0.05)	-0.94	(0.06)	0.04	(0.09)	-1.02	(0.04)	-0.68	(0.13)	**0.34**	(0.15)
	Argentina	-0.76	(0.06)	0.01	(0.13)	**0.77**	(0.15)	-0.85	(0.06)	-0.15	(0.11)	**0.70**	(0.12)
	Brazil	-1.19	(0.03)	-0.88	(0.10)	**0.31**	(0.11)	-1.28	(0.04)	-0.67	(0.10)	**0.61**	(0.12)
	Colombia	-1.29	(0.06)	-0.87	(0.12)	**0.42**	(0.15)	-1.30	(0.05)	-0.48	(0.14)	**0.83**	(0.16)
	Dubai (UAE)	0.09	(0.02)	0.56	(0.01)	**0.47**	(0.02)	0.39	(0.01)	0.48	(0.02)	**0.10**	(0.02)
	Hong Kong-China	-0.96	(0.11)	-0.78	(0.04)	0.18	(0.12)	-0.81	(0.04)	-0.82	(0.09)	-0.01	(0.10)
	Indonesia	-1.72	(0.10)	-1.48	(0.06)	**0.24**	(0.11)	-1.54	(0.07)	-1.56	(0.11)	-0.02	(0.13)
	Jordan	-0.70	(0.04)	-0.31	(0.08)	**0.38**	(0.10)	-0.65	(0.04)	-0.31	(0.08)	**0.34**	(0.10)
	Kazakhstan	-0.54	(0.04)	-0.45	(0.05)	0.09	(0.07)	-0.59	(0.05)	-0.44	(0.04)	**0.15**	(0.07)
	Kyrgyzstan	-0.51	(0.06)	-0.73	(0.04)	-0.22	(0.09)	-0.66	(0.03)	-0.57	(0.07)	0.09	(0.08)
	Panama	-1.10	(0.10)	-0.44	(0.14)	**0.65**	(0.19)	-0.92	(0.09)	-0.02	(0.20)	**0.90**	(0.23)
	Peru	-1.46	(0.05)	-0.87	(0.19)	**0.58**	(0.21)	-1.40	(0.05)	-0.94	(0.19)	**0.45**	(0.21)
	Qatar	0.46	(0.01)	0.57	(0.01)	**0.11**	(0.02)	0.49	(0.01)	0.52	(0.01)	**0.03**	(0.01)
	Shanghai-China	-0.70	(0.08)	-0.33	(0.04)	**0.36**	(0.10)	-0.53	(0.05)	-0.44	(0.07)	0.09	(0.10)
	Chinese Taipei	-0.45	(0.04)	-0.23	(0.03)	**0.22**	(0.06)	-0.26	(0.03)	-0.49	(0.06)	**-0.23**	(0.07)
	Thailand	-1.31	(0.09)	-1.31	(0.06)	0.00	(0.11)	-1.34	(0.06)	-1.27	(0.10)	0.07	(0.13)
	Trinidad and Tobago	-0.68	(0.03)	-0.48	(0.02)	**0.20**	(0.03)	-0.57	(0.02)	-0.49	(0.05)	0.08	(0.05)
	Tunisia	-1.21	(0.06)	-1.14	(0.14)	0.08	(0.17)	-1.20	(0.06)	-0.98	(0.38)	0.22	(0.38)
	Uruguay	-0.76	(0.03)	-0.19	(0.20)	0.57	(0.21)	-0.84	(0.04)	0.15	(0.13)	**0.99**	(0.15)

Note: Values that are statistically significant are indicated in bold (see Annex A3).
Source: OECD, *PISA 2009 Database*.

[Part 2/2]
Table B4.1 **Student socio-economic background, by schools with various school-admittance criteria**

Average *PISA index of economic, social and cultural status* (ESCS) in schools whose principal reported that the following factors are "never or sometimes" or "always" considered for admittance to school

		Whether the student requires or is interested in a special programme						Preference given to family members of current or former students					
		Never or sometimes		Always		Difference (always – never or sometimes)		Never or sometimes		Always		Difference (always – never or sometimes)	
		Mean index	S.E.	Mean index	S.E.	Dif.	S.E.	Mean index	S.E.	Mean index	S.E.	Dif.	S.E.
OECD	Australia	0.36	(0.02)	0.26	(0.05)	-0.09	(0.05)	0.27	(0.02)	0.44	(0.03)	**0.17**	(0.04)
	Austria	0.02	(0.03)	0.14	(0.05)	0.11	(0.08)	0.01	(0.03)	0.28	(0.08)	**0.26**	(0.10)
	Belgium	0.21	(0.02)	0.10	(0.08)	-0.11	(0.09)	0.14	(0.02)	0.53	(0.07)	**0.39**	(0.08)
	Canada	0.49	(0.02)	0.56	(0.04)	0.07	(0.05)	0.49	(0.02)	0.61	(0.04)	**0.12**	(0.05)
	Chile	-0.52	(0.05)	-0.72	(0.13)	-0.20	(0.15)	-0.66	(0.05)	-0.29	(0.13)	**0.37**	(0.15)
	Czech Republic	-0.07	(0.02)	-0.14	(0.05)	-0.08	(0.05)	-0.08	(0.01)	-0.16	(0.06)	-0.08	(0.07)
	Denmark	0.29	(0.03)	0.38	(0.08)	0.09	(0.09)	0.28	(0.03)	0.39	(0.06)	0.11	(0.07)
	Estonia	0.18	(0.02)	-0.02	(0.05)	**-0.20**	(0.06)	0.12	(0.02)	0.33	(0.04)	**0.20**	(0.05)
	Finland	0.36	(0.02)	0.57	(0.09)	**0.22**	(0.10)	0.37	(0.02)	0.47	(0.10)	0.10	(0.10)
	Germany	0.17	(0.03)	0.22	(0.07)	0.05	(0.09)	0.14	(0.03)	0.47	(0.09)	**0.33**	(0.10)
	Greece	0.00	(0.04)	-0.16	(0.17)	-0.16	(0.18)	-0.06	(0.05)	0.12	(0.07)	0.18	(0.10)
	Hungary	-0.34	(0.11)	-0.15	(0.03)	0.20	(0.13)	-0.19	(0.03)	-0.12	(0.15)	0.08	(0.16)
	Ireland	0.07	(0.03)	-0.22	(0.11)	**-0.29**	(0.11)	-0.16	(0.04)	0.20	(0.04)	**0.36**	(0.06)
	Israel	0.00	(0.03)	-0.09	(0.06)	-0.09	(0.07)	-0.02	(0.03)	0.02	(0.13)	0.04	(0.13)
	Italy	-0.10	(0.02)	-0.14	(0.02)	-0.03	(0.04)	-0.14	(0.02)	-0.07	(0.04)	0.07	(0.06)
	Japan	0.02	(0.02)	-0.08	(0.04)	**-0.10**	(0.05)	-0.01	(0.02)	0.21	(0.24)	0.22	(0.24)
	Korea	-0.12	(0.04)	-0.33	(0.10)	**-0.21**	(0.11)	-0.15	(0.03)	-0.41	(0.18)	**-0.26**	(0.18)
	Luxembourg	0.25	(0.01)	-0.11	(0.04)	**-0.37**	(0.05)	-0.06	(0.02)	0.38	(0.02)	**0.44**	(0.03)
	Mexico	-1.30	(0.03)	-0.77	(0.11)	**0.53**	(0.11)	-1.24	(0.03)	-0.92	(0.18)	**0.32**	(0.19)
	Netherlands	0.27	(0.03)	0.19	(0.09)	-0.08	(0.10)	0.27	(0.03)	0.20	(0.12)	-0.08	(0.12)
	New Zealand	0.09	(0.02)	0.01	(0.07)	-0.08	(0.08)	-0.01	(0.03)	0.24	(0.04)	**0.25**	(0.06)
	Poland	-0.32	(0.03)	0.00	(0.08)	**0.31**	(0.09)	-0.29	(0.02)	0.06	(0.30)	0.35	(0.30)
	Portugal	-0.35	(0.08)	-0.29	(0.05)	0.06	(0.11)	-0.39	(0.05)	-0.05	(0.12)	**0.34**	(0.15)
	Slovak Republic	-0.13	(0.04)	-0.07	(0.04)	0.05	(0.07)	-0.10	(0.02)	0.14	(0.08)	**0.24**	(0.08)
	Slovenia	0.29	(0.04)	0.00	(0.02)	**-0.29**	(0.04)	0.07	(0.01)	0.12	(0.18)	0.04	(0.18)
	Spain	-0.33	(0.04)	-0.15	(0.10)	0.18	(0.11)	-0.39	(0.04)	-0.13	(0.07)	**0.27**	(0.08)
	Sweden	0.33	(0.02)	0.39	(0.06)	0.06	(0.07)	0.29	(0.02)	0.57	(0.05)	**0.28**	(0.05)
	Switzerland	0.02	(0.03)	0.32	(0.07)	**0.30**	(0.08)	0.08	(0.03)	-0.05	(0.14)	-0.13	(0.14)
	United Kingdom	0.21	(0.02)	0.30	(0.07)	0.09	(0.07)	0.23	(0.03)	0.18	(0.04)	-0.05	(0.05)
	United States	0.20	(0.05)	0.00	(0.10)	-0.19	(0.12)	0.15	(0.04)	0.66	(0.18)	**0.52**	(0.19)
	OECD average	0.01	(0.01)	0.00	(0.01)	-0.01	(0.02)	-0.04	(0.01)	0.15	(0.02)	**0.18**	(0.02)
Partners	Albania	-0.97	(0.04)	-0.86	(0.12)	0.11	(0.13)	-0.99	(0.04)	-0.78	(0.12)	0.21	(0.13)
	Argentina	-0.74	(0.06)	-0.29	(0.11)	**0.45**	(0.14)	-0.74	(0.07)	-0.48	(0.08)	**0.26**	(0.12)
	Brazil	-1.17	(0.04)	-1.10	(0.12)	0.07	(0.13)	-1.19	(0.03)	-0.84	(0.16)	**0.35**	(0.18)
	Colombia	-1.23	(0.05)	-0.89	(0.15)	**0.33**	(0.16)	-1.14	(0.06)	-1.14	(0.13)	0.00	(0.16)
	Dubai (UAE)	0.41	(0.01)	0.51	(0.02)	**0.09**	(0.03)	0.31	(0.01)	0.54	(0.01)	**0.23**	(0.02)
	Hong Kong-China	-0.79	(0.04)	-1.03	(0.12)	**-0.24**	(0.12)	-0.76	(0.04)	-1.26	(0.14)	**-0.50**	(0.15)
	Indonesia	-1.64	(0.07)	-1.42	(0.08)	**0.22**	(0.11)	-1.57	(0.06)	-1.48	(0.11)	0.08	(0.13)
	Jordan	-0.64	(0.03)	-0.29	(0.10)	**0.35**	(0.11)	-0.65	(0.03)	-0.26	(0.09)	**0.39**	(0.10)
	Kazakhstan	-0.57	(0.04)	-0.39	(0.06)	**0.18**	(0.08)	-0.51	(0.03)	-0.46	(0.12)	0.06	(0.12)
	Kyrgyzstan	-0.59	(0.05)	-0.68	(0.04)	-0.09	(0.07)	-0.61	(0.03)	-0.76	(0.08)	-0.14	(0.09)
	Panama	-0.80	(0.10)	-0.75	(0.14)	0.04	(0.19)	-0.87	(0.10)	-0.44	(0.27)	0.44	(0.31)
	Peru	-1.33	(0.05)	-1.28	(0.17)	0.05	(0.18)	-1.34	(0.05)	-1.22	(0.16)	0.12	(0.17)
	Qatar	0.53	(0.01)	0.40	(0.02)	**-0.13**	(0.02)	0.46	(0.01)	0.57	(0.01)	**0.11**	(0.02)
	Shanghai-China	-0.49	(0.04)	-0.45	(0.15)	0.04	(0.16)	-0.47	(0.04)	-0.71	(0.15)	-0.24	(0.16)
	Chinese Taipei	-0.23	(0.03)	-0.51	(0.05)	**-0.29**	(0.07)	-0.29	(0.03)	-0.54	(0.10)	**-0.25**	(0.11)
	Thailand	-1.52	(0.06)	-0.99	(0.09)	**0.53**	(0.12)	-1.31	(0.05)	-1.30	(0.17)	0.01	(0.20)
	Trinidad and Tobago	-0.55	(0.02)	-0.70	(0.05)	**-0.15**	(0.05)	-0.58	(0.02)	-0.15	(0.07)	**0.43**	(0.07)
	Tunisia	-1.17	(0.06)	-1.66	(0.24)	**-0.49**	(0.26)	-1.19	(0.06)	-1.22	(0.18)	-0.03	(0.20)
	Uruguay	-0.70	(0.04)	-0.80	(0.14)	-0.10	(0.16)	-0.85	(0.05)	0.11	(0.16)	**0.96**	(0.18)

Note: Values that are statistically significant are indicated in bold (see Annex A3).
Source: OECD, *PISA 2009 Database*.

ANNEX B: DATA TABLES

[Part 1/2]
Table B4.2 **Various school-admittance criteria, by school type**

Percentage of students in schools whose principal reported that the following factors are "always" considered for admittance to school

		Student's record of academic performance, including placement test, and/or recommendation of feeder schools						Parents' endorsement of the instructional or religious philosophy of the school					
		Publicly managed schools		Privately managed schools		Difference (private – public)		Publicly managed schools		Privately managed schools		Difference (private – public)	
		%	S.E.	%	S.E.	Dif. in %	S.E.	%	S.E.	%	S.E.	Dif. in %	S.E.
OECD	Australia	32.9	(3.8)	34.3	(5.2)	1.4	(6.8)	5.1	(1.8)	67.9	(4.1)	**62.8**	(4.6)
	Austria	57.7	(3.0)	80.5	(7.8)	**22.8**	(8.8)	2.1	(1.1)	19.6	(7.8)	**17.6**	(7.9)
	Belgium	15.7	(3.7)	17.3	(2.8)	1.6	(4.5)	31.4	(5.7)	36.7	(3.6)	5.3	(6.6)
	Canada	25.1	(1.6)	80.6	(6.5)	**55.6**	(6.8)	12.1	(1.5)	43.1	(7.8)	**31.0**	(8.0)
	Chile	23.0	(4.9)	52.1	(5.3)	**29.1**	(7.2)	1.4	(1.4)	27.8	(4.6)	**26.4**	(4.8)
	Czech Republic	51.5	(2.5)	75.7	(13.5)	24.2	(13.8)	16.6	(2.7)	28.7	(10.1)	12.1	(10.4)
	Denmark	5.7	(1.8)	3.6	(2.5)	-2.1	(3.1)	3.1	(1.2)	45.4	(7.4)	**42.4**	(7.5)
	Estonia	29.1	(2.9)	47.7	(18.7)	18.6	(19.1)	16.6	(2.8)	56.9	(20.5)	40.3	(20.7)
	Finland	2.6	(1.2)	36.6	(16.7)	**34.0**	(16.8)	1.3	(0.9)	3.0	(1.0)	1.7	(1.3)
	Germany	70.7	(2.4)	100.0	(0.0)	**29.3**	(2.4)	2.0	(1.0)	53.5	(15.3)	**51.5**	(15.3)
	Greece	3.5	(1.3)	52.6	(13.2)	**49.0**	(12.9)	5.5	(1.8)	43.0	(15.3)	**37.5**	(16.2)
	Hungary	86.1	(2.3)	92.3	(4.8)	6.2	(5.2)	17.8	(3.2)	66.9	(10.9)	**49.1**	(11.4)
	Ireland	27.0	(6.6)	21.6	(4.6)	-5.4	(8.1)	3.3	(2.4)	40.7	(6.0)	**37.4**	(6.4)
	Israel	52.1	(4.4)	66.3	(8.3)	14.2	(9.1)	26.8	(3.3)	51.2	(9.4)	**24.4**	(10.2)
	Italy	42.4	(2.2)	36.1	(6.9)	-6.3	(7.5)	33.7	(1.9)	59.0	(8.7)	**25.4**	(8.6)
	Japan	92.1	(2.1)	78.3	(5.2)	**-13.8**	(5.4)	7.3	(2.3)	17.3	(5.3)	10.0	(5.4)
	Korea	49.5	(5.4)	53.5	(6.4)	4.0	(9.0)	1.0	(1.0)	13.1	(4.6)	**12.1**	(4.7)
	Luxembourg	38.2	(0.1)	69.4	(0.3)	**31.2**	(0.3)	17.8	(0.1)	5.2	(0.0)	**-12.6**	(0.1)
	Mexico	40.5	(1.9)	47.3	(6.0)	6.8	(6.5)	11.8	(1.2)	37.2	(6.1)	**25.4**	(6.2)
	Netherlands	92.4	(3.1)	86.3	(3.5)	-6.1	(4.6)	9.3	(4.3)	26.6	(4.7)	**17.3**	(6.0)
	New Zealand	24.6	(3.1)	63.8	(18.3)	**39.1**	(18.5)	17.2	(2.0)	76.7	(16.8)	**59.4**	(16.9)
	Poland	16.2	(2.6)	38.6	(9.5)	**22.4**	(10.4)	2.8	(1.2)	47.0	(14.4)	**44.2**	(14.5)
	Portugal	1.2	(0.8)	1.5	(1.1)	0.3	(1.4)	16.1	(2.8)	61.9	(9.5)	**45.8**	(10.0)
	Slovak Republic	60.6	(3.1)	83.8	(8.1)	**23.1**	(8.8)	16.2	(3.0)	45.7	(13.4)	**29.5**	(13.6)
	Slovenia	27.7	(0.3)	56.3	(0.9)	**28.6**	(0.9)	5.5	(0.1)	57.5	(0.9)	**51.9**	(0.9)
	Spain	1.7	(0.5)	4.0	(1.4)	2.3	(1.4)	2.3	(1.3)	27.5	(4.3)	**25.2**	(4.4)
	Sweden	3.8	(1.5)	2.8	(2.3)	-1.0	(2.9)	4.5	(1.7)	14.2	(8.1)	9.7	(8.3)
	Switzerland	64.2	(3.0)	78.2	(11.2)	14.0	(12.0)	1.5	(0.9)	26.2	(12.5)	**24.7**	(12.5)
	United Kingdom	13.7	(1.9)	70.2	(18.0)	**56.5**	(18.4)	11.8	(2.3)	25.9	(13.2)	14.1	(13.3)
	United States	20.2	(3.1)	100.0	(0.0)	**79.8**	(3.1)	3.4	(1.5)	74.4	(14.8)	**71.0**	(14.4)
	OECD average	**35.7**	**(0.5)**	**54.4**	**(1.6)**	**18.7**	**(1.7)**	**10.2**	**(0.4)**	**40.0**	**(1.8)**	**29.8**	**(1.9)**
Partners	Albania	50.6	(4.0)	74.2	(10.4)	**23.6**	(11.0)	12.8	(2.4)	54.8	(13.8)	**42.0**	(14.2)
	Argentina	11.3	(2.8)	37.0	(6.5)	**25.6**	(7.1)	13.6	(3.6)	73.0	(7.1)	**59.3**	(7.9)
	Brazil	8.0	(1.3)	26.1	(4.9)	**18.1**	(5.0)	15.2	(2.0)	57.7	(9.3)	**42.5**	(9.4)
	Colombia	25.7	(4.0)	63.6	(8.1)	**37.8**	(9.1)	11.4	(2.5)	51.3	(10.3)	**39.9**	(10.5)
	Dubai (UAE)	32.9	(0.1)	82.3	(0.1)	**49.4**	(0.2)	22.8	(0.0)	40.5	(0.1)	**17.7**	(0.1)
	Hong Kong-China	87.3	(7.8)	83.8	(2.9)	-3.5	(8.3)	13.2	(13.1)	27.7	(3.7)	14.5	(13.6)
	Indonesia	79.2	(4.8)	59.2	(5.6)	**-19.9**	(7.5)	21.0	(4.0)	52.4	(6.4)	**31.4**	(7.7)
	Jordan	31.1	(3.9)	49.2	(9.4)	18.0	(10.2)	24.1	(3.7)	35.7	(5.4)	11.6	(6.5)
	Kazakhstan	34.2	(3.6)	93.4	(7.2)	**59.2**	(8.4)	52.9	(3.9)	96.4	(3.9)	**43.6**	(5.8)
	Kyrgyzstan	61.2	(3.8)	43.8	(19.7)	-17.4	(20.0)	26.8	(3.8)	26.4	(17.2)	-0.3	(17.6)
	Panama	37.6	(5.8)	75.6	(9.3)	**38.0**	(10.9)	9.9	(4.0)	28.9	(7.6)	**19.1**	(8.6)
	Peru	16.7	(2.9)	45.4	(8.9)	**28.7**	(9.4)	11.8	(2.7)	36.2	(8.5)	**24.4**	(9.2)
	Qatar	25.7	(0.1)	86.9	(0.2)	**61.2**	(0.3)	52.2	(0.1)	19.3	(0.3)	**-32.9**	(0.3)
	Shanghai-China	56.3	(3.4)	62.2	(10.5)	5.9	(11.1)	39.9	(4.1)	76.8	(8.8)	**36.9**	(9.7)
	Chinese Taipei	56.4	(3.8)	48.0	(7.3)	-8.5	(8.2)	22.5	(4.5)	40.0	(7.2)	**17.5**	(8.5)
	Thailand	68.3	(3.4)	76.3	(8.2)	8.1	(8.9)	30.1	(4.1)	58.4	(8.0)	**28.4**	(9.2)
	Trinidad and Tobago	61.5	(0.4)	62.7	(0.4)	**1.2**	(0.5)	6.2	(0.2)	12.0	(0.3)	**5.8**	(0.4)
	Tunisia	20.4	(3.9)	82.2	(17.5)	**61.8**	(18.0)	1.8	(1.1)	4.6	(3.2)	2.8	(3.4)
	Uruguay	7.5	(1.9)	22.9	(6.8)	**15.4**	(7.0)	4.5	(1.6)	55.7	(9.6)	**51.2**	(9.7)

Note: Values that are statistically significant are indicated in bold (see Annex A3).
Source: OECD, *PISA 2009 Database*.

[Part 2/2]
Table B4.2 **Various school-admittance criteria, by school type**

Percentage of students in schools whose principal reported that the following factors are "always" considered for admittance to school

| | | Whether the student requires or is interested in a special programme |||||| Preference given to family members of current or former students ||||||
| | | Publicly managed schools || Privately managed schools || Difference (private – public) || Publicly managed schools || Privately managed schools || Difference (private – public) ||
		%	S.E.	%	S.E.	Dif. in %	S.E.	%	S.E.	%	S.E.	Dif. in %	S.E.
OECD	Australia	15.4	(2.7)	11.2	(3.5)	-4.1	(4.5)	27.6	(3.0)	66.1	(4.5)	**38.6**	(5.8)
	Austria	37.3	(3.8)	63.3	(9.0)	**26.0**	(9.4)	18.7	(2.9)	38.6	(10.1)	19.9	(10.3)
	Belgium	22.5	(4.3)	11.7	(2.3)	**-10.9**	(4.9)	14.2	(3.9)	16.9	(2.6)	2.7	(5.0)
	Canada	18.1	(2.2)	21.2	(6.6)	3.1	(6.9)	10.5	(1.2)	37.1	(6.6)	**26.6**	(6.8)
	Chile	21.4	(5.3)	20.2	(4.0)	-1.1	(6.6)	10.6	(3.5)	31.4	(5.6)	**20.7**	(6.6)
	Czech Republic	17.9	(2.9)	16.5	(9.2)	-1.3	(9.6)	5.6	(1.9)	6.2	(8.2)	0.5	(8.3)
	Denmark	5.0	(1.6)	20.3	(5.1)	**15.3**	(5.2)	15.2	(2.9)	30.4	(6.7)	**15.2**	(7.2)
	Estonia	17.4	(2.7)	0.0	(0.0)	**-17.4**	(2.7)	13.1	(2.5)	20.6	(18.4)	7.5	(18.6)
	Finland	6.2	(1.7)	40.0	(23.8)	33.8	(23.7)	2.8	(1.2)	1.0	(0.3)	-1.7	(1.2)
	Germany	25.7	(3.3)	21.6	(11.2)	-4.1	(11.7)	11.4	(2.4)	37.9	(15.1)	26.5	(15.4)
	Greece	13.0	(2.9)	28.2	(16.1)	15.2	(16.0)	21.4	(3.0)	28.4	(15.8)	7.0	(15.7)
	Hungary	76.7	(3.7)	87.1	(7.7)	10.4	(8.4)	6.7	(2.1)	19.2	(8.0)	12.6	(8.1)
	Ireland	10.1	(4.4)	11.3	(3.7)	1.2	(5.8)	31.2	(6.5)	67.4	(4.7)	**36.1**	(8.0)
	Israel	31.6	(4.3)	8.7	(5.0)	**-23.0**	(6.6)	4.7	(2.0)	22.2	(8.5)	17.5	(8.9)
	Italy	49.7	(2.0)	59.8	(6.5)	10.1	(7.3)	28.8	(1.6)	13.4	(4.5)	**-15.3**	(5.0)
	Japan	28.6	(3.5)	22.7	(6.2)	-5.9	(7.0)	0.0	(0.0)	5.2	(3.0)	5.2	(3.0)
	Korea	15.5	(3.2)	23.6	(5.7)	8.1	(6.1)	1.2	(1.2)	7.5	(3.6)	6.3	(3.7)
	Luxembourg	10.9	(0.1)	37.0	(0.2)	**26.1**	(0.3)	58.5	(0.1)	48.9	(0.3)	**-9.6**	(0.3)
	Mexico	13.4	(1.1)	27.7	(6.1)	**14.3**	(6.1)	6.7	(0.9)	10.5	(5.5)	3.8	(5.5)
	Netherlands	2.9	(1.9)	12.5	(3.9)	**9.5**	(4.0)	1.7	(0.9)	11.4	(3.6)	**9.8**	(3.7)
	New Zealand	12.8	(2.1)	13.4	(13.6)	0.6	(13.8)	32.4	(3.0)	83.7	(16.3)	**51.4**	(16.6)
	Poland	10.1	(2.1)	58.5	(12.5)	**48.4**	(12.6)	2.3	(1.2)	42.0	(10.0)	**39.7**	(9.7)
	Portugal	50.2	(4.1)	75.2	(9.0)	**25.0**	(10.2)	21.8	(2.9)	36.0	(12.8)	14.2	(13.0)
	Slovak Republic	43.1	(4.0)	44.6	(13.7)	1.5	(14.1)	2.2	(1.5)	0.0	(0.0)	-2.2	(1.5)
	Slovenia	76.8	(0.6)	57.5	(0.9)	**-19.4**	(1.1)	0.6	(0.3)	2.7	(0.6)	**2.1**	(0.7)
	Spain	12.6	(2.5)	15.6	(3.9)	2.9	(4.5)	25.5	(3.0)	43.5	(4.7)	**17.9**	(5.5)
	Sweden	5.1	(1.8)	5.8	(7.6)	0.7	(7.8)	10.9	(2.3)	66.6	(7.7)	**55.6**	(8.0)
	Switzerland	17.4	(2.8)	31.8	(13.2)	14.5	(13.2)	1.0	(0.3)	3.4	(4.4)	2.4	(4.4)
	United Kingdom	3.2	(1.2)	1.4	(1.5)	-1.8	(2.0)	40.2	(3.7)	19.8	(12.9)	-20.4	(13.5)
	United States	13.1	(2.9)	10.8	(7.5)	-2.4	(8.0)	3.0	(1.4)	24.8	(9.5)	**21.7**	(9.6)
	OECD average	**22.8**	**(0.5)**	**28.6**	**(1.6)**	**5.9**	**(1.7)**	**14.4**	**(0.5)**	**28.1**	**(1.6)**	**13.7**	**(1.6)**
Partners	Albania	16.6	(2.6)	41.1	(11.3)	**24.4**	(12.1)	14.1	(3.0)	25.5	(13.2)	11.4	(13.9)
	Argentina	26.5	(3.9)	27.6	(5.7)	1.1	(6.6)	42.5	(4.2)	59.0	(6.4)	**16.6**	(7.9)
	Brazil	11.8	(1.5)	19.4	(6.7)	7.6	(7.1)	9.2	(2.0)	19.0	(7.5)	9.8	(7.7)
	Colombia	18.8	(4.3)	42.1	(10.5)	**23.3**	(11.2)	18.9	(3.8)	19.0	(8.5)	0.1	(9.3)
	Dubai (UAE)	9.4	(0.0)	12.8	(0.2)	**3.4**	(0.2)	5.0	(0.0)	60.5	(0.2)	**55.5**	(0.2)
	Hong Kong-China	20.6	(16.9)	9.4	(2.5)	-11.2	(17.2)	14.4	(8.7)	10.0	(1.9)	-4.4	(8.9)
	Indonesia	41.0	(5.8)	44.2	(5.3)	3.2	(7.5)	8.2	(3.4)	26.6	(4.6)	**18.4**	(5.2)
	Jordan	19.6	(3.4)	27.0	(6.3)	7.4	(7.2)	17.8	(3.0)	33.9	(4.9)	**16.1**	(5.8)
	Kazakhstan	34.8	(3.5)	40.9	(20.6)	6.1	(20.8)	6.0	(1.7)	43.7	(21.3)	37.6	(21.4)
	Kyrgyzstan	64.4	(4.2)	45.1	(19.6)	-19.3	(20.3)	19.3	(3.2)	0.0	(0.0)	**-19.3**	(3.2)
	Panama	14.0	(4.6)	18.2	(4.9)	4.2	(6.6)	13.7	(4.8)	36.2	(9.0)	**22.6**	(10.2)
	Peru	13.2	(2.8)	21.3	(7.3)	8.1	(8.4)	16.0	(2.8)	16.1	(5.5)	0.1	(5.9)
	Qatar	20.1	(0.1)	13.8	(0.2)	**-6.3**	(0.2)	36.5	(0.1)	47.4	(0.3)	**10.8**	(0.3)
	Shanghai-China	11.9	(2.8)	11.9	(7.4)	0.0	(7.9)	7.3	(2.5)	0.0	(0.0)	**-7.3**	(2.5)
	Chinese Taipei	24.2	(4.8)	57.5	(6.9)	**33.3**	(8.4)	7.6	(2.9)	30.3	(5.9)	**22.7**	(6.6)
	Thailand	37.6	(4.5)	52.0	(8.2)	14.5	(9.7)	9.5	(2.4)	35.2	(11.5)	**25.7**	(11.8)
	Trinidad and Tobago	7.9	(0.2)	7.1	(0.3)	**-0.8**	(0.4)	3.5	(0.1)	2.4	(0.1)	**-1.0**	(0.1)
	Tunisia	4.6	(2.1)	0.0	(0.0)	**-4.6**	(2.1)	9.9	(2.3)	0.2	(0.2)	**-9.7**	(2.3)
	Uruguay	14.8	(2.4)	15.3	(6.7)	0.5	(6.8)	7.4	(1.9)	52.9	(10.9)	**45.5**	(11.1)

Note: Values that are statistically significant are indicated in bold (see Annex A3).
Source: OECD, *PISA 2009 Database*.

ANNEX B: DATA TABLES

[Part 1/2]

Table B4.3 **Socio-economic stratification, after accounting for the proportion of public funding for schools and various school-admittance criteria**

Difference in the *PISA index of economic, social and cultural status* (ESCS) between privately and publicly managed schools (private – public)

After accounting for the following school-admittance criteria and before accounting for the percentage of total school funding coming from government sources:

		Student's record of academic performance (including placement test) and/or recommendation of feeder schools		Parents' endorsement of the instructional or religious philosophy of the school		Whether the student requires or is interested in a special programme		Preference given to family members of current or former students		All four admittance criteria	
		Dif. in index point (priv. – pub.)	S.E.	Dif. in index point (priv. – pub.)	S.E.	Dif. in index point (priv. – pub.)	S.E.	Dif. in index point (priv. – pub.)	S.E.	Dif. in index point (priv. – pub.)	S.E.
OECD	Australia	**0.47**	(0.03)	**0.54**	(0.04)	**0.46**	(0.03)	**0.47**	(0.03)	**0.53**	(0.04)
	Austria	**0.22**	(0.11)	**0.34**	(0.11)	**0.34**	(0.10)	**0.29**	(0.11)	**0.22**	(0.11)
	Belgium	**0.31**	(0.04)	**0.30**	(0.04)	**0.29**	(0.04)	**0.30**	(0.05)	**0.28**	(0.05)
	Canada	**0.51**	(0.07)	**0.51**	(0.07)	**0.54**	(0.06)	**0.53**	(0.07)	**0.50**	(0.08)
	Chile	**0.63**	(0.08)	**0.58**	(0.10)	**0.79**	(0.09)	**0.75**	(0.09)	**0.48**	(0.10)
	Czech Republic	**0.23**	(0.11)	**0.29**	(0.10)	**0.28**	(0.10)	**0.28**	(0.10)	**0.22**	(0.11)
	Denmark	**0.21**	(0.06)	**0.22**	(0.07)	**0.21**	(0.06)	**0.21**	(0.06)	**0.22**	(0.07)
	Estonia	0.28	(0.14)	0.31	(0.16)	0.32	(0.19)	0.30	(0.17)	0.29	(0.19)
	Finland	0.15	(0.18)	0.16	(0.16)	0.09	(0.11)	0.16	(0.16)	0.10	(0.14)
	Germany	0.22	(0.15)	0.34	(0.19)	0.29	(0.15)	0.20	(0.14)	0.24	(0.17)
	Greece	**1.05**	(0.23)	**1.03**	(0.18)	**1.09**	(0.19)	**1.05**	(0.17)	**1.05**	(0.22)
	Hungary	**0.30**	(0.13)	**0.35**	(0.15)	**0.34**	(0.15)	**0.35**	(0.14)	**0.29**	(0.14)
	Ireland	**0.29**	(0.06)	**0.28**	(0.06)	**0.30**	(0.06)	**0.19**	(0.06)	**0.18**	(0.07)
	Israel	0.12	(0.10)	0.15	(0.10)	0.11	(0.10)	0.13	(0.10)	0.10	(0.11)
	Italy	**0.23**	(0.10)	**0.22**	(0.10)	**0.24**	(0.10)	**0.25**	(0.10)	**0.23**	(0.10)
	Japan	**0.21**	(0.04)	**0.22**	(0.04)	**0.22**	(0.03)	**0.22**	(0.04)	**0.20**	(0.04)
	Korea	0.04	(0.08)	0.07	(0.08)	0.04	(0.08)	0.04	(0.08)	0.07	(0.08)
	Luxembourg	-0.03	(0.04)	**-0.08**	(0.04)	**0.12**	(0.04)	-0.05	(0.04)	**0.20**	(0.04)
	Mexico	**1.40**	(0.09)	**1.34**	(0.10)	**1.38**	(0.09)	**1.43**	(0.10)	**1.30**	(0.09)
	Netherlands	-0.07	(0.09)	-0.06	(0.09)	-0.08	(0.09)	-0.07	(0.09)	-0.05	(0.08)
	New Zealand	**0.75**	(0.05)	**0.59**	(0.05)	**0.74**	(0.05)	**0.64**	(0.08)	**0.54**	(0.07)
	Poland	**0.95**	(0.11)	**1.05**	(0.16)	**0.95**	(0.13)	**1.03**	(0.16)	**0.96**	(0.20)
	Portugal	**0.48**	(0.14)	**0.34**	(0.15)	**0.48**	(0.14)	**0.43**	(0.13)	**0.30**	(0.14)
	Slovak Republic	0.13	(0.10)	0.15	(0.10)	0.19	(0.10)	0.18	(0.10)	0.13	(0.10)
	Slovenia	**0.54**	(0.06)	**0.66**	(0.07)	**0.58**	(0.07)	**0.63**	(0.06)	**0.52**	(0.07)
	Spain	**0.67**	(0.06)	**0.61**	(0.08)	**0.68**	(0.06)	**0.64**	(0.06)	**0.60**	(0.09)
	Sweden	**0.43**	(0.08)	**0.41**	(0.09)	**0.42**	(0.09)	**0.33**	(0.09)	**0.31**	(0.10)
	Switzerland	**0.39**	(0.14)	**0.43**	(0.15)	**0.37**	(0.17)	**0.40**	(0.15)	**0.42**	(0.17)
	United Kingdom	**0.68**	(0.08)	**0.76**	(0.06)	**0.77**	(0.05)	**0.76**	(0.06)	**0.67**	(0.08)
	United States	**0.86**	(0.15)	**0.79**	(0.21)	**0.92**	(0.15)	**0.88**	(0.16)	**0.57**	(0.20)
	OECD average	**0.42**	(0.02)	**0.43**	(0.02)	**0.45**	(0.02)	**0.43**	(0.02)	**0.39**	(0.02)
Partners	Albania	**0.85**	(0.12)	**0.80**	(0.13)	**0.84**	(0.12)	**0.83**	(0.13)	**0.82**	(0.14)
	Argentina	**0.80**	(0.14)	**0.79**	(0.16)	**0.89**	(0.13)	**0.91**	(0.13)	**0.79**	(0.16)
	Brazil	**1.62**	(0.09)	**1.54**	(0.09)	**1.61**	(0.10)	**1.60**	(0.09)	**1.52**	(0.10)
	Colombia	**1.39**	(0.12)	**1.28**	(0.13)	**1.39**	(0.11)	**1.40**	(0.11)	**1.27**	(0.14)
	Dubai (UAE)	**0.60**	(0.03)	**0.71**	(0.03)	**0.70**	(0.03)	**0.73**	(0.03)	**0.60**	(0.03)
	Hong Kong-China	-0.01	(0.09)	0.06	(0.06)	0.04	(0.07)	0.04	(0.07)	0.01	(0.07)
	Indonesia	-0.09	(0.13)	-0.15	(0.13)	-0.15	(0.12)	-0.16	(0.13)	-0.10	(0.15)
	Jordan	**0.47**	(0.10)	**0.49**	(0.09)	**0.50**	(0.09)	**0.47**	(0.09)	**0.42**	(0.09)
	Kazakhstan	**0.51**	(0.21)	**0.49**	(0.22)	**0.53**	(0.21)	**0.55**	(0.24)	**0.54**	(0.23)
	Kyrgyzstan	**1.13**	(0.24)	**1.16**	(0.26)	**1.15**	(0.24)	**1.14**	(0.25)	**1.11**	(0.26)
	Panama	**1.65**	(0.14)	**1.65**	(0.16)	**1.75**	(0.15)	**1.74**	(0.17)	**1.62**	(0.18)
	Peru	**1.28**	(0.13)	**1.33**	(0.14)	**1.36**	(0.13)	**1.35**	(0.13)	**1.28**	(0.14)
	Qatar	**0.50**	(0.02)	**0.44**	(0.02)	**0.40**	(0.01)	**0.40**	(0.01)	**0.53**	(0.02)
	Shanghai-China	0.33	(0.18)	0.33	(0.19)	0.35	(0.19)	0.33	(0.19)	0.31	(0.18)
	Chinese Taipei	-0.09	(0.05)	-0.08	(0.05)	-0.01	(0.06)	-0.06	(0.06)	0.04	(0.07)
	Thailand	0.27	(0.13)	0.27	(0.14)	0.20	(0.15)	0.29	(0.14)	0.29	(0.15)
	Trinidad and Tobago	**0.23**	(0.03)	**0.22**	(0.03)	**0.23**	(0.03)	**0.23**	(0.03)	**0.21**	(0.03)
	Tunisia	**0.52**	(0.14)	**0.54**	(0.09)	**0.52**	(0.09)	**0.54**	(0.10)	**0.48**	(0.14)
	Uruguay	**1.60**	(0.07)	**1.67**	(0.10)	**1.59**	(0.08)	**1.55**	(0.09)	**1.54**	(0.10)

Note: Values that are statistically significant are indicated in bold (see Annex A3).
Source: OECD, *PISA 2009 Database*.

[Part 2/2]

Table B4.3 **Socio-economic stratification, after accounting for the proportion of public funding for schools and various school-admittance criteria**

Difference in the *PISA index of economic, social and cultural status* (ESCS) between privately and publicly managed schools (private – public)

After accounting for the following school-admittance criteria and after accounting for the percentage of total school funding coming from government sources:

		Student's record of academic performance (including placement test) and/or recommendation of feeder schools		Parents' endorsement of the instructional or religious philosophy of the school		Whether the student requires or is interested in a special programme		Preference given to family members of current or former students		All four admittance criteria	
		Dif. in index point (priv. – pub.)	S.E.	Dif. in index point (priv. – pub.)	S.E.	Dif. in index point (priv. – pub.)	S.E.	Dif. in index point (priv. – pub.)	S.E.	Dif. in index point (priv. – pub.)	S.E.
OECD	Australia	**0.22**	(0.03)	**0.25**	(0.05)	**0.22**	(0.03)	**0.22**	(0.04)	**0.22**	(0.05)
	Austria	m	m	m	m	m	m	m	m	m	m
	Belgium	**0.30**	(0.04)	**0.30**	(0.05)	**0.29**	(0.05)	**0.30**	(0.05)	**0.28**	(0.05)
	Canada	**0.45**	(0.08)	**0.43**	(0.07)	**0.48**	(0.07)	**0.47**	(0.08)	**0.42**	(0.09)
	Chile	**0.57**	(0.10)	**0.52**	(0.11)	**0.67**	(0.11)	**0.66**	(0.11)	**0.48**	(0.11)
	Czech Republic	**0.33**	(0.14)	**0.31**	(0.13)	**0.29**	(0.13)	**0.30**	(0.13)	**0.32**	(0.14)
	Denmark	**0.36**	(0.11)	**0.37**	(0.13)	**0.36**	(0.12)	**0.33**	(0.11)	**0.38**	(0.14)
	Estonia	0.01	(0.13)	0.05	(0.15)	-0.01	(0.20)	0.04	(0.16)	-0.01	(0.15)
	Finland	0.16	(0.20)	0.16	(0.19)	0.08	(0.14)	0.16	(0.19)	0.09	(0.15)
	Germany	0.01	(0.17)	0.12	(0.20)	0.08	(0.17)	0.04	(0.15)	0.06	(0.17)
	Greece	0.28	(0.40)	0.28	(0.38)	0.38	(0.35)	0.33	(0.35)	0.38	(0.40)
	Hungary	**0.35**	(0.16)	**0.39**	(0.18)	**0.38**	(0.17)	**0.38**	(0.17)	**0.34**	(0.17)
	Ireland	**0.13**	(0.06)	**0.17**	(0.06)	**0.15**	(0.06)	0.06	(0.06)	0.10	(0.06)
	Israel	0.15	(0.10)	0.20	(0.10)	0.15	(0.10)	0.16	(0.10)	0.16	(0.10)
	Italy	-0.02	(0.10)	-0.02	(0.09)	-0.02	(0.10)	-0.01	(0.10)	-0.02	(0.10)
	Japan	-0.05	(0.07)	-0.04	(0.07)	-0.04	(0.07)	-0.04	(0.07)	-0.05	(0.07)
	Korea	0.06	(0.07)	0.10	(0.08)	0.06	(0.08)	0.07	(0.08)	0.10	(0.08)
	Luxembourg	**-0.22**	(0.04)	**-0.23**	(0.05)	**-0.16**	(0.05)	**-0.32**	(0.05)	**-0.15**	(0.05)
	Mexico	**1.38**	(0.10)	**1.35**	(0.11)	**1.39**	(0.10)	**1.44**	(0.11)	**1.30**	(0.10)
	Netherlands	-0.15	(0.09)	-0.13	(0.09)	-0.14	(0.09)	-0.15	(0.08)	-0.11	(0.09)
	New Zealand	0.05	(0.12)	-0.06	(0.12)	0.05	(0.12)	-0.02	(0.12)	-0.08	(0.12)
	Poland	0.23	(0.19)	0.35	(0.24)	0.24	(0.22)	0.34	(0.23)	0.23	(0.23)
	Portugal	0.07	(0.13)	0.05	(0.13)	0.08	(0.12)	0.05	(0.12)	0.04	(0.12)
	Slovak Republic	0.11	(0.11)	0.10	(0.11)	0.15	(0.10)	0.15	(0.11)	0.09	(0.11)
	Slovenia	**0.56**	(0.07)	**0.68**	(0.07)	**0.61**	(0.07)	**0.66**	(0.07)	**0.55**	(0.08)
	Spain	**0.51**	(0.09)	**0.45**	(0.10)	**0.50**	(0.09)	**0.49**	(0.09)	**0.46**	(0.10)
	Sweden	**0.43**	(0.09)	**0.41**	(0.09)	**0.42**	(0.09)	**0.33**	(0.09)	**0.31**	(0.10)
	Switzerland	-0.09	(0.10)	-0.06	(0.09)	-0.09	(0.11)	-0.07	(0.10)	-0.09	(0.11)
	United Kingdom	1.32	(2.57)	0.73	(2.40)	0.76	(2.40)	0.60	(2.46)	1.01	(2.58)
	United States	0.32	(0.38)	0.33	(0.40)	0.49	(0.35)	0.36	(0.37)	0.11	(0.40)
	OECD average	**0.27**	(0.09)	**0.26**	(0.09)	**0.27**	(0.09)	**0.25**	(0.09)	**0.24**	(0.09)
Partners	Albania	**0.77**	(0.20)	**0.74**	(0.21)	**0.77**	(0.20)	**0.75**	(0.21)	**0.73**	(0.21)
	Argentina	**0.75**	(0.13)	**0.75**	(0.16)	**0.87**	(0.11)	**0.89**	(0.12)	**0.78**	(0.16)
	Brazil	**0.74**	(0.23)	**0.67**	(0.22)	**0.75**	(0.23)	**0.76**	(0.23)	**0.68**	(0.23)
	Colombia	**1.01**	(0.16)	**0.99**	(0.16)	**1.02**	(0.15)	**1.00**	(0.14)	**1.00**	(0.17)
	Dubai (UAE)	0.19	(0.10)	**0.28**	(0.10)	**0.26**	(0.10)	**0.29**	(0.10)	0.14	(0.10)
	Hong Kong-China	-0.16	(0.10)	-0.08	(0.08)	-0.12	(0.08)	-0.10	(0.08)	-0.14	(0.08)
	Indonesia	**-0.44**	(0.12)	**-0.51**	(0.11)	**-0.49**	(0.10)	**-0.54**	(0.11)	**-0.48**	(0.13)
	Jordan	0.09	(0.14)	0.19	(0.17)	0.20	(0.16)	0.01	(0.19)	0.07	(0.13)
	Kazakhstan	-0.04	(0.25)	-0.03	(0.26)	-0.04	(0.28)	-0.03	(0.28)	-0.01	(0.30)
	Kyrgyzstan	**0.78**	(0.30)	**0.79**	(0.30)	**0.75**	(0.29)	**0.70**	(0.29)	**0.77**	(0.32)
	Panama	**1.79**	(0.45)	**1.74**	(0.44)	**1.87**	(0.43)	**1.86**	(0.42)	**1.72**	(0.44)
	Peru	**1.22**	(0.16)	**1.27**	(0.17)	**1.29**	(0.15)	**1.28**	(0.16)	**1.22**	(0.16)
	Qatar	**1.11**	(0.06)	**1.10**	(0.06)	**1.11**	(0.06)	**1.10**	(0.06)	**1.11**	(0.06)
	Shanghai-China	**0.68**	(0.27)	0.40	(0.34)	0.43	(0.36)	0.41	(0.34)	**0.70**	(0.28)
	Chinese Taipei	-0.25	(0.23)	**-0.40**	(0.16)	**-0.46**	(0.16)	**-0.39**	(0.17)	-0.22	(0.20)
	Thailand	-0.13	(0.12)	-0.14	(0.13)	-0.17	(0.14)	-0.15	(0.13)	-0.11	(0.14)
	Trinidad and Tobago	**-0.18**	(0.04)	**-0.18**	(0.04)	**-0.18**	(0.04)	**-0.22**	(0.04)	**-0.21**	(0.04)
	Tunisia	**1.72**	(0.58)	**1.81**	(0.58)	**1.76**	(0.59)	**1.83**	(0.59)	**1.75**	(0.59)
	Uruguay	**1.13**	(0.40)	**1.14**	(0.41)	**1.10**	(0.40)	**0.98**	(0.41)	**0.99**	(0.42)

Note: Values that are statistically significant are indicated in bold (see Annex A3).
Source: OECD, *PISA 2009 Database.*

ANNEX B: DATA TABLES

[Part 1/1]

Table B4.4 **Relationship between student socio-economic background and school autonomy, resources, climate and performance**

		Index of school responsibility for curriculum and assessment		Index of school responsibility for resource allocation		Index of the school's educational resources		Index of teacher shortage		Index of disciplinary climate		Performance in reading	
		Correlation	S.E.	Correlation	S.E.	Correlation	S.E.	Correlation	S.E.	Correlation	S.E.	Correlation	S.E.
OECD	Australia	0.05	(0.03)	**0.28**	(0.02)	**0.16**	(0.02)	**-0.14**	(0.03)	**0.23**	(0.02)	**0.40**	(0.02)
	Austria	-0.04	(0.04)	-0.01	(0.02)	0.02	(0.04)	-0.01	(0.04)	**0.14**	(0.03)	**0.44**	(0.02)
	Belgium	0.03	(0.03)	0.00	(0.03)	0.01	(0.03)	**-0.10**	(0.03)	**0.12**	(0.04)	**0.48**	(0.02)
	Canada	0.06	(0.03)	**0.15**	(0.03)	**0.08**	(0.02)	**-0.07**	(0.02)	**0.09**	(0.02)	**0.30**	(0.02)
	Chile	**0.17**	(0.06)	**0.28**	(0.04)	**0.25**	(0.04)	-0.04	(0.05)	0.11	(0.06)	**0.56**	(0.02)
	Czech Republic	0.01	(0.02)	-0.02	(0.04)	0.00	(0.03)	**-0.17**	(0.03)	**0.11**	(0.03)	**0.39**	(0.02)
	Denmark	**0.07**	(0.03)	0.07	(0.04)	0.02	(0.03)	**-0.10**	(0.03)	**0.13**	(0.03)	**0.34**	(0.02)
	Estonia	-0.03	(0.03)	-0.02	(0.04)	0.05	(0.03)	-0.02	(0.03)	0.06	(0.04)	**0.31**	(0.03)
	Finland	0.01	(0.03)	**0.09**	(0.04)	0.05	(0.03)	0.01	(0.03)	-0.01	(0.03)	**0.16**	(0.03)
	France	w	w	w	w	w	w	w	w	**0.16**	(0.04)	**0.43**	(0.03)
	Germany	**-0.10**	(0.03)	0.04	(0.03)	0.03	(0.04)	-0.05	(0.04)	**0.08**	(0.03)	**0.46**	(0.02)
	Greece	**0.15**	(0.02)	**0.17**	(0.03)	0.09	(0.05)	**-0.11**	(0.03)	0.06	(0.04)	**0.38**	(0.02)
	Hungary	0.09	(0.05)	-0.02	(0.05)	0.08	(0.06)	-0.06	(0.05)	**0.25**	(0.04)	**0.57**	(0.02)
	Iceland	-0.03	(0.01)	**-0.05**	(0.02)	0.02	(0.02)	**-0.16**	(0.02)	**0.09**	(0.01)	**0.18**	(0.02)
	Ireland	-0.04	(0.05)	**0.17**	(0.05)	0.08	(0.05)	**-0.08**	(0.04)	0.07	(0.05)	**0.33**	(0.03)
	Israel	0.03	(0.03)	**0.10**	(0.04)	**0.12**	(0.04)	-0.03	(0.04)	0.03	(0.03)	**0.37**	(0.02)
	Italy	0.02	(0.02)	**0.05**	(0.02)	**0.08**	(0.02)	0.01	(0.02)	**0.23**	(0.02)	**0.40**	(0.01)
	Japan	0.02	(0.04)	**0.12**	(0.03)	**0.09**	(0.03)	-0.02	(0.03)	**0.24**	(0.03)	**0.38**	(0.02)
	Korea	**0.10**	(0.05)	0.04	(0.04)	-0.02	(0.05)	-0.01	(0.05)	**0.18**	(0.04)	**0.40**	(0.03)
	Luxembourg	**0.17**	(0.01)	0.01	(0.01)	**0.06**	(0.01)	**-0.16**	(0.01)	**0.18**	(0.01)	**0.43**	(0.01)
	Mexico	**0.18**	(0.04)	**0.31**	(0.03)	**0.41**	(0.02)	**-0.18**	(0.03)	-0.04	(0.03)	**0.47**	(0.02)
	Netherlands	-0.01	(0.03)	0.01	(0.04)	0.03	(0.05)	0.03	(0.05)	0.00	(0.04)	**0.39**	(0.02)
	New Zealand	-0.01	(0.03)	**0.08**	(0.03)	**0.08**	(0.03)	**-0.09**	(0.03)	**0.21**	(0.03)	**0.39**	(0.02)
	Norway	-0.01	(0.03)	0.04	(0.03)	0.05	(0.03)	**-0.08**	(0.03)	0.02	(0.03)	**0.19**	(0.03)
	Poland	-0.04	(0.04)	**0.10**	(0.05)	0.03	(0.03)	-0.03	(0.03)	-0.05	(0.04)	**0.34**	(0.03)
	Portugal	**0.13**	(0.03)	0.08	(0.07)	**0.14**	(0.04)	-0.05	(0.04)	0.00	(0.05)	**0.43**	(0.03)
	Slovak Republic	-0.05	(0.04)	0.02	(0.04)	-0.03	(0.03)	**-0.11**	(0.04)	0.04	(0.03)	**0.41**	(0.02)
	Slovenia	**-0.07**	(0.01)	**-0.03**	(0.01)	**0.07**	(0.01)	-0.01	(0.02)	**0.25**	(0.02)	**0.45**	(0.01)
	Spain	**0.09**	(0.03)	**0.26**	(0.02)	**0.06**	(0.02)	-0.01	(0.03)	0.03	(0.03)	**0.38**	(0.03)
	Sweden	-0.02	(0.03)	**0.13**	(0.03)	**0.11**	(0.03)	-0.05	(0.03)	**0.14**	(0.03)	**0.31**	(0.03)
	Switzerland	**0.11**	(0.03)	0.04	(0.06)	0.05	(0.04)	**-0.07**	(0.03)	**0.10**	(0.04)	**0.35**	(0.03)
	Turkey	0.01	(0.04)	**0.18**	(0.08)	0.03	(0.03)	0.01	(0.04)	0.09	(0.04)	**0.49**	(0.03)
	United Kingdom	0.05	(0.03)	**0.08**	(0.03)	0.00	(0.03)	**-0.08**	(0.03)	**0.20**	(0.03)	**0.40**	(0.02)
	United States	0.11	(0.05)	0.05	(0.05)	0.12	(0.05)	**-0.16**	(0.05)	**0.23**	(0.05)	**0.47**	(0.03)
	OECD average	**0.04**	(0.01)	**0.08**	(0.01)	**0.07**	(0.01)	**-0.07**	(0.01)	**0.11**	(0.01)	**0.39**	(0.00)
Partners	Albania	0.01	(0.04)	**0.15**	(0.03)	**0.26**	(0.04)	**-0.23**	(0.05)	-0.05	(0.07)	**0.42**	(0.04)
	Argentina	**0.16**	(0.06)	**0.30**	(0.05)	**0.34**	(0.04)	**-0.14**	(0.05)	**-0.16**	(0.05)	**0.51**	(0.03)
	Azerbaijan	-0.08	(0.05)	-0.04	(0.04)	**0.11**	(0.05)	-0.05	(0.05)	0.02	(0.05)	**0.29**	(0.04)
	Brazil	**0.26**	(0.03)	**0.41**	(0.02)	**0.33**	(0.03)	**-0.24**	(0.02)	0.05	(0.03)	**0.48**	(0.02)
	Bulgaria	0.00	(0.05)	**-0.11**	(0.05)	0.06	(0.04)	**0.11**	(0.05)	**0.13**	(0.06)	**0.52**	(0.02)
	Colombia	**0.16**	(0.05)	**0.42**	(0.03)	**0.34**	(0.04)	**-0.20**	(0.04)	0.06	(0.06)	**0.54**	(0.03)
	Croatia	0.03	(0.06)	**0.13**	(0.07)	0.05	(0.04)	**-0.10**	(0.04)	**0.20**	(0.03)	**0.38**	(0.03)
	Dubai (UAE)	**0.33**	(0.01)	**0.32**	(0.01)	**0.21**	(0.01)	**-0.12**	(0.01)	**0.12**	(0.01)	**0.39**	(0.01)
	Hong Kong-China	0.02	(0.05)	0.07	(0.05)	0.03	(0.05)	**-0.10**	(0.04)	0.04	(0.06)	**0.29**	(0.03)
	Indonesia	0.06	(0.06)	-0.02	(0.05)	**0.29**	(0.04)	**-0.23**	(0.05)	**-0.12**	(0.05)	**0.37**	(0.05)
	Jordan	**0.17**	(0.04)	**0.28**	(0.03)	**0.14**	(0.05)	**-0.13**	(0.03)	-0.01	(0.04)	**0.22**	(0.04)
	Kazakhstan	**-0.10**	(0.04)	0.09	(0.06)	**0.12**	(0.04)	-0.04	(0.04)	**0.10**	(0.04)	**0.35**	(0.03)
	Kyrgyzstan	-0.05	(0.04)	**0.22**	(0.06)	**0.15**	(0.06)	0.04	(0.04)	0.04	(0.04)	**0.42**	(0.03)
	Latvia	0.03	(0.04)	-0.05	(0.03)	**0.08**	(0.03)	0.04	(0.04)	-0.07	(0.04)	**0.37**	(0.03)
	Liechtenstein	**0.33**	(0.04)	**0.34**	(0.04)	**-0.39**	(0.04)	**0.25**	(0.05)	-0.03	(0.04)	**0.37**	(0.04)
	Lithuania	**-0.10**	(0.03)	**-0.11**	(0.02)	-0.01	(0.03)	-0.03	(0.04)	**0.12**	(0.05)	**0.40**	(0.02)
	Macao-China	**0.17**	(0.01)	-0.01	(0.01)	**0.13**	(0.01)	-0.01	(0.01)	**0.06**	(0.01)	**0.15**	(0.01)
	Montenegro	-0.02	(0.02)	0.00	(0.01)	**-0.05**	(0.01)	**-0.05**	(0.02)	**0.12**	(0.02)	**0.38**	(0.02)
	Panama	0.07	(0.08)	**0.47**	(0.07)	**0.47**	(0.06)	**-0.17**	(0.07)	-0.10	(0.07)	**0.52**	(0.05)
	Peru	**0.14**	(0.05)	**0.43**	(0.04)	**0.38**	(0.06)	**-0.25**	(0.05)	0.06	(0.05)	**0.63**	(0.03)
	Qatar	**0.18**	(0.01)	**0.12**	(0.01)	**0.12**	(0.01)	0.01	(0.01)	**0.08**	(0.01)	**0.21**	(0.01)
	Romania	-0.06	(0.04)	-0.01	(0.05)	**0.11**	(0.04)	**-0.10**	(0.04)	**0.14**	(0.04)	**0.40**	(0.03)
	Russian Federation	-0.04	(0.03)	0.02	(0.03)	**0.14**	(0.03)	-0.07	(0.05)	-0.03	(0.03)	**0.37**	(0.03)
	Serbia	**-0.11**	(0.03)	-0.02	(0.03)	-0.01	(0.03)	**-0.14**	(0.02)	**0.18**	(0.04)	**0.38**	(0.02)
	Shanghai-China	-0.06	(0.05)	0.02	(0.05)	**0.10**	(0.05)	**-0.11**	(0.04)	**0.28**	(0.03)	**0.47**	(0.03)
	Singapore	0.05	(0.02)	**0.24**	(0.01)	**0.05**	(0.01)	**-0.13**	(0.01)	**0.19**	(0.01)	**0.36**	(0.01)
	Chinese Taipei	-0.01	(0.04)	**-0.09**	(0.03)	**0.09**	(0.04)	-0.08	(0.05)	**0.13**	(0.04)	**0.36**	(0.02)
	Thailand	-0.02	(0.05)	0.05	(0.05)	**0.28**	(0.04)	-0.06	(0.07)	-0.04	(0.06)	**0.51**	(0.03)
	Trinidad and Tobago	**0.09**	(0.02)	**0.08**	(0.01)	**0.06**	(0.02)	**-0.11**	(0.02)	**0.09**	(0.01)	**0.40**	(0.01)
	Tunisia	0.01	(0.05)	0.03	(0.01)	**0.08**	(0.04)	0.04	(0.05)	**-0.25**	(0.04)	**0.37**	(0.03)
	Uruguay	**0.29**	(0.03)	**0.42**	(0.03)	**0.21**	(0.04)	**-0.16**	(0.03)	**0.11**	(0.03)	**0.53**	(0.02)

Note: Values that are statistically significant are indicated in bold (see Annex A3).
Source: OECD, *PISA 2009 Database*.

DATA TABLES: ANNEX B

[Part 1/1]
Table B4.5 Likelihood that socio-economically advantaged students will attend privately managed schools

Socio-economically advantaged students (nationally standardised ESCS is 1) attending privately managed schools (reference group is students with ESCS being 0)

		Before accounting for school characteristics			School's average reading performance			School's quality of educational materials			School's autonomy in curriculum and assessment			School's disciplinary climate			Average student socio-economic background in school		
		Model 1			Model 2			Model 3			Model 4			Model 5			Model 6		
		Odds ratio	Coef.	S.E.	Odds ratio	Coef.	S.E.	Odds ratio	Coef.	S.E.	Odds ratio	Coef.	S.E.	Odds ratio	Coef.	S.E.	Odds ratio	Coef.	S.E.
OECD	Australia	1.92	0.65	(0.05)	1.42	0.35	(0.06)	1.83	0.60	(0.05)	1.92	0.65	(0.05)	1.74	0.55	(0.05)	1.00	0.00	(0.00)
	Austria	1.20	0.19	(0.08)	1.12	0.12	(0.06)	1.20	0.19	(0.08)	1.21	0.19	(0.08)	1.12	0.12	(0.08)	1.00	0.00	(0.00)
	Belgium	1.34	0.29	(0.04)	w	w	w	1.34	0.30	(0.04)	1.34	0.29	(0.04)	1.35	0.30	(0.04)	1.00	0.00	(0.00)
	Canada	1.20	0.18	(0.04)	1.11	0.11	(0.04)	1.18	0.17	(0.03)	1.18	0.16	(0.04)	1.18	0.16	(0.04)	1.00	0.00	(0.01)
	Chile	2.09	0.74	(0.09)	1.42	0.35	(0.09)	1.84	0.61	(0.10)	2.00	0.69	(0.10)	2.04	0.71	(0.09)	1.00	0.00	(0.00)
	Czech Republic	1.06	0.06	(0.04)	1.04	0.04	(0.04)	1.05	0.05	(0.04)	1.06	0.06	(0.04)	1.01	0.01	(0.04)	1.00	0.00	(0.00)
	Denmark	1.19	0.18	(0.06)	1.08	0.08	(0.05)	1.19	0.18	(0.06)	1.17	0.15	(0.06)	1.18	0.17	(0.06)	1.00	0.00	(0.00)
	Estonia	1.05	0.05	(0.05)	1.05	0.05	(0.04)	1.05	0.05	(0.05)	1.05	0.05	(0.05)	1.05	0.05	(0.05)	1.00	0.00	(0.01)
	Finland	1.03	0.03	(0.05)	1.03	0.03	(0.05)	1.02	0.02	(0.05)	1.03	0.03	(0.05)	1.03	0.03	(0.05)	1.00	0.00	(0.00)
	Germany	1.06	0.06	(0.06)	1.09	0.09	(0.04)	1.06	0.06	(0.06)	1.08	0.08	(0.06)	1.01	0.01	(0.06)	1.00	0.00	(0.00)
	Greece	1.24	0.21	(0.06)	1.17	0.16	(0.06)	1.22	0.20	(0.07)	1.18	0.17	(0.07)	1.23	0.20	(0.07)	1.00	0.00	(0.00)
	Hungary	1.19	0.17	(0.09)	1.19	0.18	(0.07)	1.18	0.16	(0.09)	1.16	0.15	(0.09)	1.20	0.19	(0.09)	1.00	0.00	(0.00)
	Ireland	1.40	0.34	(0.06)	1.14	0.13	(0.06)	1.39	0.33	(0.07)	1.38	0.32	(0.07)	1.38	0.32	(0.07)	1.00	0.00	(0.00)
	Israel	1.07	0.06	(0.07)	1.00	0.00	(0.06)	1.09	0.08	(0.08)	1.06	0.06	(0.07)	1.05	0.05	(0.08)	1.00	0.00	(0.00)
	Italy	1.04	0.04	(0.03)	1.13	0.12	(0.03)	1.03	0.03	(0.03)	1.04	0.04	(0.03)	1.08	0.08	(0.03)	1.00	0.00	(0.00)
	Japan	1.30	0.26	(0.04)	1.43	0.36	(0.05)	1.27	0.24	(0.05)	1.30	0.26	(0.04)	1.45	0.37	(0.06)	1.00	0.00	(0.00)
	Korea	1.04	0.04	(0.10)	0.90	-0.10	(0.08)	1.04	0.04	(0.09)	1.02	0.02	(0.09)	0.92	-0.09	(0.11)	1.00	0.00	(0.00)
	Luxembourg	0.96	-0.04	(0.03)	0.95	-0.05	(0.03)	0.89	-0.12	(0.03)	0.88	-0.13	(0.03)	0.92	-0.08	(0.03)	1.00	0.00	(0.03)
	Mexico	1.59	0.46	(0.04)	1.49	0.40	(0.04)	1.34	0.29	(0.04)	1.52	0.42	(0.04)	1.59	0.46	(0.04)	1.00	0.00	(0.00)
	Netherlands	0.92	-0.08	(0.09)	0.97	-0.03	(0.08)	0.91	-0.10	(0.09)	0.92	-0.08	(0.09)	0.87	-0.14	(0.09)	1.00	0.00	(0.00)
	New Zealand	1.24	0.21	(0.04)	1.14	0.13	(0.04)	1.18	0.17	(0.04)	1.22	0.20	(0.04)	1.17	0.16	(0.05)	1.00	0.00	(0.01)
	Poland	1.11	0.10	(0.05)	1.07	0.07	(0.04)	1.10	0.10	(0.05)	1.11	0.10	(0.05)	1.11	0.10	(0.06)	1.00	0.00	(0.01)
	Portugal	1.22	0.20	(0.07)	1.09	0.09	(0.06)	1.13	0.13	(0.07)	1.09	0.09	(0.12)	1.23	0.21	(0.07)	1.00	0.00	(0.00)
	Slovak Republic	1.07	0.07	(0.05)	1.03	0.03	(0.05)	1.08	0.07	(0.05)	1.07	0.06	(0.05)	1.04	0.04	(0.06)	1.00	0.00	(0.00)
	Slovenia	1.08	0.07	(0.03)	1.04	0.04	(0.04)	1.07	0.07	(0.03)	1.08	0.07	(0.03)	1.03	0.03	(0.03)	1.00	0.00	(0.04)
	Spain	1.82	0.60	(0.05)	1.46	0.38	(0.06)	1.80	0.59	(0.05)	1.80	0.59	(0.06)	1.83	0.61	(0.05)	1.00	0.00	(0.00)
	Sweden	1.21	0.19	(0.05)	1.12	0.11	(0.04)	1.19	0.18	(0.05)	1.21	0.19	(0.05)	1.16	0.15	(0.05)	1.00	0.00	(0.00)
	Switzerland	1.09	0.09	(0.07)	1.09	0.08	(0.06)	1.09	0.09	(0.07)	1.06	0.05	(0.08)	1.09	0.09	(0.07)	1.00	0.00	(0.00)
	United Kingdom	1.25	0.22	(0.05)	1.17	0.16	(0.05)	1.25	0.23	(0.05)	1.24	0.22	(0.05)	1.18	0.17	(0.05)	1.00	0.00	(0.00)
	United States	1.39	0.33	(0.08)	1.15	0.14	(0.07)	1.39	0.33	(0.09)	1.35	0.30	(0.09)	1.28	0.24	(0.08)	1.00	0.00	(0.00)
Partners	Albania	1.39	0.33	(0.08)	1.19	0.17	(0.07)	1.16	0.15	(0.10)	1.40	0.33	(0.08)	1.43	0.36	(0.09)	1.00	0.00	(0.01)
	Argentina	2.25	0.81	(0.11)	1.44	0.37	(0.10)	2.09	0.74	(0.11)	2.18	0.78	(0.11)	2.20	0.79	(0.11)	1.00	0.00	(0.00)
	Brazil	1.83	0.61	(0.04)	1.37	0.32	(0.05)	1.55	0.44	(0.06)	1.64	0.49	(0.06)	1.83	0.60	(0.05)	1.00	0.00	(0.00)
	Colombia	2.13	0.76	(0.07)	1.50	0.41	(0.07)	1.69	0.52	(0.09)	2.04	0.71	(0.07)	2.12	0.75	(0.07)	1.00	0.00	(0.00)
	Dubai (UAE)	1.98	0.69	(0.03)	1.56	0.44	(0.04)	1.85	0.61	(0.04)	1.58	0.46	(0.04)	1.95	0.67	(0.03)	1.00	0.00	(0.04)
	Hong Kong-China	1.00	0.00	(0.08)	1.03	0.03	(0.08)	1.00	0.00	(0.08)	1.00	0.00	(0.08)	1.00	0.00	(0.08)	1.00	0.00	(0.00)
	Indonesia	0.89	-0.12	(0.11)	1.02	0.02	(0.09)	0.95	-0.06	(0.11)	0.85	-0.17	(0.10)	0.88	-0.12	(0.11)	1.00	0.00	(0.00)
	Jordan	1.36	0.31	(0.06)	1.31	0.27	(0.05)	1.34	0.29	(0.06)	1.28	0.25	(0.07)	1.37	0.31	(0.06)	1.00	0.00	(0.01)
	Kazakhstan	1.09	0.08	(0.08)	1.05	0.05	(0.06)	1.07	0.07	(0.08)	1.09	0.08	(0.08)	1.08	0.08	(0.07)	1.00	0.00	(0.00)
	Kyrgyzstan	1.15	0.14	(0.07)	1.06	0.06	(0.06)	1.13	0.12	(0.07)	1.16	0.15	(0.07)	1.15	0.14	(0.07)	1.00	0.00	(0.00)
	Panama	3.18	1.16	(0.14)	2.19	0.78	(0.17)	2.20	0.79	(0.14)	3.24	1.18	(0.14)	3.13	1.14	(0.14)	1.00	0.00	(0.03)
	Peru	2.34	0.85	(0.08)	1.53	0.43	(0.07)	1.95	0.67	(0.11)	2.36	0.86	(0.09)	2.33	0.84	(0.08)	1.00	0.00	(0.00)
	Qatar	1.50	0.41	(0.02)	1.24	0.21	(0.02)	1.46	0.38	(0.02)	1.34	0.29	(0.02)	1.45	0.37	(0.02)	1.00	0.00	(0.03)
	Shanghai-China	1.13	0.12	(0.07)	1.08	0.07	(0.06)	1.13	0.13	(0.07)	1.15	0.14	(0.07)	1.14	0.13	(0.07)	1.00	0.00	(0.01)
	Chinese Taipei	0.88	-0.13	(0.06)	1.20	0.18	(0.06)	0.86	-0.15	(0.06)	0.88	-0.13	(0.06)	0.94	-0.06	(0.06)	1.00	0.00	(0.00)
	Thailand	1.14	0.13	(0.07)	1.27	0.24	(0.09)	0.99	-0.01	(0.08)	1.14	0.13	(0.08)	1.14	0.13	(0.07)	1.00	0.00	(0.00)
	Trinidad and Tobago	1.09	0.08	(0.03)	1.10	0.10	(0.04)	1.07	0.07	(0.04)	1.06	0.06	(0.03)	1.10	0.09	(0.03)	1.00	0.00	(0.04)
	Tunisia	1.03	0.03	(0.08)	1.07	0.07	(0.07)	1.03	0.03	(0.08)	1.03	0.03	(0.08)	1.03	0.03	(0.08)	1.00	0.00	(0.00)
	Uruguay	2.45	0.90	(0.06)	1.76	0.56	(0.05)	2.31	0.84	(0.05)	2.06	0.72	(0.06)	2.43	0.89	(0.06)	1.00	0.00	(0.04)

Note: Models are logistic regression with the dichotomous dependent variable of PRIVATE (0=public schools; 1=private schools). Model 1 includes only one independent variable ESCS (nationally standardised). Models 2 to 6 include each of the school characteristics as an independent variable in addition to the nationally standardised ESCS. All these school characteristic variables are centred around the national average, which is zero.
Estimates of coefficient indicate log-odds of socio-economically advantaged students attending private schools; and the log-odds are also converted into odds, which present the likelihood of socio-economically advantaged students attending private schools when other independent variables included in the model are at the national average.
Estimates significant at the 5% level (p<0.05) are in bold.
Source: OECD, *PISA 2009 Database*.

ANNEX B: DATA TABLES

Table B4.6
[Part 1/1]
Likelihood that socio-economically advantaged students will attend privately managed schools, after accounting for the proportion of public funding for schools

Socio-economically advantaged students (nationally standardised ESCS is 1) attending privately managed schools (reference group is students with ESCS at 0), after accounting for the proportion of public funding for schools

		Before accounting for school characteristics (Model 1)			After accounting for: School's average reading performance (Model 2)			Quality of school's educational materials (Model 3)			School's autonomy in curriculum and assessment (Model 4)			School's disciplinary climate (Model 5)			Average student socio-economic background in school (Model 6)		
		Odds ratio	Coef.	S.E.	Odds ratio	Coef.	S.E.	Odds ratio	Coef.	S.E.	Odds ratio	Coef.	S.E.	Odds ratio	Coef.	S.E.	Odds ratio	Coef.	S.E.
OECD	Australia	**1.40**	**0.34**	(0.05)	**1.25**	**0.22**	(0.06)	**1.39**	**0.33**	(0.05)	**1.41**	**0.34**	(0.05)	**1.36**	**0.30**	(0.05)	1.00	0.00	(0.00)
	Austria	m	m	m	m	m	m	m	m	m	m	m	m	m	m	m	m	m	m
	Belgium	**1.32**	**0.28**	(0.05)	w	w	w	**1.32**	**0.28**	(0.05)	**1.32**	**0.28**	(0.05)	**1.36**	**0.31**	(0.05)	1.00	0.00	(0.00)
	Canada	**1.13**	**0.12**	(0.04)	**1.08**	**0.08**	(0.04)	**1.13**	**0.12**	(0.04)	**1.13**	**0.13**	(0.04)	**1.12**	**0.12**	(0.04)	1.00	0.00	(0.01)
	Chile	**2.10**	**0.74**	(0.12)	**1.47**	**0.39**	(0.11)	**1.89**	**0.64**	(0.14)	**2.07**	**0.73**	(0.13)	**2.05**	**0.72**	(0.12)	1.00	0.00	(0.00)
	Czech Republic	1.05	0.05	(0.05)	1.01	0.01	(0.05)	1.04	0.04	(0.05)	1.05	0.05	(0.05)	0.99	-0.01	(0.06)	1.00	0.00	(0.00)
	Denmark	1.07	0.07	(0.10)	1.02	0.02	(0.03)	1.07	0.07	(0.10)	1.08	0.08	(0.09)	1.06	0.06	(0.09)	1.00	0.00	(0.00)
	Estonia	0.98	-0.02	(0.05)	1.00	0.00	(0.04)	0.98	-0.02	(0.05)	0.98	-0.02	(0.05)	0.98	-0.02	(0.06)	1.00	0.00	(0.01)
	Finland	1.01	0.01	(0.06)	1.01	0.01	(0.06)	1.00	0.00	(0.06)	1.01	0.01	(0.06)	1.01	0.01	(0.06)	1.00	0.00	(0.01)
	Germany	1.01	0.01	(0.07)	1.06	0.06	(0.05)	1.01	0.01	(0.07)	1.02	0.02	(0.07)	0.96	-0.04	(0.07)	1.00	0.00	(0.00)
	Greece	1.05	0.05	(0.07)	1.04	0.04	(0.06)	1.04	0.04	(0.07)	1.02	0.01	(0.07)	1.04	0.04	(0.07)	1.00	0.00	(0.00)
	Hungary	**1.21**	**0.19**	(0.09)	**1.23**	**0.20**	(0.07)	**1.20**	**0.18**	(0.09)	1.18	0.16	(0.09)	**1.24**	**0.21**	(0.09)	1.00	0.00	(0.00)
	Ireland	**1.18**	**0.16**	(0.08)	0.99	-0.01	(0.07)	**1.17**	**0.16**	(0.08)	**1.18**	**0.16**	(0.08)	1.14	0.13	(0.08)	1.00	0.00	(0.00)
	Israel	1.10	0.09	(0.07)	1.02	0.02	(0.06)	1.10	0.10	(0.07)	1.10	0.09	(0.07)	1.09	0.08	(0.07)	1.00	0.00	(0.00)
	Italy	1.00	0.00	(0.03)	**1.09**	**0.08**	(0.03)	0.99	-0.01	(0.03)	1.00	0.00	(0.03)	1.03	0.03	(0.04)	1.00	0.00	(0.00)
	Japan	1.03	0.03	(0.07)	**1.39**	**0.33**	(0.07)	1.02	0.02	(0.08)	1.03	0.03	(0.07)	**1.23**	**0.21**	(0.12)	1.00	0.00	(0.00)
	Korea	1.07	0.07	(0.09)	0.92	-0.09	(0.08)	1.07	0.07	(0.09)	1.06	0.06	(0.09)	0.96	-0.04	(0.10)	1.00	0.00	(0.00)
	Luxembourg	**0.89**	**-0.12**	(0.03)	**0.92**	**-0.08**	(0.03)	**0.83**	**-0.19**	(0.03)	**0.87**	**-0.14**	(0.03)	**0.89**	**-0.12**	(0.03)	1.00	0.00	(0.03)
	Mexico	**1.50**	**0.41**	(0.04)	**1.42**	**0.35**	(0.05)	**1.29**	**0.26**	(0.04)	**1.45**	**0.37**	(0.04)	**1.50**	**0.41**	(0.04)	1.00	0.00	(0.00)
	Netherlands	0.85	-0.16	(0.09)	0.92	-0.08	(0.07)	0.85	-0.16	(0.09)	0.85	-0.16	(0.09)	0.84	-0.18	(0.09)	1.00	0.00	(0.00)
	New Zealand	1.03	0.03	(0.05)	1.06	0.06	(0.05)	1.02	0.02	(0.05)	1.03	0.03	(0.05)	1.01	0.01	(0.06)	1.00	0.00	(0.01)
	Poland	1.02	0.02	(0.06)	1.01	0.01	(0.05)	1.02	0.02	(0.06)	1.02	0.02	(0.06)	1.02	0.02	(0.06)	1.00	0.00	(0.01)
	Portugal	1.04	0.04	(0.07)	1.01	0.01	(0.06)	1.02	0.02	(0.07)	1.04	0.04	(0.13)	1.05	0.05	(0.07)	1.00	0.00	(0.00)
	Slovak Republic	1.06	0.06	(0.06)	1.03	0.03	(0.05)	1.06	0.06	(0.06)	1.05	0.05	(0.06)	1.04	0.04	(0.06)	1.00	0.00	(0.04)
	Slovenia	**1.08**	**0.08**	(0.03)	1.04	0.03	(0.04)	**1.08**	**0.07**	(0.03)	**1.08**	**0.08**	(0.03)	1.03	0.03	(0.04)	1.00	0.00	(0.04)
	Spain	**1.50**	**0.41**	(0.05)	**1.27**	**0.24**	(0.06)	**1.45**	**0.37**	(0.04)	**1.51**	**0.41**	(0.06)	**1.53**	**0.42**	(0.06)	1.00	0.00	(0.00)
	Sweden	**1.20**	**0.18**	(0.05)	**1.12**	**0.11**	(0.04)	**1.18**	**0.17**	(0.05)	**1.21**	**0.19**	(0.05)	**1.15**	**0.14**	(0.05)	1.00	0.00	(0.00)
	Switzerland	0.88	-0.12	(0.09)	1.01	0.01	(0.06)	0.87	-0.13	(0.09)	0.88	-0.13	(0.10)	0.90	-0.11	(0.09)	1.00	0.00	(0.01)
	United Kingdom	1.45	0.37	(0.54)	1.07	0.07	(0.07)	1.48	0.39	(0.54)	1.35	0.30	(0.36)	1.21	0.19	(0.23)	1.00	0.00	(0.00)
	United States	1.02	0.02	(0.12)	1.00	0.00	(0.09)	0.99	-0.01	(0.13)	1.02	0.02	(0.12)	0.97	-0.03	(0.14)	1.00	0.00	(0.00)
Partners	Albania	1.19	0.18	(0.09)	1.13	0.13	(0.08)	1.11	0.10	(0.10)	**1.21**	**0.19**	(0.10)	**1.23**	**0.20**	(0.10)	1.00	0.00	(0.01)
	Argentina	**2.24**	**0.81**	(0.11)	**1.54**	**0.43**	(0.09)	**2.10**	**0.74**	(0.11)	**2.16**	**0.77**	(0.11)	**2.19**	**0.78**	(0.11)	1.00	0.00	(0.00)
	Brazil	**1.18**	**0.17**	(0.05)	**1.26**	**0.23**	(0.06)	**1.16**	**0.15**	(0.05)	**1.18**	**0.17**	(0.06)	**1.16**	**0.15**	(0.06)	1.00	0.00	(0.00)
	Colombia	**1.68**	**0.52**	(0.11)	**1.43**	**0.36**	(0.10)	**1.49**	**0.40**	(0.12)	**1.63**	**0.49**	(0.10)	**1.68**	**0.52**	(0.11)	1.00	0.00	(0.00)
	Dubai (UAE)	0.60	-0.51	(0.38)	0.54	-0.62	(0.34)	0.66	-0.41	(0.30)	0.66	-0.41	(0.23)	0.61	-0.50	(0.38)	1.00	0.00	(0.46)
	Hong Kong-China	0.92	-0.08	(0.07)	0.96	-0.04	(0.07)	0.92	-0.08	(0.07)	0.93	-0.07	(0.07)	0.92	-0.08	(0.07)	1.00	0.00	(0.00)
	Indonesia	**0.61**	**-0.50**	(0.11)	**0.80**	**-0.23**	(0.11)	**0.67**	**-0.40**	(0.12)	**0.57**	**-0.56**	(0.12)	**0.60**	**-0.51**	(0.11)	1.00	0.00	(0.00)
	Jordan	1.03	0.03	(0.07)	1.06	0.06	(0.05)	1.02	0.02	(0.10)	1.03	0.03	(0.07)	1.04	0.04	(0.07)	1.00	0.00	(0.01)
	Kazakhstan	0.99	-0.01	(0.07)	0.98	-0.02	(0.07)	0.98	-0.02	(0.07)	0.99	-0.01	(0.07)	0.99	-0.01	(0.07)	1.00	0.00	(0.00)
	Kyrgyzstan	1.07	0.07	(0.06)	1.02	0.02	(0.06)	1.06	0.05	(0.06)	1.08	0.07	(0.06)	1.07	0.06	(0.06)	1.00	0.00	(0.00)
	Panama	**2.01**	**0.70**	(0.24)	**1.72**	**0.54**	(0.24)	**1.77**	**0.57**	(0.27)	**2.13**	**0.76**	(0.22)	**1.94**	**0.66**	(0.23)	1.00	0.00	(0.05)
	Peru	**2.08**	**0.73**	(0.10)	**1.57**	**0.45**	(0.09)	**1.76**	**0.57**	(0.11)	**2.13**	**0.75**	(0.11)	**2.08**	**0.73**	(0.10)	1.00	0.00	(0.00)
	Qatar	**2.04**	**0.71**	(0.06)	**2.01**	**0.70**	(0.06)	**1.95**	**0.67**	(0.06)	**2.18**	**0.78**	(0.07)	**2.05**	**0.72**	(0.05)	1.00	0.00	(0.07)
	Shanghai-China	1.10	0.10	(0.08)	1.06	0.06	(0.07)	1.11	0.11	(0.08)	1.10	0.10	(0.08)	1.02	0.02	(0.09)	1.00	0.00	(0.01)
	Chinese Taipei	**0.61**	**-0.49**	(0.19)	0.91	-0.10	(0.16)	**0.59**	**-0.54**	(0.24)	**0.61**	**-0.50**	(0.19)	**0.68**	**-0.39**	(0.16)	1.00	0.00	(0.00)
	Thailand	0.94	-0.07	(0.09)	1.09	0.09	(0.09)	0.85	-0.16	(0.09)	0.94	-0.06	(0.09)	0.94	-0.06	(0.09)	1.00	0.00	(0.00)
	Trinidad and Tobago	**0.92**	**-0.08**	(0.04)	1.02	0.02	(0.04)	**0.91**	**-0.09**	(0.04)	**0.92**	**-0.09**	(0.04)	**0.92**	**-0.08**	(0.04)	1.00	0.00	(0.05)
	Tunisia	1.05	0.05	(0.09)	1.09	0.08	(0.08)	1.06	0.05	(0.09)	1.05	0.05	(0.09)	1.05	0.05	(0.09)	1.00	0.00	(0.00)
	Uruguay	**1.39**	**0.33**	(0.13)	**1.29**	**0.25**	(0.10)	**1.38**	**0.32**	(0.14)	**1.37**	**0.31**	(0.14)	**1.43**	**0.36**	(0.14)	1.00	0.00	(0.05)

Note: Models are logistic regressions with the dichotomous dependent variable of PRIVATE (0 = public schools; 1 = private schools). Model 1 includes two independent variables ESCS (nationally standardised) and the proportion of public funding for schools (centred around the national average within each country). Models 2 to 6 include each of the school characteristics as an independent variable in addition to the nationally standardised ESCS and the proportion of public funding for schools (centred around the national average within each country). All these variables are centred around the national average of 0.
Estimates of coefficient indicate log-odds of socio-economically advantaged students attending private schools; the log-odds are also converted into odds, which present the likelihood of socio-economically advantaged students attending private schools when other independent variables included in the model are at the national average.
Estimates significant at the 5% level (p<0.05) are in bold.
Source: OECD, *PISA 2009 Database*.

ORGANISATION FOR ECONOMIC CO-OPERATION AND DEVELOPMENT

The OECD is a unique forum where governments work together to address the economic, social and environmental challenges of globalisation. The OECD is also at the forefront of efforts to understand and to help governments respond to new developments and concerns, such as corporate governance, the information economy and the challenges of an ageing population. The Organisation provides a setting where governments can compare policy experiences, seek answers to common problems, identify good practice and work to co-ordinate domestic and international policies.

The OECD member countries are: Australia, Austria, Belgium, Canada, Chile, the Czech Republic, Denmark, Estonia, Finland, France, Germany, Greece, Hungary, Iceland, Ireland, Israel, Italy, Japan, Korea, Luxembourg, Mexico, the Netherlands, New Zealand, Norway, Poland, Portugal, the Slovak Republic, Slovenia, Spain, Sweden, Switzerland, Turkey, the United Kingdom and the United States. The European Commission takes part in the work of the OECD.

OECD Publishing disseminates widely the results of the Organisation's statistics gathering and research on economic, social and environmental issues, as well as the conventions, guidelines and standards agreed by its members.